Introduction To Holy Spirit

May blessings run and overtake you -

Dr. Betty Gilliam
5-4-2018

Introduction To Holy Spirit

THE FAITH CONNECTION

"And they were all filled with the Holy Ghost, and began to speak in other tongues, as the Spirit gave them utterance." (Acts 2:4)

Dr. Betty J. Gilliam

Copyright © 2018 Dr. Betty J. Gilliam

All rights reserved.

ISBN-13: 9781979067683
ISBN-10: 1979067686

Reviews

"WE HAVE BEEN WAITING FOR *a book like this on the Person of the Holy Spirit. Dr. Gilliam writes with clarity and authority drawn from decades of Biblical wisdom and dynamic experience in the power of the Holy Spirit. This is more than a good read. This book challenges us to rethink our relationship with the Holy Spirit and to give Him His rightful place. The end result is a new dimension of supernatural living."*

David W. Dorries, Ph.D. Director of Kairos Ministries International, an educational outreach to the body of Christ. Largo, Florida.

I have known Betty Gillam for many years and the number one thing I see in her character is a passion for His Presence. This book will not only cause you to desire to spend time with the Holy Spirit and to be filled with his power, but will also educate you on the understanding of the biblical theology of the Holy Spirit. For such a time as this has this book been written to reveal truth that arms you for the last days. I pray it will release a hunger to know the Holy Spirit as a person as it has in my life.

Terry Nance, Author, God's Armorbearer; Senior Pastor, Impact Church, Sherwood Arkansas

"We highly recommend Introduction to Holy Spirit: The Faith Connection for all who are seeking a more intimate relationship with Holy Spirit. Dr. Gilliam has masterfully articulated answers to questions many have pondered for years. We are excited about this book because the knowledge and revelation we have gained from her over the years is now available to everyone and we believe these truths will transform many lives for the Kingdom of God."

"The Tuesday Group" Faith Christian Center Church, Central Arkansas Bible College Alumni, Jacksonville, AR

"Dr. Betty Gilliam is an amazing author and teacher/professor of the Word of God. As you read these pages you will feel her heartbeat. This is a woman of God who has a passion for learning and for imparting her knowledge to the body of Christ. I received my Doctorate in Renewal Church History Studies at Central Arkansas Bible College of which she is president and professor. I gained a wealth of knowledge with a deeper understanding of God, the Early Church, and how Holy Spirit is relevant in the earth today."

Dr. Sandi Sims; Pastor, Victory Worship Center, Beebe, AR.; Regional Director, Word Churches International, Inc.

In my 40 years of full-time ministry I have studied countless books and articles dealing with faith, but Dr. Gilliam's book, Introduction to Holy Spirit: The Faith Connection, is probably the most comprehensive book I have read on that subject. She leads her readers into deep truths using straightforward and uncomplicated language. It was an honor to read and study this book from which I learned so much. No library dealing with faith can be complete without this great work included in its collections.

Don Jones, PhD., Claremont University, Th.D., North. Carolina College of Theology, Chancellor of Midwest College of Theology, President of Lifeline Ministries.

Table Of Contents

Reviews..v
Dedication......................................xi
Acknowledgments...............................xiii
Preface...xv
Introduction..................................xvii

Chapter 1	The Trinity	1
Chapter 2	What Is Man That You Are Mindful of Him?	21
Chapter 3	From Death to Life	47
Chapter 4	God Himself Would Come to Save Humanity	93
Chapter 5	First Things First: Part One	125
Chapter 6	First Things First: Part Two	153
Chapter 7	Holy Spirit Anointing of Jesus	165
Chapter 8	Glorification	183
Chapter 9	Three Baptisms	199
Chapter 10	Holy Spirit Baptism vs. Fruit of the Spirit	207
Chapter 11	Holy Spirit Baptism Doctrine	217
Chapter 12	The Unique Role of Holy Spirit Baptism	235
Chapter 13	The Unique Sign: Sounds from Heaven	245
Chapter 14	The Value of Tongues	257
Chapter 15	Love Is the Key to Power	275

Chapter 16   Holy Spirit Empowerment 287
Chapter 17   Victory in the Holy Spirit 301
Chapter 18   Fully Persuaded 317

             About the Author 329

Dedication

This book is dedicated to the loves of my life;

My husband, the loving hand that holds my world together;

My children, Anita, Cathy, Brenda, Taunya, and Barbie,

Without whom I would have no world;

My grandchildren and great grandchildren who are the spice in the mix;

My sons-in-law, and grandsons and granddaughters-in-law who complete our

family.

Most of all this book is dedicated to

The glory of the Father, Son, and Holy Spirit.

Acknowledgments

THERE ARE MANY WHO HAVE been helpful in various ways on the journey of writing this book, but there are a few who helped set me on this path and have faithfully cheered me on.

The first grateful "thank you" is to my mother, Selma Cole Thornton who taught me to: "Learn to love. Love to learn. Dream big." This has been the foundation of my life.

My sister, Donna Williams, continued the work of encouragement to push me to finish the project. She prayed much with me and for me.

My dear friends in the "Tuesday group" were always willing to read and reread the material, and offer suggestions and corrections to help me while firmly pressing me forward.

Donna Walker, thank you for more things than I can list here.

My granddaughter, McKenzie Hefley, has been there to correct form and format issues to assure the proper order and to insist that it have aesthetic pleasantness.

My mentor and close friend, Dr. David Dorries, would not let me quit.

Without my friend, Lisa Douglas, this book would not be in print.

Thank you Bob and Liz Bevis for providing the computer and program to make this venture less burdensome.

Thanks to my family for believing in me and never giving up on me.

Most importantly, thank you to my husband and best friend, Gene Gilliam, who believes in me much more than I deserve. Without him, I would still be trying to find my way and my place in life. With him, I am complete.

Preface

MOST PEOPLE SHY AWAY FROM the word "theology" because they have a misunderstanding of the meaning of the word. In its simplest meaning theology is the study of God and the outcome of that study. Everyone has their own theology whether they realize it or not. All believe certain things about God. Even if it is based on little or no actual study or facts; it is their theology.

Most important to this study is the "Doctrine" of the Holy Spirit. Doctrine is derived strictly from scripture instead of philosophical logic or reasoning as in theology. Doctrine refers to the entire body of truth that defines and describes the good news of Jesus Christ. Good and correct doctrine is based solidly on the Scriptures (I Timothy 1:10, 13-14; 4:16; 6:3; Titus 1:9).

The message in the Scriptures includes some historical facts, but doctrine is deeper than that. Jesus' death and events in his life are integral facts, but they are not doctrine. However, Jesus' death "for sins" as doctrine is important ((I Corinthians. 15:3; I John 2:7, 24; 2:26; 3:11). Doctrine tells the importance of the facts. This book will tell of the importance of the facts of Jesus' life and of the facts of the biblical statements concerning Holy Spirit, as well as, the manifestation of Holy Spirit power.

The key is making sure one's thoughts are in line with what the Bible says about the subject. My hope is that this book helps the reader to stop and consider the Scriptures concerning Holy Spirit and his involvement in the world today through believers. I've inserted many scriptures in the text for the reader's convenience.

This book is written for the layperson: yet, there are nuggets of meaty truth that are meant to challenge all who read it to grow in new knowledge or to refresh those truths that have lain dormant for too long. This book is light theology and scriptural doctrine concerning Holy Spirit written in simple terms so all may benefit from a clearer understanding with opportunity to grow and share. Scripture quotations are from the King James Version of the Bible unless otherwise stated.

Introduction

MY INTENTION FOR THE FIRST eight chapters of this book is to: (1) bring better understanding of the Trinity to the readers; (2) to inform readers of the value God placed on humanity; (3,4) to show the hopeless situation which mankind was in after the fall and to explain the full penalty for sin as being eternal death from which man could not save himself and that God must come to save him, (5 and 6) to discuss the importance of the incarnation, life, death, resurrection, ascension and glorification of Jesus Christ in the two great heavenly events: (A) redemption through the eternal covenant cut by God (Elohim) in heaven (Genesis 1:1; Revelation 13:8b), and (B) the empowerment of believers after the ascension and glorification of Jesus in heaven; to show that the earthly empowerment of Jesus was by the same Holy Spirit; and (8) to gain an understanding of the importance of the glorification of Jesus at which time he again as-sumed those things which he had laid aside to walk on earth as man. After the glorification of Jesus Christ, Holy Spirit was then poured out on all flesh to empower all who believe. Have you received Jesus Christ? Have you asked to be baptized in the Holy Spirit?

From the discussion of who God (Trinity) is, who man is, and the two outstanding events that occurred in heaven (i.e. the eternal covenant of Revelation 13:8b and the glorification of Jesus), we can see how paramount, crucial, and consequential these events are to man's standing with God. These two heavenly events had to be revealed to man in order for him to participate in the provisions of God. Because of these two events, we can come into a personal relationship with the Father through his Son, Jesus Christ. We can then be baptized in Holy Spirit for empowerment to live victoriously and be witnesses of the truth that Jesus Christ is the way, the truth, and the life. There is no other Savior. Do you know him personally? Have you personally asked him into your heart? If so, have you asked Jesus to baptize you in the Holy Spirit which is provided for your victorious living and empowerment to witness? It is a glorious experience and amazing empowerment that we will discuss more fully in the following chapters. God has designed a redemption plan that totally enables humanity to be all that God initially created us to be.

Because of the incarnational birth, God's Son came and dwelt among man and though he was God, he lived 100% as man in order to qualify to pay man's penalty for sin. He lived a sinless life and therefore, sin had no hold on him and he could rise again having paid the penalty. Jesus is our substitute and because of this, "whosoever will" can choose Jesus as their Redeemer and Savior. God accepts us on the merits of Jesus. When the Lamb was brought to the priest, he examined the lamb to see if the Lamb was without spot or blemish. When we go to God, we take the "Lamb of God, Jesus Christ" who, when examined in our stead, is found without spot or blemish. It is not by our own righteousness but by and through the righteousness of Jesus Christ as our sacrifice that we come boldly into the throne room of grace. You become the child of God by faith in what Jesus did to purchase your salvation. Believe and receive.

Chapters 9-18 cover more specifically the baptism in the Holy Spirit. Chapter 9 distinguishes between the three baptisms revealed in the New Testament: baptism into Christ, water baptism, and baptism in the Holy Spirit. The discussion continues in chapter 9 by distinguishing between baptism in the Holy Spirit and fruit of the Spirit. The anointing of Jesus at his water baptism is the time of his revelation to Israel as their long awaited Messiah. In chapter 10, we see that miracles and supernatural activities began only after the Holy Spirit anointing of Jesus by God which occurred at his water baptism. At his ascension, Jesus commanded his follow-ers to wait for the Holy Spirit outpouring before going forth to minister. Holy Spirit doctrine is revealed in Scripture as is seen in chapter 11. The unique role and unique sign of the baptism of the Holy Spirit is discussed in chapter 12 and 13. In chapter 14 we discuss the value of speaking in unknown tongues (i.e. your prayer language). Chapter 15 reveals that love must be the motivation behind the desire for spiritual gifts because love is the key to Holy Spirit power in the church. Holy Spirit baptism is the coming of the special presence and power of God on believers (Ch. 16). Holy Spirit gives believers victory in life (Ch. 17). Are you fully persuaded? (Ch.18)

Chapter One: The Trinity

Introduction

Elohim: The Trinity Revealed in the Earth

Is Jesus Deity?

The Nicene Creed (325 A.D.)

Is Holy Spirit Deity?

The Nicene Constantinopolitan Creed (381 A.D.)

Essence of God: Father, Son, and Holy Spirit

The Trinity: Three in One

The Trinity: God in Three Persons

The Trinity: Eternality: Jesus Christ: In the Beginning

The Trinity: Eternality: Holy Spirit: In the Beginning

Uniqueness of Each Person of the Trinity

The Trinity in Covenant

CHAPTER 1
The Trinity

INTRODUCTION

THIS BOOK IS DIFFERENT. It is written in table talk as opposed to academic speech. It is written in conversation much like what occurs when friends are sharing a cup of coffee. There is repetition throughout not because I did not realize it, but because in my long career as a teacher I have found repetition to be necessary to learning and its reinforcement. If you enter into this dialogue with me, when you finish reading this book, you will be amazed at your spiritual growth. If you read and discuss the many scriptures I have included, your knowledge will be doubly strong and your faith will be strengthened because it will be based on God's word not man's assumptions or opinions. Come let us reason together. One of my main goals is to cause you to think and reason more deeply while relying on Scripture to be your guide. The intention of this book is to minister a scriptural basis for your truth about the Holy Spirit and the Church today.

In *Introduction to Holy Spirit*, we will immediately discuss the Trinity to gain a better understanding of the meaning of the term "Trinity" and "unity in diversity and diversity in unity." We will examine the relationship between the Father's will in heaven and his will in Earth for humanity using the words that Jesus taught us to pray in Matthew 6: 9-13: *"Thy kingdom come, thy will be done in earth as it is in heaven."* Based on this prayer, we will discuss two major events revealing God's will that occurred in heaven out of the sight and participation of humanity, but of necessity were in time made manifest in the Earth to reveal God's will for humankind. Both of these events have to do with the active role of Holy Spirit in the earth since the initial outpouring on the Day of Pentecost. Without both of these events there would be no Holy Spirit indwelling and manifestations through believers as we know it today. The remaining chapters will contain scriptural basis for the doctrine of Holy Spirit baptism as a subsequent experience, the value of tongues, a discussion of tongues as evidence, and how to receive the Holy Spirit. Finally, we will discuss the question, "What are you fully persuaded of?"

As I stated above, this book is written in table-talk as opposed to academic speech. It is in conversational mode that we will approach the main subject of this book which is Holy Spirit.

However, to more fully examine the role, works, gifts, etc. of the Holy Spirit, we will first talk about the Father and Jesus Christ, his Son. Better understanding of the Trinity will bring clearer understanding about the work of the Holy Spirit. Therefore, in the first chapter, I will call attention to the relations between and among the Father, Son, and Holy Spirit while hopefully presenting a clearer picture of the Trinity.

Much remains to be said about Holy Spirit, but in order to understand Holy Spirit we must understand some things about Jesus and how he provided the way for Holy Spirit to be poured out into the earth. To understand about Jesus and Holy Spirit we need to talk about the Trinity.

"What is the Trinity?" "Who is Elohim?" The following discussion of the Trinity and the name "Elohim" will enhance the understanding of the two events to be discussed later in this book.

ELOHIM: THE TRINITY REVEALED IN THE EARTH

"The Trinity is that which has been given to you to know and experience of the totality of God."

God spoke this to me in 2004 as I was struggling to find words to express the concept of Trinity.

The Trinity consists of the Father, the Son, and Holy Spirit. The <u>Father</u> gave his <u>Son</u>, Jesus, to make eternal life available to those who believe, and then he sent <u>Holy Spirit</u> to indwell those believers. There was a process, an order. It was only <u>after</u> the Father had given his only begotten Son that the work of redemption could be accomplished. It was only <u>after</u> the finished work of Jesus, the Son of God who had been given, that Holy Spirit could be poured out upon all flesh. It is only <u>after</u> a person is cleansed by the blood of Jesus that Holy Spirit can indwell them (John 3:1-6; Mark 2:22). We will begin with the question: "Who is Jesus?"

IS JESUS DEITY?

Since the beginning of Jewish history, Jews believed in the existence of the Father God. Therefore, in the later years, when the early Church was birthed, Christian Jews had no doubt about the existence of the Father God (Deuteronomy 6:4). However, there was a sense of uncertainty pertaining to the actual deity of Jesus. They had known of the humanity of Jesus Christ who had walked among them, but what about his deity? Thus, one of the first questions that the early church had to deal with concerned Jesus. They had seen the supernatural healings, demonic deliverances, walking on water, stilling the storm, and many miracles that Jesus did. But was he fully God? Was he fully human? What about his nature? Did he assume man's fallen nature? Did the divine and human natures mix so as to produce a completely new creature in Jesus?

There were several heresies that sprang up in the Christian community in response to the questions concerning the humanity and divinity of Jesus. These heresies included Gnosticism, Arianism, Apollinarism, and Nestorianism. These wrong teachings had to be dealt with in order for the church worldwide to know and to speak the same truths. These issues were dealt with in church councils in which Church leaders came together to discuss, debate, search the Scriptures, fight, yell, struggle with each other's beliefs, and pray together to come to truth. The early church councils set a precedent for assuring that early Christian Church theology, beliefs, creeds, confessions, and doctrines were all based on scriptural truth. By this, Christians everywhere would all know, believe, and speak the same basic tenets of faith. It was at these councils that Christian "orthodoxy" was established.

Orthodoxy (*Gr. orthodoxia*) is sound or correct doctrine or right believing. The early councils' main goal was to make sure that Christian beliefs and confessions were solidly grounded in truth. The questions concerning Jesus' deity were dealt with in the first ecumenical council in Nicene in A.D. 325. This council confirmed that Jesus was God. That was the orthodox statement of truth.

The Nicene Creed (325 A.D.)
We believe in one God, the Father Almighty, maker of all things visible and invisible. And in one Lord Jesus Christ, the Son of God, begotten of his Father, only begotten, that is, of the substance of the Father.

God of God; Light of light; very God of very God; begotten, not made; being of one substance with the Father, By whom all things were made, both things in heaven and things in the earth:

Who for us men and for our salvation came down, and was incarnate, and was made man: He suffered, and rose again the third day: and ascended into heaven: and shall come again to judge the quick and the dead. And in the Holy Ghost.

Is Holy Spirit Deity?
The Nicene Creed acknowledged that Jesus is God, but they only acknowledged Holy Spirit's existence. They did not acknowledge him as of the same substance as the Father and the Son. They simply said: "And in the Holy Spirit." It was almost like an afterthought as being important, but not yet knowing his position or what to say about him. Remember that the thought of a Godhead or Trinity was new to their thinking processes.

The early church dealt with the question of the deity of Jesus because that had everything to do with whether he was to be worshipped and if he was truly the propitiation for sin. If Jesus is God, he is the final once for all sacrifice for sin, and therefore, they were free from the law. If Jesus is God, then he could indeed bring full redemption and baptize believers in the Holy Spirit. The council said "Yes. He is deity. He is one with the Father."

But what of Holy Spirit? This was another major issue for the Church to deal with. They had confirmed that Jesus was deity, but now the early Church had to deal with questions concerning the Holy Spirit. Many questions had to be answered about Holy Spirit. However the first questions were "Who is Holy Spirit? From whence did he come? Is he God? The early Church struggled with questions concerning the Holy Spirit. These were dealt with at the Nicene-Constantinopolitan Council in 381A.D. They articulated the answers and formed a creed for the church. The council confirmed that Holy Spirit is indeed God; that he proceeds from the Father; and that he is to be worshipped and glorified with the Father and the Son.

The Nicene-Constantinopolitan Creed (381 A.D.)

We believe in one God, the Father Almighty, Maker of heaven and earth, and of all things visible and invisible;

And in one Lord Jesus Christ, the Son of God, the <u>Only-begotten.</u> Begotten of the Father before all ages, Light of Light, Very God of Very God, Begotten, not made; <u>of one essence</u> with the Father, by whom all things were made: Who for us men and for our salvation came down from heaven, and was incarnate of the Holy Spirit and the Virgin Mary, and was made flesh; And was crucified also for us under Pontius Pilate; and suffered and was buried; And the third day He rose again, according *to the Scriptures; And ascended into heaven, and sits at the right hand of the Father; And He shall come again with glory to judge the living and the dead, Whose kingdom shall have no end.*

And we believe in the Holy Spirit the Lord, and Giver of Life, Who <u>proceeds from</u> the Father, Who with the Father and the Son together is worshipped and glorified, who spoke by the Prophets.

And we believe in one holy, Catholic and Apostolic Church. We acknowledge one Baptism for the remission of sins. We look for the Resurrection of the dead, And the Life of the age to come. Amen.

In this council, the concept of the Trinity was clarified and articulated. The Father is God; The Son is God; Holy Spirit is God: Three in One. The orthodox Christian belief declared by this council was that Holy Spirit is God. He is one with the Father and the Son. He is of the same essence.

Essence of God: Father, Son, and Holy Spirit

Essence is the fundamental nature of something apart from which the thing would not be what it is. It is the core of what makes something what it is without being something else. Each person of the Trinity is said to share the same essence---the God essence. The word "essence" communicates immutability and changeless being.

Essence is that which distinguishes one creature from another. A dog is a dog and will ever be a dog. A cat is a cat and will ever be a cat. A human is a human and will ever be a human. Why? Because of that which we call essence. Essence is that which God declared would cause every seed to produce "after its own kind." Humans will always produce humans. Dogs will always produce dogs, etc. Within a species, there is variation, but there can be no cross over to birth and perpetuate something other.

The Trinity: Three in One

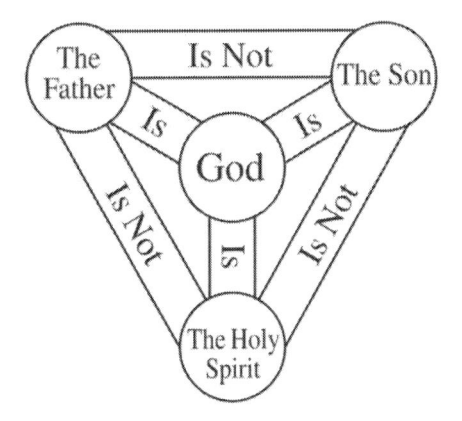

```
         Is Not
  The ───────────── The Son
 Father             
    \   Is    Is   /
     \    God     /
   Is \          / Is
   Not \   Is   / Not
        The Holy
         Spirit
```

After the Nicene and Constantinopolitan Councils, the questions of the deity of Jesus and the Holy Spirit were settled. Both were declared to be God by much evidence and Scripture. How could this be? Is there more than one God? The following discussion is meant to help one understand the concept of Trinity better.

Throughout the Old Testament, God revealed himself to mankind through his names. In other words, God is revealed in the Hebrew Scriptures. Each name reveals a special attribute or aspect of God. There are several "Jehovah" names such as Jehovah-Jireh, and Jehovah Rapha. Also there are several "El" names such as El Shaddai or Elohim. The revelation to man of who God is was given initially through the use of names beginning in Genesis 1:1.

The Hebrew name *Elohim* is used in Genesis 1:1: *"In the beginning God (Elohim)....* *Elohim* is a "uni-plural" noun describing one who stands in covenant relationship ratified by an oath. (Andrew Jukes, *The Names of God*) The very first name of the Creator God revealed unity in plurality and plurality in unity. Elohim is a uni-plural noun that describes God in a way similar to how the word "stalk" describes several bananas joined together as one stalk or several grapes joined together as one "cluster."

The concept that "God is One" is much more than this "stalk" or "cluster" illustration could ever portray, but it gives an idea of the revelation in the word *Elohim* as being "plurality in unity" and "unity in plurality."

The same concept can be seen in an egg. There is the shell, the yoke, and the white. None by itself is "the egg" but each is "egg." Apart each has a name: shell, white, yolk. The shell is egg. The white is egg. The yoke is egg. Yet, none is the whole by itself. In truth each is "egg," but without the composite truth of what makes up an egg, there would be a conflict in calling each part "egg." Each part is not the complete "egg." It takes all three parts to be what is defined as an egg. It is the special attributes or functions of each that contribute to a certain inter-relation and action of each one to the other and to that as a whole which makes an egg, an egg.

Nothing can be added to it and it remain an egg and nothing can be subtracted from it and it remain an egg. Without any one part you do not have an egg. If you do not have the whole together as an egg then there is no definition for any part to be "egg." The white has a relation to the yoke and one to the shell; the yoke has a relation to the shell and the white; and the shell has a relation to the yoke and white. Each is distinct but needs the other to be identified as egg. It is the relation to each other and among them that distinguishes it as an "egg." Remove any part and it would be something else because each element is uniquely what it is. It is that uniqueness that makes the interrelations within an egg uniquely what it is.

Likewise, each person of the Trinity is uniquely who they are. The Father is uniquely the Father. The Son is uniquely the Son. Holy Spirit is uniquely Holy Spirit. Part of their individual uniqueness has to do with each one's roles or that in which each specifically functions. For example, the Son is the Redeemer who became flesh and dwelt among humanity. The Son was given by the Father. Holy Spirit who proceeds from the Father, indwells believers. Their uniqueness defines them individually and their uniqueness also defines their interrelations one with the other. The interrelationship within the Trinity, one to and with the other, is known by the Greek term *perichoresis* or the Latin-derived term of *circumincession*.

We can see that their individual uniqueness determines their inter-relation with one another (*perichoresis*). And this unique inter-relation in the godhead helps determine the composite definition of "God." Although we can see their individual uniqueness in their individual roles, there are also certain shared divine attributes such as omnipotence, omniscience, omnipresence, eternality, holiness, immutability, and infinity. He is almighty, all-powerful, has all wisdom, justice, goodness, etc. Only God possesses these attributes.

In the shared attributes, individual roles, and *perichoresis*, we find the definition of God. The Father is God. The Son is God. Holy Spirit is God. Together they are God. Individually they are God, but they can only be known as "God" individually because of the composite definition of God (i.e. individual roles, *perichoresis*, plus their shared attributes).

Therefore, we can see how the "uniqueness" of each (Father, Son, and Holy Spirit) determines the inter-relationship each one has to and with the other in the godhead (*perichoresis*). As stated, the individual roles, individual and corporate inter-relationships, plus the shared "attributes" determine the composite definition of "God," thus providing the right to call each "God."

These analogies fall so very far short of the reality of the Trinity, but perhaps it helps to form a useful picture of the word. There is no analogy that suffices completely to describe the Trinity, but this gives a visual illustration that we can understand.

The Trinity: God in Three Persons

Only the Father gave his only begotten Son. Only the Son became flesh, dwelt among humanity, and became the propitiation for our sins. Only Holy Spirit came to dwell in mankind to empower them to be restored to the image and likeness of God and to use the breath given by God to humanity to be witnesses of Jesus Christ (Genesis 1:26-28, 2:7; Acts 1:8; Acts 2:4; I Corinthians 3:19).

The Father is God. The Son is God. Holy Spirit is God. How? There is only one God: one divine essence. The essence of God is infinite; therefore, it cannot be subdivided. It cannot be added to, nor subtracted from. There is one God as our "one egg" and "egg" in our example above. It is not just three elements such as the yoke, white, and shell. What makes the three individual egg parts an egg is the inter-relationship of one element to and with the other which is unique and cannot be duplicated with any other element and continue to remain "egg." So too, it is not just that the Father alone, or the Son alone, or the Holy Spirit alone makes each God and all God. It is the inter-relationship and interaction between and among the Godhead that causes us to be able to declare that there is one God and only one God. This *perichoresis* or interworking among and between each in the Godhead is what makes each uniquely God and it is what makes all one God. The Trinity: Three in One.

Each shares the same essence and each is involved together in every creative and redemptive act. They are all distinct; they are all equal. They are the Godhead: three in one. There are "three persons" (i.e. Father, Son, and Holy Spirit) but only one God. Just as if you removed the yoke from an egg, you would not have "an egg." In the same way, if you removed any one of the three persons from the Godhead, you would not have "God." The word "person" describes the three members of the Godhead. A "person" is self-aware, can speak, love, hate, say "you," "yours," "me," "mine," etc. Each of the three persons of the Trinity can do that. They are in absolute harmony consisting of one essence. Whatever one does is not a lone act but is shared by all in harmony and unity. Each has a part, but each part includes all; yet, each has a unique role. The Trinity is indivisible because essence is indivisible. The thing being defined ceases to be what it is when it is broken into its constituent parts because what one part is defines the other parts as a whole.

The Trinity: Eternality: Jesus Christ: In the Beginning

One attribute of God is eternality. That means that there is no beginning and no end. Notice that John 1:1 says *"In the beginning was the Word and the Word was with God and the Word was God."* This is referring to the Son of God as being with God from the beginning and was therefore already God before Genesis 1:1. Jesus became flesh in time and space, but he had always been. He was not created in time. Jesus has always been, but he came to earth as a man in time and space to pay a debt for mankind that mankind could not pay. Jesus paid a debt for mankind that Jesus himself did not owe. Jesus became flesh over 2000 years ago, but he already was the eternal God who "became flesh" (John 1:14 and Galatians 4:4).

The Trinity: Eternality: Holy Spirit: In the Beginning

In Genesis 1:2 we see Holy Spirit's presence as he moved upon the face of the deep. Here we again see "plurality in unity and unity in plurality." Holy Spirit has no beginning nor ending. "In the beginning" Holy Spirit was with God and was God (Genesis 1:2). There is no beginning for God. Genesis records man's beginning, not God's beginning.

In Matthew 3:11-17, we see the eternal Trinity. The Father speaks, Holy Spirit descends, and Jesus receives. Jesus is God's eternal Son. Jesus came "into time" when he became flesh and dwelt among men, but he was not created at any point in eternity past. He assumed flesh in the incarnational virginal birth, but he is the eternal Son of God. He is God. There is only one God in three persons who each and all share eternally and fully in one essence: no beginning and no end.

UNIQUENESS OF EACH PERSON OF THE TRINITY

S. **Father God did NOT come to indwell mankind.** Only the Father has an only begotten Son which he gave to redeem mankind. The Father has given to his Son everything that belongs to him except being Father. Also, it is the Father from whom the Holy Spirit proceeds (John 14:26).

T. **Jesus, the Son of God, did NOT come to indwell man** in the literal sense that Holy Spirit indwells. (1) Only Jesus is the only begotten Son. (2) Only Jesus was made flesh and dwelt among us (Incarnation). (3) Only Jesus came to reveal the Father. (4) Only Jesus came to redeem all mankind (John 1:14, 18). (5) And only Jesus is the only way to God.

U. **Holy Spirit DID come to indwell believers.** Only Holy Spirit came to lead and to draw all mankind to Jesus Christ. He had been "with" man, but now he is "in" all those who receive him. He is the new wine that has been poured out to us, upon us, and in us. Only Holy Spirit leads, teaches, reveals, councils, comforts, convicts, and draws us to the Father God. He develops fruit and gives gifts to the Church to edify, instruct, heal, reveal, and to do what man alone cannot do.

THE TRINITY IN COVENANT

Elohim means "One who stands in covenant relationship ratified by an oath." Genesis 1:1 reveals that God (*Elohim*) was already in covenant <u>before</u> man was even created. "In the beginning, *Elohim*..." In the beginning (before anything was spoken in creation), Elohim was already 'one who stands in covenant relationship ratified by an oath. That is what God (Elohim) is for us today. God was Elohim "in the beginning" before anything else. From this name of God we can see that the Father, Son, and Holy Spirit were already in covenant together <u>before man was created</u> and that this covenant cut in heaven was for mankind's provision and eternal good (Revelation f13:8b)..

The Genesis revelation of God as "Elohim", (i.e. one who stands in covenant relationship ratified by an oath) laid the groundwork for the unfolding of the truth of "the Lamb slain from the foundation of the world" (Revelation 13: 8b) in heaven in the eternal past. The name "God" in Genesis1:1 began the revelation in earth of the covenant cut in heaven by the creator as recorded in Revelation 13:8b. How wonderful it must have been for Adam to call the name of God knowing that each time he said that name he was saying "one who stands in covenant relationship ratified by an oath." This was the eternal heavenly blood covenant which was finalized by the shed blood of Jesus in earth "in the fullness of time."

Revelation 13:8b *says "the lamb slain <u>FROM THE FOUNDATION OF THE WORLD."</u>* (When? Before mankind was even created, this covenant was cut in mankind's behalf).

Ephesians 1:4 says we were chosen in Christ <u>BEFORE THE FOUNDATION OF THE WORLD</u>. When? Before mankind was created, God was in covenant to bring salvation and redemption to humankind should he choose to sin and go away from God. Even before mankind was created, God made a covenant together to redeem us should Adam fall.

I Peter 1:18-20 *Forasmuch as ye know that ye were not redeemed with corruptible things, as silver and gold, from your vain conversation received by tradition from your fathers; but with <u>the precious blood of Christ, as of a lamb</u> without blemish and without spot: who verily was <u>ORDAINED BEFORE THE FOUNDATION OF THE WORLD, but was manifest in these last times for you.</u>*

II Timothy 1:9 *Who hath saved us and called us with a holy calling not according to our works, but according to his own purpose, which <u>was given us in Christ Jesus BEFORE THE WORLD BEGAN.</u>*

As shown in Revelation 13:8b, *Elohim* God--Father, Son, and Holy Spirit--covenanted together in eternity past. God used various names to reveal certain aspects about himself to humanity. The first name God used was *Elohim*. This name reveals that the triune God was in an eternal covenant together before any creative act occurred in Genesis. God was already *Elohim*. He was God in covenant before he created man or any part of the creation. The provision was made in eternity past for redemption of all creation even before God brought order out of chaos and created man to oversee it. God's covenants with men in Genesis revealed this heavenly covenant.

Covenants are about relationship. *Elohim* loves by virtue of relationship which can be seen in covenants God made with man and the *perichoresis* within the godhead. The godhead is plurality in unity and unity in plurality. We see glimpses in the Trinitarian relationship of "unity in plurality" through the mention of Holy

Spirit in Genesis 1:2 where *Elohim* (Father, Son and Holy Spirit) brings order out of chaos. We see glimpses of the unity in plurality again in Genesis 1:26 when *Elohim* said, *"Let US make man in OUR image..."* and also in Genesis 11:7 when God said, *"Let US go down..."* This does not indicate three Gods, but there is definitely God in oneness and unity in which reference is made to plurality.

Through this discussion of the Trinity, we have seen the involvement of the Trinity–Father, Son, and Holy Spirit—in covenant together and in creation of heaven, earth, and all things therein, but the crowning act was the creation of mankind (Ps. 8; Genesis 1:26-28; Genesis 2:7). Mankind was made in the image and likeness of God, and God breathed his own breath into the nostrils of man and man became a living soul. God made nothing else in his image and likeness, nor did he breathe his breath into any other creature causing them to become a living soul. The Trinity was there in creation. The Trinity was aware of the fall of man and the Trinity is revealed in the acts of redemption and empowerment of mankind.

Chapter Two: What Is Man That You Are Mindful of Him?

Introduction

Mankind: Made in God's Image and Likeness, but Not His Essence

What is Man?

God's Breath Became Man's Life

Breath and Words

Humankind: Spirit and Soul and Body

Spirit

Soul

Body

The Disconnect

The Reconnect

Salvation before Holy Spirit Baptism

Subdue and Have Dominion

Before the Fall

After the Fall

Summary

CHAPTER 2
What Is Man That You Are Mindful of Him?

Introduction
In chapter one, we discussed the Trinity, and the fact that Father, Son, and Holy Ghost, were all present in the creation event as revealed in Genesis One. God created the heaven and earth and all that is therein including animal life. Then he created Adam in his own image and likeness and placed him in the Garden of Eden to dress and keep it. He told the first man, Adam, to subdue the earth and have dominion over all creatures. Through Adam, God delegated authority over earth to all mankind.

Mankind Made in God's Image and Likeness, but Not His Essence.
Though man is created in God's image and likeness, and though God's very own breath brought life to mankind's body and soul, humans will never be God (Genesis 1:26-28; 2:7.17). Those who receive Jesus Christ as their Savior by faith are "adopted" by God and are spiritually "born-again" but they remain human. Why?

Because what anything is, is determined by the essence of the perpetuating seed. Essence is the blueprint in the seed.

Essence is the intrinsic or indispensable properties that serve to characterize or identify something. Intrinsic means "of or relating to the essential nature of a thing; inherent." Essence is the intrinsic or inherent unchanging nature of a thing or class of things. It can be said to be the most important ingredient or crucial element. The thing or being is what it is from the core or inside out.

Putting on a costume or mask does not make a human something other than a human. Demons "putting on" or "possessing" a human body does not make demons "human." Jesus did not "put on" flesh; he "became" flesh. He was born of a human (Mary) as a human with a human nature. Jesus was fully man… fully human.

There are male and female humans. Both are human, but each has distinguishing physical and emotional traits. The physical difference is that which is used to identify which gender a human is at birth. Chemicals such as estrogen and testosterone within the body are responsible for development of the distinguishing male/female bodily parts. They also affect and effect the distinguishing emotions.

We are all equal in humanity and we are made in the image and likeness of God, but we are not God or gods. God did not create gods. God created humans to be humans. He created mankind in his own image and likeness but they were created human. He breathed his own breath into mankind, but mankind was still human. He crowned man with glory, but he was still human. When man sinned, he lost the covering of glory, and the image and likeness of God were forever tainted, but he remained human. Because of sin, the glory, image, and likeness were affected, and man's nature was 'at best' tainted and 'at worst' totally depraved, but he remained human. After the fall and in the fullness of time, God provided salvation and redemption for all humanity through Jesus Christ, his only begotten Son. Through Jesus, the image and likeness of God can be restored once again, and the breath God breathed into man can once again be used to declare the good news of Jesus Christ (Romans 10:6-13). Though man has been restored to God; still, he remains human.

According to Genesis 1:26-28, we were created as humans to live in a physical body to subdue and have dominion on earth and over all its creatures. The essence of our humanity does not change when we receive Christ, nor shall it change at any point in the future. In addition, a person does not become God or an angel when he or she dies. When a believer receives a glorified body at the resurrection, it will be a glorified human body just like Jesus had/has after his resurrection (I Timothy 2:5). We shall be like him in his humanity, but we will not be like him in his Deity. We are not innately supernatural as is God. Anything supernatural we do as humans is not through our own abilities as humans, but only through the power of the indwelling Holy Spirit.

WHAT IS MAN?

Genesis 1:26-28 *And God said, let us make man in our image, after our likeness: and let them have dominion over the fish of the sea and over the fowl of the air, and over the cattle, and over all the earth, and over every creeping thing that creepeth upon the earth. (27) So God created man in his own image, in the image of God created he him; male and female created he them. (28) And God blessed them, and God said unto them, be fruitful, and multiply, and replenish the earth, and subdue it: and have dominion over the fish of the sea and over the fowl of the air and over every living thing that moveth upon the earth.*

Genesis 2:7, 17-25. *(7) And the Lord God formed man of the dust of the ground, and breathed into his nostrils the breath of life; and man became a living soul. (16) And the Lord God commanded the man, saying, Of every tree of the garden thou mayest freely eat, (17) but of the tree of the knowledge of good and evil, thou shall not eat of it: for in the day that thou eatest thereof thou shalt surely die. (18) And the Lord God said, It is not good that the man should be alone; I will make him an helpmeet for him. (21) And the Lord God caused a deep sleep to fall upon Adam, and he slept: and he took one of the ribs, and closed up the flesh instead thereof; (22) and the rib, which the Lord had taken from man, made he a woman and brought her unto the man. (23) And Adam said, This is now bone of my bones, and flesh of my flesh and she shall be called Woman because she was taken out of Man. (24) Therefore shall a man leave his father and his mother and shall cleave unto his wife: and they shall be one flesh. (25) And they were both naked, the man and his wife, and were not ashamed.*

Genesis 5:2. *Male and female created he them; and blessed them, and called their name Adam, in the days when they were created.*

Isaiah 42:5 *Thus saith God the Lord, he that created the heavens, and stretched them out; he that spread forth the earth, and that which cometh out of it; he that giveth breath unto the people upon it, and spirit to them that walk therein:*

Psalms 8:4-8 *What is Man, that thou art mindful of him? And the son of man, that thou visitest him? (5) For thou hast made him a little lower than the angels, and hast crowned him with glory and honor. (6) Thou hast made him to have dominion over the works of thy hands; thou hast put all things under his feet: (7) all sheep and oxen, yea, and the beast of the field; (8) the fowl of the air, and the fish of the sea, and whatsoever passeth through the path of the sea. (9) O Lord, our Lord, how excellent is thy name in all of the earth.*

God's Breath Became Man's Life

The Hebrew word *ruach* means "air in motion, wind, breath, spirit." In Scripture, this concept of breath is involved especially in Genesis 2:7 when God "breathed" the breath of life into Adam.

When we speak or make sounds, we form our lips, tongue, and vocal cords in certain fashions to make distinctive sounds, it is then that the breath of life takes the form of words. That's important to understand. When God speaks, his "breath" comes forth full of his life and there you have 'the Word of God' (Matthew 4:4; Isaiah 55:11; John 1:1). The Father breathes forth life and when that breath goes forth, the Word which is spoken "becomes." In Genesis 1, God "says" and it "becomes." "Let there be..." and "There was..."

God speaks words using his own breath, and these spoken expressions or words reveal the mind, thoughts, and desires of God.

Isaiah 55:10-11 *For as the rain cometh down, and the snow from heaven, and returneth not thither, but watereth the earth, and maketh it bring forth and bud, that it may give seed to the sower, and bread to the eater: (11) So shall my word be that goeth forth out of my mouth: it shall not return unto me void, but it shall accomplish that which I please, and it shall prosper in the thing whereto I send it.*

Jeremiah 29:11 *For I know the thoughts that I think toward you, saith the Lord, thoughts of peace, and not of evil, to give you an expected end.*

Breath and Words

God's breath gives life to the images of his thoughts of us by virtue of the zoe life in the breath by which his words are ushered forth (Jeremiah 29:10-14). In John 3, Jesus uses the analogy of the wind blowing and while you cannot see the wind, you do see the results of its movement. He relates this to a person being "born of the Spirit" i.e. being "born again." The Greek New Testament word used for wind in John 3:1-6 is *pneuma* which means "a current of air, breath, or a breeze."

Jesus likened Holy Spirit to wind or movement of air. Breath is the movement of air. Words shaped by the possessor of that breath are formed to reveal the images of their thoughts and desires. Jesus marveled at the centurion's faith which was revealed by his statement of how words had commanding power and were obeyed when uttered. The centurion added, "*Speak the word only and my servant shall be healed.*" He understood how words and faith are connected. Words are moved forward by breath. "*Speak (or breathe) the word only, Lord, and it shall be done*" (Matthew 8:8 with Isaiah 55:10-12).

John 6:63 *It is the spirit that quickeneth; the flesh profits nothing: the words that I speak unto you, they are spirit, and they are life.*

Acts 17:28 ... *in him we live and move and have our being.*

God's words carry within them the clear images of the fullness of the meaning of his thoughts, and by the life, power, and authority of God these invisible images, upon God's verbal command, become visible in the physical realm. When he said "Let there be," there was. God said "Let us make man in our own image and likeness" and God formed man of the dust of the earth THEN he breathed his own breath into that form, and man became a "living" soul in the image and likeness of God. There was no death in the first man, Adam, until he sinned. When sin and death entered into man's spirit, man's body was appointed then to die. This was not by God's will, but by man's choice (Genesis 2:17). Spiritual death brought separation from God's life and that separation from life eventually brought death to the body.

Humankind: Spirit and Soul and Body

Too often, people are not aware that Jesus provided full redemption which includes not only provision for our spirit being born-again, but also provision for our bodies and souls which includes our minds, wills, emotions, and passions. Man is not just spirit, but spirit, soul, and body as can be seen in I Thessalonians 5:23 and Romans 8:11-17. Our whole being of spirit, soul, and body was the creation of God and all was fully redeemed through Jesus Christ. When we accept Christ as our Savior, our spirit is born again and we qualify for full redemption of our soul and body.

First Thessalonians 5:23 *And the very God of peace sanctify you wholly; and I pray God your whole spirit and soul and body be preserved blameless unto the coming of our Lord Jesus Christ.*

Romans 8:11-17 *But if the Spirit of him that raised up Jesus from the dead dwell in you, he that raised up Christ from the dead shall also quicken your mortal bodies by the Spirit that dwelleth in you. (12) Therefore, brethren, we are debtors, not to the flesh, to live after the flesh. (13) For if you live after the flesh you shall die: but if ye, through the Spirit, do mortify the deeds of the body, you shall live. (14) For as many as are led by the Spirit of God, they are the sons of God. (15) For ye have not received the spirit of bondage again to fear; but ye have received the Spirit of adoption, whereby we cry, Abba, Father. (16) The Spirit itself beareth witness with our spirit, that we are the children of God. (17) And if children, then heirs; heirs of God, and joint-heirs with Christ: if so be that we suffer with him, that we may be also glorified together.*

The makeup of man is <u>spirit and soul and body</u> as can be seen from the above Scripture. That is who you are. Your <u>spirit</u> is eternal and connects with the spirit realm and, as a born-again believer in Jesus Christ, fellowships with God. Your <u>soul</u> is eternal. When God created man and breathed his own breath into the nostrils of Adam, he became a <u>living soul</u>. That is who humanity is. Your spirit and soul are as one making you distinctly you. Your <u>soul</u> is your mind, intellect, will, emotions, reason, and passions. This is how we interact with others. There is no one like you. You are unique. Your <u>body</u> is how you interact with the physical world through your five senses. "Flesh" is how your body and soul interact.

In I Thessalonians 5:23, Paul said he prayed that our "whole" spirit, soul, and body be preserved blameless unto the coming of the Lord. "Whole" means complete or all inclusive. Each is separate, but each is a part of the whole without which there would be no "you." God knows we need to be whole. Our spirit and soul and body need to be in unity through total agreement with the Creator's words of instruction for life that we see in the Bible (i.e. the Word of God). God created us and knows exactly what we need to know, believe, say, and do to fulfill God's design for humanity.

SPIRIT

Your spirit is that which touches and communes with the realm of the Spirit. This is that of man's makeup which must be "born again" in order to be reunited with and commune with God. When we believe on and accept by faith, the Lord Jesus Christ as God's only-begotten Son who died for our sins and was resurrected after three days, then we are born-again (Romans 10:8-10). It is a spiritual act in the spirit realm done only by God.

John 3:3 *Jesus answered and said unto him: Verily, verily, I say unto thee, except a man be born again, he cannot see the kingdom of God*

I Peter 1:23 *Being born again, not of corruptible seed, but of incorruptible, by the word of God, which liveth and abideth forever.*

One function of your spirit is to worship and commune with God. Sin separated man from God, but Jesus made a way back to him. Another function of our spirit is to keep our bodies alive. James says, *"As the <u>body without the spirit is dead</u>..."* Your spirit is eternal. It will never not be. You will spend eternity in heaven or in hell. The choice is up to each individual. Both heaven and hell are real. Jesus talked about both of them as being real (Matthew 6:9; Luke 16:15-31; Hebrews 9:27). The choice must be made prior to death because we are told by Paul that after death is the judgment

(Hebrews 9:27). There is no second chance to accept Christ after death. It is a "now or never" choice. When you are born- again God fills your spirit with his life, and the God-given breath can now be used by you to bring life.

According to II Corinthians 5:17, when you are born again, you "become a new creature in Christ Jesus." You become "a new creation" – something that never before existed. "All things are new." You get a new beginning. The past is forgiven and you are cleansed. All things are new. Guilt has no place because your sins are gone; all your sins are washed away. You could say that the old person is gone and you are a brand-new person born again. You have a new beginning.

Soul

Your soul is your mind, will, intellect, reasoning, perceptions, expressions, passions, and emotions. It is all that makes you uniquely you. It is through your soul that your personality is expressed. After your spirit is "born again," then your mind (way of thinking and believing) must be renewed to think and believe as mankind was initially created by God to think and believe (i.e. like God). Until a person is born again, they cannot obey Ephesians 5:1 which says: *Be ye followers of God as dear children.* What this means is that you are to be imitators of God, and in order to do that, your mind, will, emotions, passions, etc. must be retrained to make the choices that bring life and not death. This is the responsibility of the individual <u>after</u> they are born again. God will not "renew your mind" for you, however, he does empower you by the Holy Spirit to do so.

Both your good and bad experiences in life affect your soul (i.e. your mind, will, intellect, reasoning, perceptions, expressions, passions, and emotions). After being born again, healing and deliverance from hurtful memories of the past are available to those who seek it. Some years ago as I was preparing to do an inner healing workshop, God said to me, "Sins must be forgiven, but wounds must be healed." Your wounds do not get forgiven nor did they disappear automatically. Only God can forgive your sins; only God can heal the wounds of the soul. Part of that healing occurs with the renewing of the mind. Jesus said he came to heal the brokenhearted, the bruised, the wounded, and those in bondage.

God wants to make us "whole" spirit, and soul, and body (I Thessalonians 5:23). To be "whole" is to be at peace in your whole being with a peace that passes understanding. To be whole, sins must be forgiven and wounds healed. God forgives the sin and God will heal your wounds. Some healing of wounds comes with the renewing of the mind. But others must be touched by the power and presence of Holy Spirit. Let him heal you.

Romans 12:1-2 I beseech you therefore, brethren, by the mercies of God, that you present your bodies a living sacrifice, holy, acceptable unto God, which is your reasonable service. (2) And be not conformed to this world: but be ye transformed by the <u>renewing of your mind</u>, that you may prove what is that good, and acceptable, and perfect, will of God.

Who does Paul say must renew the mind? You. Not God. The mind is not automatically renewed when you are "born again." Paul was talking to Christians and he said, "YOU (who have already been born-again) present your bodies a living sacrifice. Who is to present it? YOU. Renew your mind. Who is to renew your mind? You. YOU renew your mind. You are to present your body a living sacrifice unto God and you are to renew your mind. These actions are only possible by the power of the Holy Spirit in you, assisting you, leading you, guiding you, and encouraging you.

How do you renew your mind? You begin to diligently pray and read the Bible as never before knowing that therein are words of life and that reading them will feed your spirit. The first step is to read. Soon understanding will come as you renew your mind with the Word. Next, begin to say the words of God out loud to yourself and to others. Then write them on paper and post them all around in your daily environment. Speak the scriptures aloud and declare out loud that you believe the words of God because God does not lie, he is no respecter of persons, and he does not change. Next, do what the word says. Put actions to your faith in God's word of truth.

You can depend on the Word of God being truth because God made a covenant and swore by himself because he could swear by no greater than himself to guarantee the words of the covenant. He said he was a covenant keeper and that he would not break his covenant with man. If God were to break his covenant then he would have to destroy himself. Think about this. In essence, when God said he had sworn by himself he was saying that if he broke covenant, he would have destroyed himself as God by having lied, because *God is not man that he should lie* (Number 23:19). We have the strongest blood covenant guarantee possible. God meant what he said and said what he meant. We can depend on our covenant that is based on better promises than the Old Covenant. We have entered into this eternal blood covenant through Jesus Christ, the

Word, who was born of a woman (i.e. of water); born under the law (Galatians 4:4). Jesus became flesh so he could be our intermediary. He fulfilled the old covenant and instituted a new covenant for mankind. Jesus did for mankind what he could not do for himself.

The eternal blood covenant was cut in heaven in eternity past (Revelation 13 8b), and was then revealed and sealed on earth by the shed blood of the incarnate Son of God who became flesh to pay the price of sin FOR mankind. He who knew no sin, became sin for us. This is not easy to understand, but the Word of God has proven to be true in our lives. The peace that comes to those who know God is proof in itself. Do you know Jesus? Do you have that peace in your soul?

Our minds are created in a way that equips us to be able to appreciate and be fascinated by God's creation which displays his glory. Sad to say, people have become "fascinated by fantasy" (that which is not real or true), and which does not declare God's glory. It is filled with grave danger for those who participate in this fascination in today's society. This is what Jude was referring to.

Jude 1:4-8 *For there are certain men crept in unawares, who were before of old ordained to this condemnation, ungodly men, turning the grace of our God into lasciviousness, and denying the only Lord God, and our Lord Jesus Christ. (5) I will therefore put you in remembrance, though you once knew this, how that the Lord, having saved the people out of the land of Egypt, afterwards destroyed them that believed not. (6) And the angels which kept not their first estate but left their own habitation, he hath reserved in everlasting chains under darkness unto the judgment of the great day. (7) Even as Sodom and Gomorrah and the cities about them in like manner, giving themselves over to fornication, and going after strange flesh, are set forth for an example, suffering the vengeance of eternal fire. (8) Likewise also the filthy dreamers defile the flesh, despise dominion, and speak evil of dignities.*

Body

John 3:3-6 Jesus answered and said unto him, verily, verily, I say unto thee, except a man be born again, he cannot see the kingdom of God. (4) Nicodemus saith unto him, How can a man be born when he is old? Can he enter the second time into his mother's womb, and be born? (5) Jesus answered, Verily, verily, I say unto thee, except a man be born of water and of the Spirit, he cannot enter into the kingdom of God. (6) That which is born of the flesh is flesh; and that which is born of the Spirit is spirit.

Your <u>body</u> is the physical earthly house of your spirit and soul. Only those with a human body have authority in the earth. When man sinned and was separated from spiritual life, his body was doomed to die. When a person departs from their body, they no longer have authority in the earth. Spiritual life must be restored to guarantee resurrection to a new body. God created man for the earth. He was to rule over the earth in a body for and with God.

Since sin entered, man's propensity is toward fulfilling the lust of the eye, lust of the flesh, and the pride of life. These are lived out through the body and soul. The interaction between your body and soul make up what Paul refers to as "flesh." The life of fallen humanity is influenced by strong desires, passions, and emotions of the fallen soul. Wrong decisions and choices are made in the un-renewed mind and lived out through the body.

The body is that which experiences the world through the five senses whether good or bad. Your body can experience sickness and disease or fitness and health. God desires for your body to be in health so that you can be whole: spirit, soul, and body. If one of these elements is not whole, then all cannot be whole. Physical health is part of being whole.

Third John 2 *Beloved, I wish above all things that thou mayest prosper and <u>be in health even as <u>your soul prospers</u></u>.*

Isaiah 53:5 *But he was wounded for our transgressions, he was bruised for our iniquities; the chastisement of our peace was upon him: and <u>with his stripes we are healed</u>.*

Matthew 8:16-17 *When the even was come, they brought unto him many that were possessed with devils: and he cast out the spirits with his word, and <u>healed all that were sick</u>: (17) <u>that it might be fulfilled which was spoken by Esaias (Isaiah) the prophet, saying, Himself took our infirmities and bare our sicknesses.</u>*

First Peter 2:24 *Who his own self bare our sins in his own body on the tree that we, being dead to sin, should live under righteousness: <u>by whose stripes ye were healed</u>.*

The Disconnect

Mankind is the only creature said to have God's breath breathed into them giving them a life superior to all other creatures. Man was given eternal spiritual life that day which gave them eternal physical life. Man was not created to die. That would be a choice that he would make.

God told Adam that he could choose life or death. Death would only come in the day that he disobeyed God. When man sinned, he was instantly cut off from God who is the "source of life." An analogy could be that of how a river would in time dry up if the source of that river was cut off. Because of being cut off from the source of life (i.e. God), man could only live a limited time and limited quality physical (*bios*) life because spiritually he was separated from eternal (*zoe*) life. Man's spirit sustains the body. Because man was separated from spiritual life, eventually his body would die and his spirit would become disembodied. James said that the body without the spirit is dead and a dead spirit cannot keep a physical body alive forever. Humanity was separated from spiritual (*zoe*) eternal life until Jesus came and redeemed us, thereby, giving us a choice to be reconciled to God and to his eternal life.

All humans have breath, have spirit. When man rebelled in the Garden, his spirit was separated from God and therefore, from eternal life. Mankind's spirit, in essence, died. His what? His spirit. To 'die' means to be separated from life. In other words, man, through sin, became the 'walking dead.' They were still breathing air as sentient biological beings (i.e. thinking thoughts, having feelings, emotions, passions, and consciousness). They still had a will and ability to reason and choose, but mankind's spirit was separated from the SOURCE of eternal life and God's holiness. From that time, man had a propensity to choose sin over righteousness (i.e. death over life).

THE RECONNECT
The breath of God breathed into Adam imparted life to him and he became a "living" soul. The creation of man and God breathing life into him is a visual akin to the post-resurrection appearance

of Jesus to his disciples (John 20:21-22). Jesus *"breathed on them"* and said, *"Receive ye the Holy Spirit."* By this, Jesus revealed that the breath/eternal zoe life of God was once again made available in the earth to those who believed on Jesus Christ, the Son of God. Jesus was the fulfillment of all the types, shadows and symbols of redemption in the Old Testament. His breathing on the disciples that day revealed the restoration of eternal life that would be available to all mankind. It had true purpose and significance. Whether one believes this breathing was done symbolically or in reality, it is obvious that his life came through his breath that day just as it did in the Garden of Eden when God breathed his breath into Adam. By this, Jesus revealed that the breath of God/eternal life of God was now available to those who would believe on Jesus Christ, the Son of God. Breathing on the disciples that day was the occasion of the birth of the Church into the earth just as God breathed life into Adam in the Garden.

Salvation before Holy Spirit Baptism

A person must be born again before they are baptized in the Holy Spirit. I Peter 1:23-25 says that believers are born again of the incorruptible seed of the WORD of GOD. We are "born again" of the Word (breathe of God) in a way not unlike Adam initially becoming a living soul when God breathed the breath of life into him, and not unlike Jesus breathing on the disciples. Holy Spirit is referred to as "wind or movement of air" throughout Scripture. What a glorious thought!

Notice that even though Jesus "breathed" on these disciples, still they needed the empowerment of the Holy Spirit to live victoriously and to be witnesses that Jesus Christ is alive today.

When Holy Spirit was poured out into the earth on the day of Pentecost, there was a sound in the upper room that day accompanying his entry. It was the sound as of a rushing mighty wind (Acts 2:2). But the sound of the rushing mighty wind in the upper room did not fill them. The flames as of tongues of fire sat on the head of each, but the tongues of fire did not fill them (Acts 2:3). It was Holy Spirit himself that filled them that day and they spoke in tongues as the Spirit gave them utterance. The sound as of a rushing mighty wind and the cloven tongues of fire were symbols. Holy Spirit was the reality. Holy Spirit is the wind and the fire.

John 3:3-8 *Jesus answered, verily verily I say unto thee, except a man be born of water and of the Spirit, he cannot enter into the kingdom of God. (6) That which is born of the flesh is flesh, and that which is born of the Spirit is spirit. (7) Marvel not that I said unto thee, ye must be born again. (8) The wind bloweth with where it listeth, and thou hearest the sound thereof, but canst not tell whence it cometh, and whither it goeth; so is everyone that is born of the Spirit.*

I Peter 1:23-25 *Being born again, not of corruptible seed, but of incorruptible, by the word of God, which liveth and abideth forever. (24) For all flesh is as grass, and all the glory of man as the flower of grass. The grass withereth, and the flower thereof falleth away. (25) But the word of the Lord endureth forever. And this is the word which by the gospel is preached unto you.*

When Adam sinned, death entered his spirit and he immediately became, spiritually corrupt. The breath God had breathed into him to equip him to subdue, have dominion, and rule over the earth, was now breathed forth out of a dead spirit because his spirit was separated from God who is the source of life. Humankind's thoughts and ways became perverted and were not God's thoughts and ways because he moved from under the influence of God to the influence of Satan (Isaiah 55:8-11).

Man began to use his God-given breathe to corrupt God's creation. We see immediately how sin affected mankind. Soon after the fall, we see in Genesis 4 the first murder. This was a perversion of God's plan for man and all creation. Because God is a just God, he gave Cain every opportunity to make the right choice, but instead he rebelled and killed his brother, Abel.

SUBDUE AND HAVE DOMINION
Genesis 1:26 *And God said, Let us make man in our image, after our likeness: and let them have dominion over the fish of the sea, and over the fowl of the air, and over the cattle, and over all the earth, and over every creeping thing that creeps upon the earth. (27) So God created man in his own image, in the image of God created he him; male and female created he them. (28) And God blessed them, and God said unto them, be fruitful, and multiply, and replenish the earth, and subdue it: and have dominion over the fish of the sea, and over the fowl of the air, and over every living thing that moved upon the earth.*

This is the creation scene of mankind. God told man to subdue the earth and have dominion over all living creatures that moved upon the earth. The word subdue means "to put in its place beneath your feet and keep it in line with its intended purpose." Dominion means "to tread down as a winepress with the feet; to subjugate, rule, and reign. To prevail against." Think on this.

God had given humankind all they needed to have dominion and to subdue the earth. They were given authority to rule in the earth. They were given authority over any enemy. God had told them to "keep the Garden" which means "to hedge about and protect." If God told them to do it, he also equipped them to do it. They would subdue, have dominion, protect and rule by the same principle in the law of words that the centurion knew about and that Jesus confirmed as being a great confession of faith.

Matthew 8:5-10, 13 *When Jesus was entered into Capernaum, there came unto him a centurion, beseeching him, (6) and saying, Lord, my servant lieth at home sick of the palsy, grievously tormented. (7) And Jesus said unto him, I will come and heal him. (8) The centurion answered and said, Lord, I'm not worthy that thou shouldest come under my roof: but speak the word only, and my servant shall be healed. (9) For I am a man under authority, having soldiers under me: and I say to this man, Go, and he goeth; and to another, Come, and he cometh; and to my servant, Do this, and he doeth it. (10) When Jesus heard it, he marveled, and said to them that followed, Verily I say unto you, I have not found so great faith, no, not in Israel. (13) And Jesus said unto the centurion, Go thy way; and as thou hast believed, so be it done unto the, and his servant was healed in the selfsame hour.*

This same spiritual law of words is activated today by the breath and sound of mankind's voice, thus, releasing power and authority through their words. Jesus illustrated that law.

Mark 11:22-23 *And Jesus answering saith unto them, Have faith in God. (23) For verily I say unto you, that whosoever shall say unto this mountain, be thou removed, and be thou cast into the sea; and shall not doubt in his heart, but shall believe that those things which he saith shall come to pass; he shall have whatsoever he saith.*

The "law of the seed" was established in Genesis from the very beginning and 'words' are clearly revealed by Jesus as being "seed" (Mt13:1-23 and Mk 4:14-20). Words (like all seed) produce the blueprint in them. They reveal the desire, intent, power, and authority of the speaker.

Before the Fall

Before the fall, Adam's words were ushered forth by the very breath of God within him untainted by sin and death. That breath resided within a human body, but it was still the creative breath of God. Before sin entered, man was equipped to keep everything in order and to keep everything in line with its intended purpose by the power of his words.

After the Fall

After sin entered, the seed became corrupted and man's thoughts were no longer pure and in line with God's purposes. Death entered on the heels of sin. Since in Adam were all the seed of all humanity to come, Satan now had entry to influence the mind, will, emotions, desires, passions and words of every human being. After the fall, in Adam there was sin and death, and this was passed on throughout all generations giving Satan access to each human born into the earth.

This discussion so far has revealed that man was initially created in the image and likeness of God and had the very breath of God within him with which to rule and reign as God had designed him to do. Then we saw how man rebelled and in that sin, he was separated from God, the very source of his life. Because of that sin, death entered and the image and likeness of God became tainted at best and depraved at worst. While those who accept Jesus Christ have definitely been restored to God and his life, still the effects of death linger in humankind's body and soul and it is *"appointed unto man once to die"* (Hebrews 9:27). But God did not leave us helpless or hopeless. He provided healing of the soul and body through Jesus Christ's full redemption and the indwelling Holy Spirit.

Summary

We can see from this discussion that the makeup of man is spirit, soul, and body. Man was created in God's image and likeness, but fell away from God and was separated from eternal life. When one comes to God, he/she needs a totally new birth of their spirit, renewing of the mind, and health for the body. One's spirit is born-again when he/she accepts Christ. They are born-again spiritually. Spiritual rebirth is a crisis event (i.e. something that happens the very moment we believe and confess Jesus Christ). At that moment, we are born again of the incorruptible seed of the Word of God (I Peter 1:23). This is done only by an act of God based upon one's confession of faith in Jesus Christ. One's soul (of which the mind is integral) must also be renewed to think and reason like God (Romans 12:1-3; II Corinthians 10:5; Isaiah 55:8-9). When we think and reason like God, we will speak and act like God in life's situations. We learn how God thinks and speaks through reading and meditating on his word and through prayer. Our bodies are exposed to death daily through sickness and disease, but God has provided healing and health through Jesus Christ. Opportunity for humankind to be made "whole" is only possible because of the covenant that was cut in heaven by God and revealed on earth when God gave his Son, Jesus, to redeem us. He was resurrected for our justification and ascended to heaven and is seated at the right hand of the Father ever interceding for us.

Romans 8:11 *But if the Spirit of him that raised up Jesus from the dead dwell in you, he that raised up Christ from the dead shall also quicken your mortal bodies by his Spirit that dwelleth in you.*

Chapter Three: From Death to Life

Introduction

The Law of Sin and Death

Penalty for Sin: Three Deaths: "In Dying Thou Shalt Die"

Choose You This Day Whom You Will Serve

Definition of "Life"

Definition of "Death"

Definition of Eternal Life and Eternal Death

The Home of the Spirit Is the Body

The Effect of the Law of Sin and Death on Human Nature

The Power of Forgiveness

Definition of Sin, Trespass, Transgression, and Iniquity

From Life to Death

Man Must Have a Mediator: From Death to Life

Jesus's Resurrection Guarantees Mankind's Resurrection and a New Body

They Died in Faith, but They Needed a Body

Love Fulfills the Law

Death through Adam – Blood Poisoning

The Value of the Blood

Forgiveness and Resurrection

Life through Christ: The "Body" and Christ

Double Ownership: Creation and Redemption

Satan's Plan and Purpose

Disobedience: Man's Sin

CHAPTER 3
From Death to Life

*The thief cometh not, but for to steal, and to kill,
and to destroy: I am come that they might have life,
and that they might have it more abundantly.*

JOHN 10:10

*For the law of the Spirit of life in Christ Jesus hath
made me free from the law of sin and death*

ROMANS 8:2

INTRODUCTION

TO UNDERSTAND WHO HOLY SPIRIT is and the importance of his dwelling in believers, we are laying a solid foundation of his deity and of mankind's creation and fall. Without understanding man's plight after the fall, there is only limited understanding and appreciation of redemption and the need of Holy Spirit baptism. Fallen mankind was doomed to eternal separation from the only source of eternal spiritual life. At death, his spirit was disembodied without hope of ever having a physical body in which to dwell again. The eternal human spirit had the mark of sin and death and could only be held somewhere out of the presence of God.

Without redemption through Jesus Christ, there was no hope for a person once they left their bodies. This chapter will show the plight of fallen man and his journey from death to forgiveness, eternal life, and Holy Spirit indwelling.

Through prophecies, God revealed that in time the Redeemer would come who would pay the penalty of sin and thereby defeat death. But much more, he would defeat Satan who had man's spirit captive because of the law of sin and death. Upon physical death, those who believed the messianic prophecies and trusted in him who was to come, went to Abraham's bosom. Those who refused to believe went to the torment chamber of hell.

When God created man and placed him in the Garden, death was not present. God breathed his own breath into the nostrils of Adam, and Adam became "a living soul" (Genesis 2:7). Adam was to dress and keep the Garden in which God had placed him. The garden was filled with beauty and provision. God then created Eve so that Adam would have a helpmeet to complete him. When God told Adam to keep the Garden, he was in essence telling him to protect and guard it by hedging it about. Having been told that, Adam realized that there was potential trouble because you do not tell someone to protect something or keep it if there is no possibility of any trouble or problems. Adam failed to do that and Satan entered in through the serpent. Through the temptation presented by Satan through the serpent, Eve was deceived and she sinned as did Adam who was with her. Sin opened the door to death. God had warned Adam that disobedience would bring death. Disobedience set the spiritual law of sin and death into motion.

The Law of Sin and Death

Romans 8:1-2 says there is a spiritual law called "the law of sin and death." Whether it be a spiritual or physical law, when something activates its principles, that law goes into effect. Consider gravity which is an ever-working physical law. Even though gravity cannot be seen, you can immediately see the results of the law that rules gravity if you release an object from your hands. Because of the law of gravity the object always falls downward; it will never rise upward. The law of gravity does not change, is no respecter of persons, and it works the same today as it ever has or ever will. You cn count on it.

Gravity is a physical law which operates in the physical world, but it helps us understand the spiritual law of sin and death which operates in the spirit realm. Just as gravity becomes active when its principles are invoked by a dropped object, in the same way, the spiritual "law of sin and death" functions. When sin occurs (an object is dropped), death results (the object always falls downward). Thus, you have the law of sin and death. Where there is sin; there is death. Life will never result from sin any more than a dropped object will rise upward. The penalty or the result of sin will always be death. God did not hide that fact from Adam. The correct choices activate the law of the Spirit of life in Christ Jesus. Wrong choices activate the law of sin and death (Romans 8:2). You are responsible for your choices because you make your own choices. God does not make your choices.

God was very clear that there was a choice to be made and through that choice life or death would result. Adam's choice for death was not only for himself, but for all generations to come because Adam was the fountainhead of all humanity (Romans 5:12-21; Romans 11:32). The seed of all mankind was in the loins of Adam. You and I were in the loins of Adam when he sinned.

Sin corrupted the seed in Adam's loins, and all humanity was declared dead because they would have no access to God (i.e. no access to *zoe* eternal life). Humans would be born into the earth through natural procreation, but death through sin had corrupted Adam's seed, therefore, physical life would be limited and in time their bodies would die. Upon physical death, the spirit of man is disembodied. Sin may be enjoyed for a season, but there is a payday. The wages of sin is death (Romans 6:23).

Humankind has free will. We are not puppets. We can choose and we do. God is not responsible for our choices, but he tells us what to choose in order to live life to the fullest. God told Adam to choose life. He told him that he must not eat of the tree of the knowledge of good and evil because if he did, he would die. He did. He died.

PENALTY FOR SIN: THREE DEATHS: "IN DYING THOU SHALT DIE"

Genesis 2:17 *But of the tree of the knowledge of good and evil, thou shalt not eat of it: for in the day that thou eatest thereof thou shalt surely die.*

Choose You This Day Whom You Will Serve

Man was created with a free will. He was not a puppet. He was created with the ability to make his own decisions and choices: whether good or bad. God had given them a choice between life and death. He told them the day that they ate of the tree of the knowledge of good and evil, they would die. They clearly understood his instructions and all the implications because God is a just God and will not judge unjustly. That day in the Garden, Adam and Eve believed the lies of Satan and of their own free will, chose to sin. On the heels of sin came death. God said in the day they chose to rebel against him in disobedience, they would die. They would not die because God killed them. They would die because they chose to do what they knew would separate them from the eternal (*zoe*) life of God. They chose to disobey God. In essence, they chose to die.

It was a human, Adam, who chose to sin and open the door to death. Therefore, a man himself must pay the penalty. In Genesis 2:17, God told Adam and Eve that "in the day" they ate of the fruit of the tree of the knowledge of good and evil, they would surely die. This could read, *"in dying thou shalt die."* The word "surely" emphasizes the fact of death as being an absolute imminent truth. God withheld no information from Adam concerning the result of rebellion. Adam ate, the penalty went into effect. Man died. Although Adam and Eve did not drop down dead physically the very moment they partook of the fruit of the tree of the knowledge of good and evil, they did immediately die spiritually and that spiritual death sentence was for eternity because no fallen man could redeem himself.

Spiritual death (i.e. separation from God and *zoe* life) resulted in death for the total man: spirit and soul and body. Physical death is a picture of what it is to be spiritually dead. When one is dead physically, he or she is separated from life. Without *zoe* (eternal) life, there is limited sentient life to sustain the soul and body. A person's physical (*bios*) and soulical life (*psuche*) are sustained by their spirit wherein dwells either life or death.

When sin entered, it entered into the spirit of man. Spiritual death brought physical death. Upon physical death, the spirit becomes disembodied. In other words, a person's eternal personal spirit does not remain in his or her dead body. Where the spirit goes for eternity after leaving the body depends on the life or absence of life therein. Before Jesus came, restoration of spiritual life was not possible. Before Christ died for mankind's sin, the departed eternal spirits of all humans either went to the peaceful chamber of Abraham's bosom or to the torment chamber of hell. Those in Abraham's bosom had believed the word of God concerning the Redeemer who was prophesied to come. They had hope of deliverance through the coming Redeemer. Those in the torment chamber of hell as seen in Luke 16 had no hope. The decision for where one will spend eternity is made while residing in the physical body. After death is the judgment (Hebrews 9:27).

Luke 16:19-31. *(19) There was a certain rich man, which was clothed in purple and fine linen, and fared sumptuously every day: (20) And there was a certain beggar named Lazarus, which was laid at his gate, full of sores, (21) And desiring to be fed with the crumbs which fell from the rich man's table: moreover the dogs came and licked his sores. (22) And it came to pass, that the beggar died, and was carried by the angels into Abraham's bosom: the rich man also died, and was buried; (23) And in hell he lifted up his eyes, being in torments, and seeth Abraham afar off, and Lazarus in his bosom. (24) And he cried and said, Father Abraham, have mercy on me, and send Lazarus that he may dip the tip of his finger in water, and cool my tongue; for I am tormented in this flame. (25) But Abraham said, Son, remember that thou in thy lifetime receivedst thy good things, and likewise Lazarus evil things: but now he is comforted, and thou art tormented. (26) And besides all this, between us and you there is a great gulf fixed: so that they which would pass from hence to you cannot; neither can they pass to us, that [would come] from thence. (27) Then he said, I pray thee therefore, Father, that thou wouldest send him to my father's house: (28) For I have five brethren; that he may testify unto them, lest they also come into this place of torment. (29) Abraham saith unto him, They have Moses and the prophets; let them hear them. (30) And he said, Nay, father Abraham: but if one went unto them from the dead, they will repent. (31) And he said unto him, If they hear not Moses and the prophets, neither will they be persuaded, though one rose from the dead.*

DEFINITION OF "LIFE"

In the New Testament, there are three different Greek words with three distinct meanings which are translated by the one English word "life." This one English word does not reflect the various distinctions expressed by those three Greek words. The Greek words are: *bios, psuche,* and *zoe. Bios* refers to the life of the physical body and it is where we get the word biology. *Psuche* refers to the psychological life of the human soul which includes the mind, will, and emotions. From this Greek word, we get our English word psychology. *Zoe* refers to the uncreated, eternal life of God. It speaks of the divine life uniquely possessed by God.

We know that Adam and Eve had the *zoe* life of God within them because God said that only if they ate of the tree of the knowledge of good and evil would they die. Only by their willful sin would the door be opened to death. Zoe life cannot be held or overcome by death; it must be forfeited. Adam knowingly and willingly forfeited this life (I Timothy 2:14).

DEFINITION OF "DEATH"

Death is "separation from life" whether it be physical or spiritual life. James said that *"the body (bios) without the spirit (pneuma) is dead."* (James 2:26). The *bios* (body) life and *pneuma* (soulical, mind, will, and emotions) life are sustained by *zoe* (eternal) life. Where there is no *eternal uncreated zoe* life of God, there is limited and eventually no *pneuma* or *bios* life.

If only physical (*bios*) death was the penalty for sin, then man could pay his own penalty simply by living and then dying physically. If only spiritual death (man's spirit separated from the *zoe* life of God while in the body) was the penalty, they could have lived out their lives spiritually dead; thus paying the penalty of spiritual death (i.e. separated from life in their spirit while in the body). Then having paid the penalty, their spirit would have been released back to the presence of God where they would have received the eternal *zoe* life of God again. However, when Adam sinned, the penalty could not be paid by simply being separated from God for a period of time. The actual cause of death had to be dealt with. The cause of death was sin. It was sin that separated man from God. Death was simply the result. Sin was and is the problem. Adam not only gave up eternal life, but in its place, through sin, he then received eternal death into himself. Eternal death came as a result of sin. Therefore, sin had to be dealt with in order to defeat eternal death.

Sin separated man from his creator and sustainer of life with no way to make things right with him. Man was incapable of paying the penalty of death and ever living again because sin separated him eternally from the only source of life. Spiritual death brought physical death with no hope of resurrection and a new body. The physical body returns to the dust when it dies. Separation from the body means that the person is eternally separated from the place for which he was created, namely, in his body on earth. Unless sin was dealt with, the door to death would perpetually be open and upon physical death the spirits of all mankind would eternally be separated from God, their bodies, and from earth for which they were created. Jesus came to die in man's stead, once for all, thus dealing with sin through providing forgiveness, eternal life, and an immortal body.

Definition of Eternal Life and Eternal Death

Eternity or eternal life or death is more than just an unlimited progression of years. A common New Testament word for "eternal" is *aionios* which carries with it the idea of quality as well as quantity. Eternal life functions beyond time, as well as, in it. A good example is the story of the rich man and Lazarus in Luke 16 where we see a visual of "eternal life" and "eternal death." Both deal with forever, but they both also deal with the conditions of that existence. One is in torment. The other is in comfort.

Though eternal death speaks of death in a time frame, it is more than just length of time. In it there is no quality of life for time-everlasting. Eternal death speaks of torment, horror, lack, and no good thing forever and ever time without end.

On the other hand, eternal life not only speaks of life in a time frame, but also, high quality of life for time-everlasting. This life speaks of bliss, joy, peace, provision, and all things good forever and ever time without end.

The penalty was not just physical or spiritual separation from God while in a body on earth. The penalty of sin was to be separated from eternal life even after physical death, therefore, man's spirit would be existing eternally separated from God and his body with no hope. The penalty for sin was <u>death and separation from eternal life for all mankind because all humanity was counted under sin. There was no way for any man to redeem himself and live again. That meant all would be forever eternally separated from the *zoe* life of God with no access to it.</u> Because humans are eternal spirits, they would forever be in existence. In other words, they would never not be.

Eternal death is the result of the presence of sin and absence of any possibility of reconnecting to the *zoe* life of God. That was the position in which fallen man was found: ETERNAL separation from God who is the only source of *zoe* life. After physical death, sinful man would be ETERNALLY separated from God having no access to *zoe* life. If man has no access to the eternal spiritual life of God while still residing in the body, then the spirit of man is dead eternally once his spirit leaves his body. Eternal death cannot stand in the presence of God. Through Adam's sin, all mankind was eternally dead. The only hope was in the Redeemer who would provide forgiveness for sin.

Sin is a spiritual matter. Death entered man's spirit through sin and had a trickle-down effect. Spiritual death caused physical death. Mankind would remain in his fallen state forever because he could never finish paying the penalty and live again. The debt could not be ignored, it must be paid. Sin had to be eradicated once and for all.

When sin entered, mankind became separated from the uncreated, eternal *zoe* life of God. Where there is no life, death reigns. Where there is death, there is no quality of life. The first man, Adam, made the decision for all humanity as to whether to retain or forfeit this gift of eternal (*zoe*) life from God. God is the only source of *zoe* life and therefore, only God can give this eternal life. This is the right and privilege of God. Receiving eternal life again was contingent upon the penalty of sin being paid. The penalty for sin could only be paid through forgiveness.

Forgiveness came when Jesus died for all mankind and undid what Adam had done. We are saved by grace through faith. Through Jesus Christ, God offered redemption to all humanity so that we may be reconnected or rejoined to the only source of eternal life. When the reconnection to God is made by faith in Jesus Christ, eternal *zoe* life flows to the believer. Jesus reversed the curse of death which was upon us being made a curse for us.

Galatians 3:13 *Christ hath redeemed us from the curse of the law, being made a curse for us: for it is written, cursed is everyone that hang up on a tree.*

John 1:4 *In him was life (zoe) and the life (zoe) was the light of men.*

John 10:10 *The thief cometh not but for to steal, kill, and to destroy;* <u>*I am come that they might have life (zoe)*</u> *and that they might have it more abundantly*

The Home of the Spirit Is the Body

Mankind's spirit was created to live and thrive on earth in a human body forever. Each person's personal spirit's dwelling place is in a body. However, sin limited the years a physical body would live and sustain a human spirit because on the heels of sin, came spiritual and therefore physical death. Sin separates mankind's spirit from his body because it opens the door to death.

Your spirit will never not be. You will always be. Your spirit will either have eternal life or eternal death in it. You choose. Sin brought death to the physical body, therefore, provision must be made for where your spirit will spend eternity once it leaves your body. The provision must be made while resident in your body. You choose. You decide.

After physical death, your eternal spirit is without a body in which to dwell on earth. While the body is alive, each person makes their own personal decision as to where they will release their spirits when they die. As revealed in the story of the rich man and Lazarus in Luke 16, before Jesus redeemed humanity through his death and resurrection, disembodied spirits either went to Abraham's bosom or to the torment chamber of hell.

Since Jesus has come, if we trust in him as our Savior while we are living, we receive eternal life into ourselves then upon physical death, our spirits are released to spend eternity with God. If one does not trust in Jesus, eternal death reigns through sin. Then upon physical death, the spirits of unbelievers are released from their bodies to spend eternity in hell and torment with Satan. God sends no one to hell. Each person makes their own decision about eternity. Where will you spend eternity?

The Effect of the Law of Sin and Death on Human Nature

Human nature is distinct from the nature of animals and all other creatures. Humans reason on a higher plane which enables us to reflect on our own human nature, as well as, the nature of God, and to derive knowledge of God's will for his creation.

Human nature is the fundamental disposition and traits of humans. Human nature includes the capacity to create, reason, love, and experience a wide range of emotions. It is a unique creation that in some ways reflect the Creator. <u>It is that which makes us distinctly human.</u> While man's nature is distinctly human, initially, man's human nature was in some ways like God's nature. Humans were created in God's image and likeness; therefore, man has some understanding of God and his vast, complex design.

After the fall in the Garden of Eden, human nature "fell away" from and was separated from God and has since been inclined towards sin being influenced by Satan and the flesh through the lust of the eyes (*bios*), lust of the flesh (*psuche*), and pride of life (elevation of self above God I John 2:16). Humans' fallen nature with its propensity to sin in word, thoughts, and deeds can only be changed by the power of God. This is done when we believe and submit ourselves to Jesus Christ as our Lord and Savior. Our spirit is then "born again" by the Word of God (John 3:3-8; I Peter 1:23). We then have access to the nature of God.

Second Peter 1:4 *Whereby are given unto us exceeding great and precious promises: that by these you might be <u>partakers of the divine nature</u>, having escaped the corruption that is in the world through lust.*

When Adam fell away from the life of God, human nature no longer reflected the image and likeness of God, nor was the God-given breath used to glorify God in the earth. Mankind's fallen human nature can only be changed when the eternal *zoe* life of God once again flows in his/her spirit. How does one get from eternal death to eternal life? The answer is forgiveness for sin.

The Power of Forgiveness

Forgiveness means to release from the sin (offense) committed and to not demand repayment. Sin is the enemy that opened the door to death. Death reigned through Adam, but thanks be to God that a provision of forgiveness was made through the covenant cut in heaven as seen in Revelation 13:8b. That covenant was revealed in the earth through Jesus Christ who provided for total forgiveness and eradication of mankind's sin. Now whosoever will may choose heaven as their eternal destination. Choose life. Choose Jesus Christ. Jesus not only forgives, but he also blots out the death sentence that was against us.

Through forgiveness and remission of sins, Christ blotted out the "handwriting of ordinances" that was against us.

Colossians 2:14 *Blotting out the handwriting of ordinances that were against us, which were contrary to us, and took it out of the way, nailing it to his cross.*

Today this "handwriting of ordinances" would be a formal written order of a death sentence issued after the evidence against the accused criminal had been examined. All were guilty and deserving of death, and a death warrant was rightfully issued because mankind had sinned thereby transgressing God's spiritual law.

Romans 5:17-21 *For if by one man's offense death reigned by one; much more they which receive abundance of grace and of the gift of righteousness shall reign in life by one, Christ Jesus. (18) Therefore as by the offense of one, judgment came upon all men to condemnation; even so by the righteousness of one, the free gift came upon all men unto justification of life. (19) For as by one man's disobedience many were made sinners, so by the obedience of one shall many be made righteous. (20) Moreover the law entered, that the offence might abound. But where sin abounded, grace did much more abound: (21) that as sin hath reigned unto death, even so might grace reign through righteousness unto eternal life by Jesus Christ our Lord.*

I Corinthians 15:57 *But thanks be to God, which giveth us the victory through our Lord Jesus Christ.*

Matthew 26:28 *For this is my blood of the New Testament, which is shed for many for the remission of sins.*

I John 3:4 *Whosoever committed sin transgresseth also the law: for sin is the transgression of the law.*

Definition of Sin, Trespass Transgression, and Iniquity

<u>Sin</u> means "to miss the mark." It can refer to doing something against God or against a person or doing the opposite of what is right. It can mean doing something that will have negative results or failing to do something you know is right. James said that to

know to do good and to not do it is sin. Sin is a general term for anything that falls short of the glory of God. Man's fallen nature causes him to have a propensity to sin. If it is not kept in check, it continues on a downward spiral.

To trespass may be intentional or unintentional. It means "to fall away after being close beside." It means to cross the line or climb across a fence where you are not supposed to go.

Transgression refers to presumptuous sin. It means to choose to intentionally disobey. It is willful trespassing. When a person knowingly runs a stop sign, tells a lie, or blatantly disregards authority, they are transgressing.

Iniquity is more deeply rooted. It refers to a premeditated choice; to commit iniquity is to continue without repentance. God forgives all types of sin when we repent. However, iniquity left unchecked leads to a state of willful sin with no fear of God. Continued iniquity leads to unnatural affections, which produces a reprobate mind. Romans 1:28-32 outlines this digression in vivid detail.

All these types are lumped under the word "sin." Sin is the transgression of the law. Man sinned and was in the grips of death because of sin. He was dead without access to life. Mankind needed a Redeemer who could reconcile and restore connection to *zoe* life. To do this, the penalty or sentence of the death penalty must be paid and the curse must be reversed. When Jesus came to earth, his main mission was as Redeemer. Adam had disobeyed God and had brought death into the earth. Now death would pass on to all generations because man could not save himself. Death was in the seed from whence all mankind would be born. Man could die but he could not raise himself from the dead because sin had been entered into willingly and knowingly by Adam. Sin held him captive to death. Only through forgiveness of sin could man live again.

Through Adam, all humanity was separated from God who is the only source of eternal *(i.e. zoe)* life. To ever live again, mankind must be forgiven and redeemed. There was no human born of the seed of Adam who could give life again because mankind had no life for himself nor life to give others. Only God, the possessor and giver of eternal *zoe* life, could do that. God himself must redeem mankind because only in and through God can *zoe* life be given.

Forgiveness and the uncreated eternal zoe life of God is the only antidote to sin and death.

Only the Redeemer could provide that antidote for the total man: spirit and soul and body. This antidote is applied by the impartation of eternal *(zoe)* life to the spirit of man. *Zoe* life is received through Jesus Christ.

Galatians 3:13 says we were redeemed from the curse of the law because Jesus was made a curse for us. What were we redeemed from? We were redeemed from the law of sin and death because the curse of the law was death.

Genesis 2:17 *But of the tree of the knowledge of good and evil, thou shall not eat of it: for in the day that thou eatest thereof thou shalt surely die.*

Ephesians 4:7-10 (7) *But unto every one of us is given grace according to the measure of the gift of Christ. (8) Wherefore he saith, When he <u>ascended up on high</u>, he <u>led</u> <u>captivity captive</u>, and gave gifts unto men. (9) (Now that he ascended, what is it but that he <u>also descended first into the lower parts of the earth</u>? (10) He that descended is the same also that ascended up far above all heavens, that he might fill all things.)*

Colossians 2:13-15 says *"And you, being dead in your sins and the circumcision of your flesh, hath he quickened together with him, <u>having forgiven you all trespasses</u>; Blotting out the handwriting of ordinances that was against us, which was contrary to us, and took it out of the way, nailing it to the cross; And having spoiled principalities and powers he made a show of them openly triumphing over them in it.*

Acts 3:19 *Repent ye therefore, and be converted, <u>that your sins may be blotted out</u>, when the times of refreshing shall come from the presence of the Lord.*

First John 1:9 *If we confess our sins, he is faithful and just <u>to forgive us our sins</u>, and to <u>cleanse us</u> from all unrighteousness.*

First John 2:1-2 *My little children, these things write I unto you, that ye sin not. For if any man sin, we have an advocate with the Father, Christ Jesus the righteous: (2) and he is the propitiation for our sins: and not for ours only, but also for the sins of the whole world.*

Ephesians 1:7 *In whom we have redemption through his blood, <u>the forgiveness of sins</u>, according to the riches of his grace.*

Ephesians 4:32 *And be ye kind one to another, tenderhearted, <u>forgiving one another</u>, even as God for Christ's sake <u>hath forgiven you</u>.*

From Life to Death

When sin entered through the disobedience of Adam and Eve in the garden, death resulted. Adam and Eve knew the result of eating of the fruit of the tree of the knowledge of good and evil. It was the only tree of which God forbade them to partake. They were surrounded by beauty and provision of every kind. There was no lack. However, they chose to disobey God and the consequence resulted. They had been well informed by God that in the day they partook of that particular tree, they would die. They knew exactly what that meant because God does not judge us on things of which he has not informed us. It could not have been any clearer. They understood. They knowingly partook. They died. When they sinned, the penalty of death occurred. Spiritual death took place. They instantly knew that they had been separated from their source of life. What a horrible moment for them and all mankind.

When God came to walk with them in the cool of the day, Adam told him that they were hiding because they were naked. The glory with which God had clothed them was gone.

Psalms 8:4-5 *What is Man, that thou art mindful of him? and the son of man, that thou visited him? (5) For thou hast made him a little lower than the angels (Elohim), and <u>hast crowned him with glory and honor.</u>*

After disobeying God, and receiving the result of sin (death) they were separated from the eternal uncreated zoe life of God.

The plan for redemption was revealed to Adam and Eve by God right there in the Garden. They learned that in time the Redeemer would come (Genesis 3:15, 21). He would die and defeat their enemy, Satan. Man could not save himself from death. A Redeemer was needed who could reconcile God and man.

God instituted animal sacrifices as a visual – a type – to impress upon man the horror of separation from not only physical life but eternal life. These animal sacrifices could never redeem or reconcile anyone to God or make *zoe* life available to mankind. Sin separated God for man. Job recognized the seriousness of the situation. An animal could not mediate between God and man. Only one who was equal to both could mediate between God and man.

Man Must Have a Mediator: From Death to Life

A mediator is a reconciler. It is one who can understand and satisfy justice. It is the one who is concerned with and for both parties.

Job 9:33 *Neither is there any <u>daysman</u> betwixt us, that might <u>lay his hands upon us both</u>.*

The New Living Translation says it this way: "*If only there was <u>a mediator</u> between us, someone <u>who can bring us together</u>.*"

There needed to be a mediator between God and man because sin had separated the two. A mediator has to be qualified and accepted by both parties. God accepted Jesus as the mediator and then send him to earth to "become flesh" and be fully man so as to offer himself as man's mediator.

The mediator for man (the offender) must be able to satisfy the demands of the one offended (i.e. the Creator). Man was guilty and all men were counted as sinners because of Adam's disobedience. The penalty for sin was death. Sin and death cannot stand in the presence of God. Since all men were guilty and unable to pay the penalty, there was no hope of reconciliation without a mediator. A mediator could bring peace between God and man. Isaiah 53 says the chastisement of our peace was upon the Redeemer. The word chastisement means the correction of our peace. Jesus is our peacemaker.

God sent his Son to be the mediator on earth. He would be the perfect Lamb of God that would satisfy justice. The lamb would take away the sins of the world. Justice would be done. Jesus was/is accepted by God as the payment for sin. Because Jesus was sinless, he could not only die for mankind, but he could rise again with an immortal body; thereby, guaranteeing that those who accept Jesus as their Redeemer, Mediator, and High Priest would likewise rise again and receive a new and immortal body. The question became, "Will mankind receive Jesus as their Mediator Redeemer?"

Jesus's Resurrection Guarantees Mankind's Resurrection and a New Body

Resurrection is a crucial part of redemption because any sinful man could die, but no sinful man could physically rise again with an immortal body until sin was dealt with and until the Redeemer became the firstfruits of the resurrection and a new body. The physical resurrection of Jesus as "first fruits" guarantees those who trust in Jesus Christ a new immortal body untouched by sin and death (I Corinthians 15:20; Romans 8:10; Ephesians 3:17; I John 4:4; I Thessalonians 4:13-18).

Humanity needed a Redeemer who would be resurrected in an immortal body to guarantee us eternal life in an immortal body. It was by Holy Spirit that God raised Jesus from the dead and it will be by the same Holy Spirit that believers will be raised from the dead to receive a new body in which to dwell eternally.

Romans 8:11 *But if the Spirit of him that raised up Jesus from the dead dwell in you, he that raised up Christ from the dead shall also quicken your mortal bodies by his Spirit that dwelleth in you.*

It was crucial that Jesus pay the debt as our substitute because if our sins were not forgiven we would live forever separated from God and would never again have a body in which to live. Jesus not only provided eternal life for our spirits, but he also provided for us to have an eternal immortal body in which we will dwell forever. Man was created to live in a body. We know that Jesus's work on earth as the Son of Man and mediator was accepted by God because when the work was finished, God glorified him (Acts 3:13). Mankind knew that God had accepted the sacrifice because Holy Spirit was poured out in the earth (Acts 2:1-4). Jesus said this outpouring would occur after he was glorified (John 7:37-39). Jesus was glorified when his precious blood which had been shed for man's sin was sprinkled on the mercy seat in heaven (Hebrews 9 below).

God accepted Jesus as the sacrifice and the mediator. Now, the decision lies with mankind. The question became, "Will man except Jesus as his mediator and Redeemer?"

John 3:16 *For God so loved the world, that he gave his only begotten Son that whosoever believeth in him should not perish but have everlasting life.*

In the fullness of time, the Redeemer came to earth born of a virgin, born under the law (Galatians 4:4). He lived without sin thereby defeating sin and death. He died and rose again and he is alive forevermore. He ever lives to make intercession for us as our High Priest. He is still our High Priest mediator. Jesus made the way for all mankind to have eternal life. Because of his death for the sins of man and his resurrection for our justification, we can go from death to life by accepting the terms of the way to God which is through faith in Jesus Christ. This can occur because God approved of the mediator and has forgiven mankind through Jesus Christ. "…by his own blood he (Jesus) entered in once into the holy place having obtained eternal redemption for us" Therefore, by accepting Jesus Christ as our Savior, the way to life is restored to our spirit, and upon physical death we can now enter eternally into the presence of Almighty God, and one day we will have a new immortal body (I Thessalonians 4:13-17).

Hebrews 9:11-28 *(11) But Christ being come an high priest of good things to come, by a greater and more perfect tabernacle, not made with hands, that is to say, not of this building;(12) Neither by the blood of goats and calves, but <u>by his own blood he entered in once into the holy place, having obtained eternal redemption for us.</u> (13) For if the blood of bulls and of goats, and the ashes of an heifer sprinkling the unclean,* *sanctifieth to the purifying of the flesh:(14) How much more shall the <u>blood of Christ, who through the eternal Spirit offered himself without spot to God</u>, purge your conscience from dead works to serve the living God? (15) And for this cause he is the mediator of the New Testament that by means of death, for the redemption of the transgressions that were under the first testament, they which are called might receive the promise of eternal inheritance. (16) For where a testament is, there must also of necessity be the death of the testator. (17) For a testament is of force after men are dead: otherwise it is of no strength at all while the testator liveth. (18) Whereupon neither the first testament was dedicated without blood. (19) For when Moses had spoken every precept to all the people according to the law, he took the blood of calves and of goats, with water, and scarlet wool, and hyssop, and sprinkled both the book, and all the people, (20) Saying, This is the blood of the testament which God hath enjoined unto you. (21) Moreover he sprinkled with blood both the tabernacle, and all the vessels of the ministry. (22) And almost all things are by the law purged with blood; and without shedding of blood is no remission. (23)<u> It was therefore necessary that the **patterns** of things in the heavens should be purified with these; but the heavenly things themselves with better sacrifices than these.</u> (24) For Christ is not entered into the <u>holy places made with hands, which are the figures of the true</u>; but into heaven itself, now to appear in the presence of God for us: (25) Nor yet that he should offer himself often, as the high priest entereth into the holy place every year with blood of others; (26) For then must he often have suffered since the foundation of the world: but now once in the end of the world hath he appeared to put away sin by the sacrifice of himself. (27) And as it is appointed unto men once to die, but after this the judgment: (28) So Christ was once offered to bear the sins of many; and unto them that look for him shall he appear the second time without sin unto salvation.*

They Died in Faith, but They Needed a Body

Hebrews 11:13 *These all died in faith, not having received the promises, but <u>having seen them afar off, and were persuaded of them, and embraced them, and confessed</u> that they were strangers and pilgrims on the earth.*

Ephesians 4:8 *Wherefore he saith, when he ascended up on high, <u>he led captivity captive</u>, and gave gifts unto men.*

Who were these captives? The list of those who died in faith not having yet received the promises are listed in Hebrews 11:1-12. Those whom he "led captivity captive" were those named here plus all others who believed on the Redeemer who was yet to come. Before Jesus came, reconciliation had not been made between God and man. Therefore, after death, those who died in faith remained in Abraham's bosom (i.e. Paradise) until the time that Christ would be manifested in the earth and finish the work of redemption. When Jesus came, died, and descended into hell, he rescued them and presented them to God as first fruits. They had been held as captives in Abraham's bosom (Luke 16) not being able to stand in the presence of God until the blood of Jesus had been sprinkled on the mercy seat in the temple in Heaven. (Hebrews 9:11-28).

Luke 16:20-31 above tells the story of the rich man and Lazarus and shows the plight of those believers dying in faith before the Redeemer, Jesus Christ, had provided a way back into the presence of God. Until the finished work of Jesus Christ here on earth as the supreme sacrifice, those who died in faith believing in the coming Messiah were held in captivity in the bosom of Abraham. However, from the time that the penalty was paid by Jesus and his blood sprinkled on the mercy seat in heaven, those who die in faith in the Messiah immediately enter into the presence of God redeemed, cleansed, and justified.

Prior to the shedding of the blood of Jesus it was a dark picture compared to life after the sealing of the covenant with the blood of Jesus. His blood sealed the covenant in the last act of sprinkling it on the mercy seat in heaven. Prior to this, even those who had died believing in the coming Messiah/Redeemer could not stand in the presence of God.

Before Jesus came, died, was resurrected, and ascended no one was born-again; none yet had God's uncreated eternal zoe life restored to them. Therefore, they were held away from and out of God's presence until Jesus could come and redeem them. He finalized that redemption when *"He entered in once into the holy place,"* and sprinkled His blood on the mercy seat in Heaven (Hebrews 9:11-25). Now, upon death, believers go directly to heaven.

II Corinthians 5:6-8 tells us: *(6) Therefore [we are] always confident, knowing that, whilst we are at home in the body, we are absent from the Lord: (7) (For we walk by faith, not by sight) (8) We are confident, [I say], and willing rather <u>to be absent from the body, and to be present with the Lord.</u>*

Today, if one is dead in trespasses and sin when he/she dies, like the rich man in the story of Lazarus in Luke 16: 19-31, they go directly to hell eternally separated from God because they refused the only way to escape eternal damnation—Jesus Christ.

I Corinthians 15:55-56 says *"O death where is thy sting? O grave, where is thy victory? The sting of death is sin: and the strength of sin is the law."*

The sting of death is sin: No sin, no sting. No sting, no death. The strength of sin is the law. No law, no strength for sin. Jesus Christ, the Son of Man, had no sin in Him and he fulfilled the law through agape love.

Hebrews 4:15 *"For we have not an high priest which cannot be touched with the feelings of our infirmities; but was in all points tempted like as [we are, yet] without sin."*

Love Fulfills the Law

The <u>sting of death is sin</u> according to II Corinthians 15:56 and the <u>strength of sin is the law</u>. The law condemns one to death if they do not keep all of it, BUT it cannot change or renew or empower the spirit of man to keep the law. The law is unable to justify man before God, but Jesus fulfilled the law. How? The same way he told us to fulfill the Law which is by love.

Think on this. Jesus dealt with sin by fulfilling the law through love and shedding his own blood for our sins.

Romans 13:8-10 *Owe no man anything, but to love one another: <u>for he that loveth another hath fulfilled the law.</u> (9) For this, Thou shall* *not commit adultery, Thou shall not kill, Thou shall not steal, Thou shall not bear false witness, Thou shall not covet; and if there be any other commandment, it is briefly comprehended in this saying, namely, Thou shall love thy neighbor as thyself. (10) Love worketh no ill to his neighbor: therefore love is the fulfilling of the law.*

Galatians 5:13-14 *For, brethren, ye have been called unto liberty; only use not liberty for an occasion to the flesh, but by love serve one another. (14) For all the law is fulfilled in one word, even in this; thou shall love thy neighbor as thyself.*

Galatians 6:2 *Bear ye one another's burdens, and so fulfill the law of Christ.*

Jesus died as a representative of mankind. He qualified as humanity's representative and substitute because he was fully human just as was Adam. He was son of man, and he lived under the law without sin. Since there was no sin, there was no sting of death so Satan had no authority to hold Jesus in hell (Acts 2:24). Through love Jesus fulfilled the law of God. Jesus had eternal life in himself because he had no sin. Through love, Jesus did not sin.

The Old Testament speaks of mankind's Redeemer being none other than God Himself, but justice demanded that only a man could atone for a man's rebellious act. But how could he die for sinful man if he was God? The incarnation was the answer. Through the incarnational birth, he became flesh. He became man. He BECAME sin who knew no sin, (II Corinthians 5:21), but he did not sin himself. He was our precious innocent Passover lamb and substitute. Because he was sinless, Peter said it was impossible for

Jesus to be held in hell by death (Acts 2:24). Death only enters and has authority to enter where sin is present. No sin equals no death. Jesus laid his life down of his own accord. It was not, (indeed, it could not be), taken from him because he had no sin.

John 10:17-18 *Therefore doth my Father love me, because I lay down my life, that I might take it again. (18) <u>No man taketh it from me</u>, but I lay it down of myself. I have power to lay it down, and I have power to take it again. This commandment have I received from my Father*

DEATH THROUGH ADAM-- BLOOD POISONING

Even though man was fallen, still his blood has the highest quality of life in it of all creation. The life given to satisfy justice must be a quality of life equal to or greater than that which was lost. The life in the blood of sacrificial animals was not eternal nor life-giving. It merely "atoned" or "covered" the sin. It could not eradicate sin. The value of the blood is equal to the quality of life in it. A life-giver must possess life and be the source of it to give it away to anyone. Jesus is a life-giver because he is the source of life (I Corinthians 15:45). The blood of Jesus is "precious" blood. Only one man had life in his blood and could give his life so that ALL humanity could be forgiven. That One man is Jesus – fully God – fully man – with no confusion between the two natures (Chalcedonian Definition).

THE VALUE OF THE BLOOD

Leviticus 17:11 <u>*For the life of the flesh is in the blood: and I have given it to you upon the altar to make an atonement for your souls: for it is the blood that maketh an atonement for the soul.*</u>

<u>The value of the blood is equal to the quality of life that is in it.</u> For instance, you think nothing of stepping on bugs or killing mosquitoes, and it is very sad to run over a cat or dog. But it is devastating to hear of the death of a human. Why? The value of the blood is equal to the quality of life that is in it. The quality of life in man's blood is the highest quality of all creatures because God's breath of life flows through mankind. No bull, no goat, no sheep, no animals' blood is equal to or greater than the life in man's blood; therefore, they could not redeem man once for all. Justice required the same or greater quality of life than that forfeited in the Garden of Eden by Adam and Eve.

<u>The life of the flesh is in the blood and I have given it to you upon the altar to make an atonement for your souls: for it is the blood that maketh an atonement for the soul.</u> (Leviticus 17:11).

Only the life in man's blood could totally satisfy and fulfill the penalty of death. Only a man born into earth like all others would qualify to die for mankind's wrong doing because it was man who sinned; man whose life was forfeited. (Genesis 3:15; John 10:1-18). How could a man die for himself or for others since every human born on earth was of the seed of Adam, and thereby, the law of sin and death was passed on to every generation? Every man's blood carried death in it after the fall. Every man's spirit was separated from the eternal life of God. Mankind was doomed and without hope. But God had a plan from eternity.

Remember Rev.13:8b "... *the lamb slain from the foundation of the world.*"

Ephesians 1:4 says that humanity was chosen in him from the foundation of the world. (Hebrews 1; 2) When the covenant was cut in heaven as depicted in Revelation 13:8b, even before mankind was created, humanity was already chosen for redemption should he fall. Forgiveness of sin and a new immortal body was the answer.

Forgiveness and Resurrection

The only hope of forgiveness, resurrection, and a new body was for one who had no sin in himself to die as a substitute. If there was no sin in him then life was present and death had no way of holding him neither legally nor vitally because life cannot be held by death any more than darkness can overcome light. "No sin" means there is life present. Sin chosen over righteousness brings death. Righteousness chosen over sin brings life. Jesus was sinless because he chose life and righteousness.

In the Old Testament, God made provision for forgiveness and the covering of man's sin by blood sacrifices. These animal sacrifices for sin had to be made year after year after year. Until the Redeemer came, year after year after year the blood of bulls, goats, and lambs had to be sprinkled on the mercy seat in the temple because death was the penalty for Adam's sin in the garden. When God saw the blood he "passed over." He accepted the substitute.

In the New Testament, the Son of God is revealed as the Lamb of God who takes away the sins of the world through dying in fallen man's place. He died, but because he had no sin, he rose again thus providing the way for man to be resurrected with a new immortal body. This was sealed when he ascended to heaven and as our high priest, sprinkled his blood on the mercy seat in heaven.

Hebrews 9:23-26 *It was therefore necessary that <u>the patterns of the things in heaven</u> should be purified with these; <u>but the heavenly things themselves with better sacrifices than these</u> (24) For <u>Christ is not entered into the holy places made with hands, which are the figures of the true; but into heaven itself,</u> now to appear in the presence of God for us: (25)Nor yet that he should offer himself often, as the high priest entereth into the holy place every year with blood of others; (26) for then must he often have suffered since the foundation of the world: <u>but now once in the end of the world hath he appeared to put away sin by the sacrifice of himself.</u>*

LIFE THROUGH CHRIST: THE "BODY" AND CHRIST

Satan understood the law of the seed and the law of sin and death. He knew if he could cause the first man, Adam, to sin in disobedience to God that there would be no way for man to save himself. Satan knew that all future generations of humanity would come from the loins of Adam and if Adam was fallen then all future generations of humanity would be born with a fallen nature and under the law of sin and death. Satan knew that God was a just God and does not lie. God told Adam that if he ate of the fruit of the tree of the knowledge of good and evil, he would die. Therefore, the seed in and of Adam would be contaminated (Genesis 1:26-28; Genesis 2:7, 15-17). But God is never caught by surprise.

Double Ownership: Creation and Redemption

#1. Primary Ownership by Creation

Who created the earth? Genesis 1:1 tells us that God did. If you create something out of nothing, it belongs to you. Psalms 24:1 says "The earth is the Lord's and the fullness thereof." It is his.

God created Earth. Then he took the dust of the earth and formed man. Man's body is of the earth that God created, but it was an immobile, unthinking, non-talking, non-reasoning, non-feeling, non-passionate lump of dirt. Then God did something grand. God gave man life--his own uncreated eternal life--by breathing his own breath into that lifeless form. Man became a living, mobile, thinking, talking, reasoning, feeling, passionate being made in God's image and likeness. Man belongs to God by right of creation. The earth is the Lord's and mankind is the Lord's by creation. God gave man authority over earth and ability to subdue it and have dominion. God had that right to give authority by virtue of ownership.

Satan was not created for earth. But he was created. He was created an angel, a cherub (Ezekiel 28:14). He is not a god of any sort. He was created by God. He does not have a physical body, therefore he has no authority on earth except via a human's body. God gave Adam authority to rule in the earth...not Satan This authority is perpetuated through procreation. Only humans have bodies and; thereby, they have authority in earth. Man was created in the image and likeness of the Creator. Satan was not made in the image and likeness of God nor was he given an earthly body; therefore, he has no authority on earth.

However, Adam and Eve submitted themselves to Satan through disobedience to God. By disobedience, they were separated from God who is the source of life. They were dead spiritually, soulically, and eventually physically with no way to ever finish paying the penalty. Sin brought the penalty of "eternal" death to man because sin can never stand in the presence of God or receive eternal life. That meant they would be eternally separated from life. Sin made the way for eternal death to enter (Romans 5:12).

After the fall, all humans produced through Adam and Eve and all succeeding generations would have the law of sin and death working in them. They had sentient life, but not spiritual eternal life. Sentient life is limited by time. Because fallen humans had no *zoe* (uncreated, eternal) life of God in themselves, there was no way to pay the penalty and ever live again. Sin had to be dealt with in order to stop death. Sin required forgiveness.

Through one man, Adam, all mankind was doomed. Satan knew that God was just and would not lie. God said that if man ate of the fruit of the tree, he would die: therefore, mankind would die. The real problem was not in dying, because all men were doomed to die after sin entered. <u>The real problem was that after physical death all mankind was separated from God and was not able to be resurrected and have another body in which to live.</u>

Humankind was created with design and purpose. Mankind's true and intended place is in a body where they can subdue and have dominion over the earth as God designed them. On earth, man is superior in authority to anything that does not have a human body. Satan knew that if he could get man to sin, that sin would eventually kill the body. Once man is disembodied, he has no more authority in the earth. Only a person with a body has rights and authority in the earth. No body equals no rights or authority in earth. Those inalienable rights of which our Constitution speaks were recognized by those who framed the document as being rights given to man by God, not by man. We have the right to life, liberty, and the pursuit of happiness. You have certain authority in the earth by virtue of being human, but once you die physically, you have no rights on earth because you have no body. A body is necessary to claim rights. Satan does not have a body of his own, so he walks about as a roaring lion seeking whom he may devour. He knows if he can disembody a human, they will not only lose their rights on planet earth, but they have no power to rise up again and have a new body.

#2. Ownership by Redemption

Mankind was doomed, because once he stepped out of his own body in death, he had no way to ever live again; to ever have a body again in which to execute his purpose and design on earth. Dying was not the problem. The problem was being eternally separated from life and never again having a body in which to live. Until sin was dealt with even if man received another body. That body would also die because of sin and the cycle would go on and on. <u>Mankind would be the walking dead.</u>

Satan thought he had it all figured out. God is just. God said if man ate of the tree, he would die. If man died in sin, he would be eternally separated from his earthly body and the life of God. No human 'body' meant no right, authority, or ability to function on earth. Before Christ's coming as Redeemer of mankind, even if a person died believing in the coming Redeemer, they could not enter into God's presence until the penalty for the offense was paid because they had the marks of sin in their spirit. In addition, they could never attain to a new body. Man's spirit is eternal. It will exist somewhere eternally. After sin entered, man's earthly body was separated from life and upon death his spirit would no longer have an earthly dwelling.

Sin's penalty had to be paid so forgiveness could be given. Forgiveness brings restoration of life. Forgiveness can only be giv-en by the one who has been offended. Forgiveness means to stop being angry and to not demand payment for the wrong done. The one who commits the sin is the one who must pay the debt unless a former agreement has been made as to one who would pay the debt as a substitute for the offender. The Lamb of God would be man's substitute. Jesus Christ was declared to be the Lamb of God who qualified as mankind's substitute and Redeemer (Revelation 13: 8b; Revelation 5:6 -14; John 1:36).

Man sinned on earth in rebellion to God, and man was responsible to pay a penalty he could never finish paying. That is why Jesus had to come as man. God would be unjust and a liar if he came as God and paid man's penalty. Because all mankind was guilty and all had sin in themselves, no one qualified to die for themselves, much less all humanity and take up his life again. Death has the right to hold the sinner until sin is dealt with. How was man to ever live again? Only God himself could save fallen mankind.

Satan's Plan and Purpose

Satan knew that if he could get Adam to sin then there would be no possibility of redemption by humankind because a spiritually dead man could not redeem himself much less be the Redeemer of all mankind. The sin in the Garden placed all humanity under the law of sin and death and separation from God. There would be no man of the lineage of Adam left without sin and death. Therefore, the penalty could not be paid. Satan knew it would be required for man to pay his own death penalty. In Satan's mind Adam's disobedience to God would be the end of mankind, and he would be victorious over God. Satan would be the ruler of earth and all humankind through the law of sin and death. The authority God had given Adam to subdue and have dominion in the earth, would be used by Satan through and against fallen man (Genesis 1:26-28).

Satan assumed authority when Adam submitted to him. Satan would rule through man, but not for man's benefit. He would rule through the lust of the eye, the lust of the flesh, and the pride of life (I John 2:16). We see this in Genesis 3 where Eve was tempted when she <u>saw</u> that the fruit was good to eat. If she had turned away at that moment the problem would have been solved. But she continued to look until her <u>desire</u> had grown and at this point her flesh (including her senses, the images in her mind, and her emotions) became involved. Even though it would have been harder, had she turned away at that time, she could still have saved the day. But she did not, and as a result, her desire grew until she believed the lies of Satan. At this point, she believed that God was a liar at worst or at least she believed that he would not keep his word and allow her to die even if she disobeyed him and ate of the fruit.

This was <u>the pride of life</u>. When she was convinced of the lie, she took the fruit and ate it in disobedience, and gave to her husband who was with her who took it and ate also. When this occurred, it was the signal that they had turned their allegiance from God to God's enemy, Satan. Satan usurped the authority on earth and used it to rule and reign over humanity and all creation through lies and fear.

There was no hope for them until God gave them the substitutionary blood of an animal right there in the Garden. However, the blood of an animal did not fix the eternal problem after a person's death. The blood of an animal was of lesser value than the blood of a human because the value of the blood is equal to the quality of life that is in it. Man's blood carried within it the highest of all life superior to all created beings. Therefore the lesser quality of life in the blood of an animal could not pay the required debt that would allow the person to live in God's presence after physical death. Even though a person might, by faith, have chosen God's way of animal sacrifices to cover his sins temporarily, he still could not enter into the presence of God after physical death. His sin had been only covered and not yet eradicated (Colossians 2:14). Therefore, after death all believers on the coming redeemer were held in a place called Abraham's Bosom (Luke 16:19-31) until the time of Jesus's death whose blood not only covered man's sin, but totally eradicated it so that man could stand justified in the presence of God.

Adam represented all humanity in his disobedience, so would it be possible for another man, another Adam, to represent all humanity through his obedience? The answer is yes. But there was a problem. There was no man who was sinless who could die for sinful man. No fallen man could save himself much less save the human race because ALL had sinned and come short of the glory of God. But God had a redemption plan: a plan that included God identifying with man and becoming fully man and walking on earth as fully human and not as God. Though it would be God who would become fully human (would become fully flesh) yet, he would not walk as God on earth. He would be the second Adam. He would be the last Adam. He would come to redeem humanity himself. But how could this be? How could God redeem man if the debt had to be paid by a man? God had a plan. That plan was the incarnational birth of God's only begotten Son.

The <u>incarnational birth</u> of Jesus was the chosen means used by God to fulfill his promise of redemption even from the time of man's fall (Genesis 3:15). (Also see Hebrews 2:1-8). To understand Christ's role in humankind's redemption fully one must look at the incarnation and understand its importance in redemption. God came to save man, but not as God. John 1:14 says God "became flesh." This is the key to man's redemption. God did not break the covenant, man did. Therefore man must pay his own debt of sin. Jesus had to have a physical body. His body, like all humans, was the dwelling place of his spirit. Jesus was like mankind in every way.

Philippians 2:5-7 teaches that Jesus laid aside those attributes that are possessed only by God, and he walked as fully and truly man on earth.

Disobedience: Man's Sin

The declaration in Genesis 2:17 was that "man" would die if "man" sinned. Man sinned and man died "in the day" he ate of the fruit. It was not that the fruit was poisoned in a literal sense, but their sin of disobedience was a covenant-breaking act that opened the door to death. Humankind was separated from the source of his life through sin. Upon the heels of sin, came death. Death reigned through sin. All humans were fallen, therefore, no man could die for himself and live again much less could he die for others. Only the covenant partner – God – could save him. But God is a just God. He does not lie. He does not change. God had said, "You shall surely die" – therefore, man must surely die if God is just, honest, and never changes. Disobedience to the blood covenant was the sin. God was the covenant partner and so it was God that was sinned against.

Because of the sin of disobedience, man died – was separated from life. In the day he disobeyed God in the Garden and ate of the fruit in rebellion to God's warning (Genesis 2:17), he died. This rebellious act of disobedience in essence revealed that Adam and Eve believed that God was withholding something from them that they could get by eating of the forbidden fruit of the tree of knowledge of good and evil. But man was wrong. He was dead wrong.

Through Adam, humanity died that day and was without hope. After disobeying God, Adam could not save himself. He needed one like himself in every way to be his Savior. God had the answer: God, the covenant partner, himself would come to earth and become flesh to save humankind. As the covenant partner he had that right. He did not 'become LIKE" flesh. He became flesh and all that we as humans are in every aspect of our being even to our fallen human nature. If he left anything out then that which he did not assume of fallen humanity, he did not redeem. In essence this says that human nature has been redeemed because it has been united with divinity, through the union of the two in Christ. (Cappadocian Father, Gregory of Nazianzus, and Irenaeus of Lyons).

The Adamic covenant was broken by Adam in the Garden of Eden and because all future generations were in his loins, spiritual death passed on to all humanity (Romans 5:12-21).

Adam (as a human), fell (as a human) and was separated from God who is the only source of life. Without God there is no life. As a result of the defiant disobedience, death reigned in Adam and all future generations. However, Jesus became flesh and because he was sinless and obedient to the covenant, life remained in him. He was not separated from life because he did not sin. Because there was no sin in Jesus, there was no guilt. Because there was no guilt, there was no death. Because there was no death, there was life. Because there was life, Jesus could not be held by death. Satan had not planned on the incarnation and substitutionary death of Jesus Christ.

First Corinthians 2:7-8 *But we speak the wisdom of God in a mystery, even the hidden wisdom, which God ordained before the world unto our glory: (8) which none of the princes of this world knew: for had they known it, they would not have crucified the Lord of glory.*

Acts 2:24 *(Jesus) whom God hath raised up, having loosed the pains of death: because it was not possible that he should be holden of it (death).*

Jesus did not deal with the symptom (death) but with the cause (sin). He did this as mankind's substitute. Jesus defeated death when he defeated sin because sin is the cause of death.

Eternal life is made available by faith in the finished work of Jesus Christ to whosoever will. It is offered to all, but forced on none. When one chooses Jesus as Savior, he or she enters into the eternal covenant with God through his only begotten Son. We rely on Jesus because of his vicarious death, burial, and resurrection. He did in the flesh what no other man could do – he redeemed us and made us partakers of the nature of God (II Peter 1:4) through our faith in his finished work.

One outstanding thing we see in Romans 5:1-11 is that man can choose his destiny by receiving Christ and his finished work, or he may choose to remain in his fallen state. Unlike Adam, through Jesus, God offers everyone a choice. He sets before each person life and death, and encourages each as he did Joshua to "choose life" (Deuteronomy 30:19).

The very first step in accepting Christ as Savior by faith is to know who he is and what he did to provide a salvation of peace for all. Jesus is God's only begotten Son who became flesh and dwelt among us. He was fully God; yet fully man, but he laid aside the privileges of deity when he became flesh and walked as man on planet Earth so as to identify fully and totally with humanity. His full humanity was lived out in total obedience to God and the resulting sinlessness qualified him to be the propitiation for fallen man (I John 2:2; 4:10). In other words, Jesus Christ became our substitute and assumed our obligations; thereby, clearing us of guilt by the vicarious punishment which he endured (Hebrews

2:17 "reconciliation" in the KJV could/should be "propitiation" as in the NAS version as well as other translations). The point is that the incarnational birth provided the way for Jesus to be born into the earth and to live and to die as fully human to pay humanity's penalty.

Through obedience to God, personal sin is conquered in our personal lives. Jesus overcame sin and provided forgiveness for all mankind through his shed blood on the cross. He is our Passover Lamb. God has forgiven us and has given us eternal life. This eternal life is not based on good work. However, when we sin there is a consequence that results. But that sin or consequence cannot separate us from God if we repent.

If a person claims to believe on Jesus as his or her personal Savior, but there is no change in them and they continue to sin habitually, I would advise them to examine their first works (I John 3:9). If there is no commitment to obey God, there is doubt that the relationship is even there. Each one must answer for themselves. I'm not referring to works as making a person perfect, I am speaking of desiring to please God and obeying him in right living. Where there is a true relationship, there is no desire to bring pain to the other person by doing the opposite of what that person desires. God's desires for his children will only bring life and not death into their lives. We are blessed when we walk in obedience to God. We have life in us through Jesus Christ and life cannot be held by death.

In Acts 2:24, Peter said it was not possible for Jesus to be held by death. Life cannot be held by death. Life was in Jesus through his sinlessness, when he paid the penalty for mankind's sin therefore, he took up his life again. These things were all accomplished because the incarnational birth of God's only begotten Son, Jesus Christ.

The incarnation brought Jesus from heaven to earth to live fully and truly as a human. It was the first step in the earthly manifestation of the covenant cut by God (Elohim) in heaven. Revelation 13:8b. "...the lamb slain from the foundation of the world." God himself would redeem mankind.

Chapter Four: God Himself Would Come to Save Humanity

Introduction

Mankind's Redeemer Must Have a Body

Only God Could Save Humanity

Christ Emptied Himself to Become Flesh

Seed of Woman Manifested in Earth: The Incarnational Birth of Jesus Christ

What is Incarnation?

Holy Spirit in the Incarnation

The Holy Ghost Shall Come upon Thee

The Power of the Highest Shall Overshadow Thee

What Does "Flesh" Mean?

Why Jesus Came

Thy Will Be Done on Earth As It Is in Heaven

Immanuel: God with Us

God's Will in Heaven Revealed in Earth

There Was Never a Time When Christ Was Not

One Spirit: Same Spirit

Death, Hell, and the Grave

The Holy Spirit of Resurrection

Christ's Life, Death, and Resurrection Revealed God's Will in Heaven

God Must Become Flesh

Adam Broke the Law, but Jesus Fulfilled the Law

Jesus, Lamb of God

Jesus, Baptizer in Holy Spirit

CHAPTER 4
God Himself Would Come to Save Humanity

Introduction

Because of sin, humanity was totally separated from God and from uncreated eternal (*zoe*) life and therefore, there was no way for his body to be sustained eternally. When the body dies, the spirit of man no longer has a house in which to dwell on earth. Because of sin, no one had the right or power to rise up from the dead and assume a new body. Without a body, one has no presence or authority on earth. Without life, one is eternally separated from God (i.e. separated from the source of life). Things were hopeless. Man needed a Redeemer to restore him to God and life.

Mankind's Redeemer Must Have a Body

Before Christ came, the departed spirits descended directly to either Abraham's bosom or to hell and torment. Since man could not save himself because of the law of sin and death, God himself would have to come as man and die for man as his substitute. To pay mankind's penalty of death, he must lower himself and become one with man. To redeem mankind, God must become flesh, live, and die in a flesh and blood body without sin.

From the beginning, God delegated the authority in the earth to man and did not take it back when man fell. Humans still have the authority in the earth to subdue and have dominion. Because authority was given to humanity, God himself must also become flesh (i.e. become human) and live as all humans live in a physical body in a physical world in order to have the right to exercise man's God-given authority to subdue and have dominion. God gave humans authority to rule over earth and to keep any enemies out. A human has a spirit, soul, and body. Therefore, only those who have a spirit, soul, and body have the right to exercise authority here.

Jesus came to earth as man and paid the penalty for sin as a representative of all humanity; therefore, we can live again by receiving his life, death, and resurrection by faith as substitutionary. Jesus was our representative who brought us life through obedi-ence just as Adam had been our representative and brought us death through his disobedience. Jesus undid what Adam had done. This is called recapitulation (to undo) (Romans 5:17; I Corinthians 15:20-22, 45).

Ephesians 1:4 says humanity was chosen in Christ before the foundation of the world. This is confirmed in Hebrews 2 where it clearly declares that Jesus did not come to redeem angels (including Lucifer who chose to rebel against God). He chose to redeem mankind. Adam did not give his seed an opportunity to make their own individual choice. Jesus came to redeem mankind as a whole and to allow each to choose life or death.

Each time we receive the elements of communion (i.e. bread and wine or juice), we celebrate the body and life of Christ. We celebrate his physical life, death, burial, and resurrection. We celebrate because, as believers, we will never be left without a body again. Because he lives, so too, we live. God wants your body to be healthy and able. He wants you to live a full life. A full life is a high- quality life which is filled with health, safety, provision, and peace.

He took the stripes on his physical body which represents to us that our physical healing has been purchased. The horrible beatings Jesus endured is a visual to remind us that sin has a price and through Christ, we have the right to be healed physically. We have that right through Jesus and we have the power to enforce that right through Holy Spirit. We receive healing by faith just as we receive salvation through Christ by faith, and in the same way, by faith, we receive Holy Spirit baptism.

Sin and sickness does not have any authority (right) nor power (might) to reign in you anymore because of what was done by Jesus Christ, the baby born in a manger. This is *Immanuel*, God with us. O Come let Us Adore Him who defeated sin and sickness and made a way for us to live a victorious and healthy life. We will receive a new body in which to rule and reign with Christ eternally. The Spirit of God dwells in you and ministers healing and health to your body now. Your body is the temple of the Holy Ghost!

Through Jesus Christ, we have been restored to the place God intended us to be. As children of God, we have access to the Holy Ghost power to keep sin and sickness away because Jesus came in the flesh to provide a way back to God. Joy To the World The

Lord Has Come, Let Earth Receive Her King. He gave us Holy Spirit power to overcome sin, sickness and eternal death.

First Corinthians 6:19-20 *What? Know ye not that your body is a temple of the Holy Ghost which is in you, which you have of God, and <u>you are not your own</u>? (20) For you are <u>bought with a price therefore glorify God in your body, and in your spirit, which are God's.</u>*

First Peter 1:18-19 *Forasmuch as you know that you were not redeemed with corruptible things, as silver and gold, from your vain conversation received by tradition from your fathers; (19) but <u>with the precious blood of Christ, as of a lamb without blemish and without spot.</u>*

Only God Could Save Humanity

Several Old Testament Scriptures confirm that because God knew mankind could not save himself, that he, himself, would come to redeem mankind. Once a person understands Revelation 13:8b, then it does not surprise them to read the Old Testament Scriptures revealing the Savior of mankind as being God himself. Revelation 13:8b will be addressed in detail later in this book.

<u>Psalms 49:7</u>, *<u>No man can by any means redeem his brother, or give to God a ransom for him.</u>*

<u>Isaiah 9:6-7</u>, *<u>For unto us a child is born, unto us a son is given</u>: and the government shall be upon his shoulder: and his name shall be called Wonderful, Counselor, <u>The mighty God, The everlasting Father</u>, The Prince of Peace. (7) Of the increase of his government and peace there shall be no end, upon the throne of David, and upon his kingdom,*

to order it, and to establish it with judgment and from henceforth even forever. The zeal of the Lord of hosts shall perform this.

Isaiah 43:11, <u>I, even I, am the Lord: and beside me there is no savior.</u>

Isaiah 45:21, *Tell ye, and bring them near: yea, let them take counsel together: who hath declared this from ancient time? Who hath told it from that time? Have not I the Lord?* <u>And there is no God else beside me; a just God and a Savior; there is none beside me.</u>

Isaiah 59:15-16 *Yea, truth faileth, and he that departeth from evil maketh himself a prey: and the Lord saw it, and it displeased him that there was no judgment. (16) And he saw that there was no man, and wondered that there was no intercessor:* <u>therefore his arm brought salvation; and his righteousness, it sustained him.</u>

Hosea 13:4 *Yet I have been the Lord your God since the land of Egypt; and you were not to know any god except me,* <u>for there is no savior besides me.</u>

Christ Emptied Himself to Become Flesh

The question then arises as to how God himself could come to earth as the Redeemer since the Redeemer must be a human like all humanity?

Philippians 2:5-8 *Let this mind be in you, which was also in Christ Jesus. (6) Who* <u>being in the form of God</u>, *thought it not robbery to be equal with God. (7) But* **made himself of no reputation**, *and* <u>took upon him the form of a servant</u>, *and* <u>was made in the likeness of men.</u>

(8) And being found in fashion as a man, he humbled himself, and became obedient unto death, even the death of the cross.

The phrase "made himself of no reputation" could be translated "emptied or stripped himself." Of what did he empty or strip himself?

(1) Glory (John 17:5).
(2) Independent authority. Though equal with the Father, he became uniquely submissive to him (John 5:30).
(3) Laid aside his divine attributes, and was instead anointed by the Holy Spirit as a man (Acts 10:38).
(4) At a crucial moment he gave up intimate fellowship with his Father (Matthew 27:46).

Thus it was that God's only begotten Son "became flesh" (John 1:14). He was the Incarnate Son of God.

> David W. Dorries stated that "The purpose of the Incarnation was to redeem Adam's fallen race. The flesh that had become corrupted and alienated from God had to be cleansed from its sin and reconciled with God. This redemptive motive led the Son of God to leave His place of majesty and glory in heaven and descend to earth to take to Himself the lowly flesh of Adam. This kenosis (self-emptying) of His deity was not an abdication of His divine nature, but rather a self-limitation to live within the boundaries of finite humanity." (David W. Dorries, Ph.D. Spirit-Filled Christology (San Diego: Aventine Press, 2006), 108).

In a paper on the Incarnation, concerning the phrase "Made himself of no reputation" (*Kenosis*) Dr. Donna Walker stated:

"He voluntarily put aside his glory with the Father in order to become like us. We cannot fully understand the cost of the cross without understanding the cost of the incarnation, the magnitude of what Jesus left, and his willingness to totally humble himself to the Father's will."

SEED OF WOMAN MANIFESTED IN EARTH: THE INCARNATIONAL BIRTH OF JESUS CHRIST

God would use woman to bring the Redeemer into Earth, and as a result, Satan would hate all women. The fact that God said there was to be a "seed of woman" who would defeat Satan brought into the equation a mystery because a woman produces an egg, not seed (sperm). This prophey was another glimpse into the unfolding eternal covenant. The Lamb of God would be born of a woman.

This was a mystery, but the mystery began to be unfolded when God said to Isaiah, *"Therefore the Lord himself shall give you a sign: behold, a virgin shall conceive, and bear a son, and shall call his name Immanuel."* (Isaiah 7:14)

How could there be a "seed of woman?" How could a virgin give birth? The answer is because this virgin would not conceive naturally, but miraculously by God's intervention through the incarnational conception of His Son. This virgin birth mystery would be a "sign." Who was going to give the sign? God himself. God Himself would be involved in this conception. "There will be a "virgin" (one who has never known a man sexually) who will conceive. How can a woman conceive if she does not know a man who provides the seed? She cannot. She cannot UNLESS God gets involved. God got involved. Isaiah 7:14 prophesied that it would be <u>a son </u>that this virgin would produce and that she would call him *Immanuel*. *Immanuel* means: "God with us" (Luke 1:26-37 and Matthew 1:23).

God's words recorded in Genesis 3:15, 21 placed before the eyes of Adam and Eve a visual of the blood covenant cut 'by God with God" in eternity past (Revelation 13:8b). God revealed that the eternal covenant had provided that there would be a supernatural seed that would be born of a woman (thereby being human) who would defeat Satan. Later, God revealed in Isaiah 7:14, that this seed would be a son, born of a woman; born of a virgin. To Mary, the chosen virgin, God revealed that this would be his own Son, therefore, this son would also be God. God in the flesh. This required incarnational conception. Mary was a virgin before conception and a virgin after conception.

What is Incarnation?

Incarnation is the union of divinity with humanity in Jesus Christ. Incarnation is the doctrine that the second person of the Trinity assumed human form in the person of Jesus Christ and is completely both God and man. To incarnate means "to be enfleshed or become flesh." It was a voluntary act of Jesus to humble himself so that he might become flesh and die for our sins (I Peter 3:18).

Holy Spirit in the Incarnation

The incarnational event is explained in Luke 1:35 when it is said *"The Holy Ghost shall come upon thee, and the power of the highest shall overshadow thee therefore* (because of those facts) *that holy thing that shall be born of thee shall be called the Son of God."* This conception was due to the direct action of God. This Son of God/son of man would be the Savior of the world.

To be the Savior: (1) He must be a human because God or an angel could not justly die for our sins. He must truly share fully in our humanity. (2) He must be a man of eternality. He must possess eternal life because a person of death could not pay the price of eternal death for himself, much less for all of mankind. If he had sin then he would have death instead of life in him and therefore, he could not give anyone life...even himself. (3) He must be a sinless innocent man because a sinner can not die for other sinners because he would have death in himself (Romans 6:23). The incarnational virgin birth guaranteed all three of these conditions.

To understand how the Savior was to be the Son of God, we must understand the incarnational event. This event is recorded in Luke 1 which says that the Holy Spirit would *come upon* Mary and the presence of the Most High would *overshadow* her.

THE HOLY GHOST SHALL COME UPON THEE

When it says that the *"Holy Spirit shall come upon thee,"* we can refer back to Genesis 1:2 where Holy Spirit *"hovered"* over the earth and brought life out of chaos. The word used in Genesis 1:2 is the same verb used in the Greek translation and as that used in Luke 1:35. Holy Spirit brought life to Mary's womb. This is a miracle and inexplicable to the human mind, but we know that it is true through the witness of the birth, life, death, resurrection, ascension, and glorification of Jesus Christ and the subsequent outpouring of Holy Spirit through this one born of the Virgin Mary: Jesus Christ, Son of God, and Son of Man.

Genesis 1:2 *And the earth was without form, and void; and darkness was upon the face of the deep. And the Spirit of God <u>moved upon</u> the face of the waters.*

THE POWER OF THE HIGHEST SHALL OVERSHADOW THEE

What does <u>overshadow</u> mean? For a visual, we can look at Exodus 40:35 and Psalms 91:4 which use this same verb in the Greek translation. The images in these two Scriptures give us an idea or picture of what happened with Mary. The *"power of the most high"* completely surrounded her just as the cloud surrounded, covered, and filled the tabernacle.

Exodus 40:35 *And Moses was not able to enter into the tent of the congregation, because the cloud <u>abode thereon</u>, and the glory of the Lord filled the tabernacle.*

Psalms 91:4 *He will <u>cover you</u> with his feathers, and under his wings you will find refuge; his faithfulness will be your shield and rampart*

WHAT DOES "FLESH" MEAN?

John 1:14 *And the Word was made <u>flesh</u> and dwelt among us, (and we beheld his glory, the glory as of the only begotten of the Father,) full of grace and truth.*

In John 1:14, the Greek word *Sarx* is translated flesh. This word does not mean a cloak of human physical bodily flesh, but instead it means the sphere of earthly human life in its totality.

It embraces the whole of human existence; including physical, intellectual, emotional, and reasoning functions. Jesus embraced all that we are as humans. What he did not assume, he could not and did not redeem (Dorries, p.108). Jesus truly and fully became flesh.

Jesus became fully, truly human without ceasing to be fully, truly divine. There was a corporate merger between a divine being and human nature. The divine side of the equation had to limit itself and take on certain limitations in order to be truly and fully human. To be fully human is to be mortal and have limitations of time and space and knowledge and power, and, of course, to be tempted. Jesus was tempted like us in every respect, but he did not sin (Hebrews 4:15). From this we can see that is not necessary to sin in order to be truly and fully human.

Why Jesus Came

In the "fullness of time," Jesus became flesh in the earth as the Lamb of God. The incarnation, crucifixion, and resurrection were the physical manifestations of that eternal blood covenant that was cut in heaven when the Lamb was slain "from the foundation of the world" (Revelation 13:8b). Jesus came to declare (reveal) God and his eternal blood covenant to humanity. Jesus came to earth and became flesh because of the covenant cut in heaven in eons past (Revelation 13: 8b).

John 3:16 *For God so loved the world that he gave his only begotten son, that whosoever believeth in him should not perish but have everlasting life.*

John 10:10 *The thief cometh not, but for to steal, and to kill, and to destroy: I am come that they might have life, and that they might have it more abundantly.*

John 1:18 *No man hath seen God at any time; the only begotten Son, which is in the bosom of the Father, he hath declared him.* (Declare means to reveal).

I Peter 1:20 *Who* (Jesus Christ) *verily was <u>foreordained before the foundation of the world,</u> but was manifest in these last times for you.*

Ephesians 1:4 *According as he hath chosen us in him <u>before the foundation of the world,</u> that we should be holy and without blame before him in love.*

Galatians 4:4-5 *But when the <u>fullness of time</u> was come, God sent forth his son; made of a woman, made under the law. (5) To redeem them that were under the law, that we might receive the adoption of sons.*

John 1:14 *And the <u>Word was made flesh,</u> and dwelt among us, (and we beheld his glory, the glory as of the only begotten of the Father,) full of grace and truth.*

John 1:33 *And I [John] knew him not: but he that sent me to baptize with water, the same said unto me, "Upon whom thou shalt see the Spirit descending, and remaining on him, the same is <u>he which baptizes with the Holy Ghost.</u>*

John 1:36 *...looking upon Jesus as he walked, he saith, <u>Behold the Lamb of God</u>.*

Revelation 13:8b "...*the lamb slain from the foundation of the world.*"

These very important verses reveal that in eternity past the Lamb of God was slain in heaven in the heart and counsel of God before being made manifest in the earth for humanity to know and experience.

Thy Will Be Done On Earth As It Is in Heaven (Matthew 6:10).

God's will for humanity's redemption in heaven was revealed and accomplished on earth through Jesus Christ, God's only begotten Son. The result of the lamb slain is seen in the book of Revelation.

Read Revelation 5 slowly and take time to think about the result of the Lamb of God slain from the foundation of the world. The Lamb slain from the foundation of the world became the Lamb who was slain on earth for the salvation of mankind. Because he came and died as a man for mankind, he is qualified to receive glory and honor and power, as well as, to open the seals on the Book that no one else qualifies to open.

God's will in heaven was revealed in earth to Old Testament prophets and to Mary by Gabriel, the arch angel, (Luke 1:26-35). God's will was revealed to Joseph by an angel in a dream (Matthew 1:18-21). God's will in heaven was revealed in earth by Jesus when he was made flesh and dwelt among men through the incarnational birth (John 1:14, 18). God's will in heaven was revealed on earth when he poured out Holy Spirit to indwell believers (Acts 2:1-4).

God's will for the end times was revealed to John the apostle on the Isle of Patmos (Revelation 1:10).

IMMANUEL: GOD WITH US
John 1:14 says *"And the word was made flesh and dwelt among us..."*

Luke 1:26-35 *And in the sixth month the angel Gabriel was sent from God unto a city of Galilee, named Nazareth, (27) to a virgin espoused to a man whose name was Joseph, of the house of David; and the virgin's name was Mary. (28) And the angel came in unto her and said, Hail thou that art highly favored, the Lord is with thee: blessed art thou among women. (29) And when she saw him she was troubled at his saying and cast in her mind what manner of salutation this should be, (30) And the angel said unto her, Fear not Mary; for thou hast found favor with God. (31) And, behold, thou shalt conceive in thy womb and bring forth a son, and shalt call his name Jesus. (32) And he shall be great, and shall be called the Son of the Highest and the Lord God shall give unto him the throne of his father, David: (33) And he shall reign over the house of Jacob forever; and of his kingdom there shall be no end. (34) Then said Mary unto the angel, How shall this be, seeing I know not a man? (35) And the angel answered and said unto her, the Holy Ghost shall come upon thee, and the power of the Highest shall overshadow thee; therefore also that holy thing which shall be born of thee shall be called the Son of God.*

Matthew 1:18-25 *Now the birth of Jesus Christ was on this wise: when as his mother Mary was espoused to Joseph, before they came together, she was found with child of the Holy Ghost. (19) Then Joseph her husband, being a just man, and not willing to make her a publick example, was minded to put her away privily. (20) but while he thought on these things, behold, the angel of the Lord appeared unto him in a dream, saying, Joseph, thou son of David, fear not to take unto thee Mary thy wife; for that which is conceived in her is of the Holy Ghost. (21) And she shall bring forth a son, and thou shalt call his name JESUS: for he shall save his people from their sin. (22) Now all this was done, that it might be fulfilled which was spoken of the Lord by the prophet, saying, (23) behold, a virgin shall be with child, and shall bring forth a son, and they shall call his name Emmanuel, which being interpreted is, God with us. (24) Then Joseph being raised from sleep did as the angel of the Lord had bidden him, and took unto him his wife: (25) and knew her not until she had brought forth her firstborn son, and he called his name JESUS.*

God fulfilled all of the messianic "types" of the Old Testament in Jesus Christ. These fulfillments began with the flesh and blood bodily manifestation through the incarnational birth of the Son of God in the earth (John 1:14). This was the initial physical manifestation in the earth of the eternal plan of Elohim made in heaven in eternity past (Revelation 13:8). According to John 1:36, the Son of God, Jesus Christ, was the Lamb of God of Revelation 13:8. According to John 1:18, the "Son of God" came to earth as man to declare (reveal) the heavenly eternal covenant of God to man. Jesus came to reveal a heavenly covenant that was God's will for mankind on earth. The heavenly covenant was revealed through Jesus' birth, life, death, and resurrection in the flesh on earth.

God's Will in Heaven Revealed in Earth

Of the Trinity, only the Son became flesh and assumed our fallen human nature. (John 1:1-4, 14.) He is 100% God. He is 100% human. He did not cease to be God when he became human. Jesus did not cease to be God, but he walked on earth within the limitations and boundaries of humankind. He was born, lived, and died as a human. He suffered physically, mentally, emotionally, and in every area of humanity. Through the incarnational birth, God became flesh and dwelt among humanity. He was fully man then and was/is even called "man" after his ascension.

I Timothy 2:5-6 *For there is one God, and one mediator between God and men,* **the man** *Christ Jesus, who gave himself a ransom for all, to be testified in due time.*

When he became flesh on earth, Jesus functioned only as you and I function as a human. He came to reveal God and to be an example to us as to the plan of God for humanity. He had a human nature fully as our human nature in all its fallenness; yet, he never ceased to be God. God came in the flesh to function in the earth as 100% human by laying aside his unique rights and privileges as the Son of God. He emptied himself and became one with us. He was God come in the flesh (Philippians 2:6-8). He never ceased to be God, but He lived as 100% human and yet, without sin. He restricted himself to the limitations of a human body. (See Chapter 1 on Trinity).

There Was Never A Time When Christ Was Not.

Philippians 2:5-9 *Let this mind be in you, which was also in Christ Jesus. (6) Who, being in the form of God, thought it not robbery to be equal with God: (7) but* <u>*made himself of no reputation*</u>, *and took upon him the form of a servant, and was made in the likeness of men: (8) and being found in fashion as a man,* <u>*he humbled himself,*</u> *and became obedient unto death, even the death of the cross. (9) Wherefore God also hath highly exalted him, and given him a name which is above every name.*

The Son of God was not created. He has no beginning or end just as the Father and the Holy Spirit have no beginning or end. He possesses the attribute of eternality. Jesus was made flesh, but he was still God (John 1:1-4, 14, 18). He was/is eternally God. The Son did not come into existence at the time of His incarnation. His incarnational birth is when he was made flesh and humbled himself to the limitations of the human body.

The Father God is eternal-past and future. The Son of God is eternal past and future. Holy Spirit is eternal past and future. We know according to Rev. 13:8 that the Lamb was slain in heaven from the foundations of the world in the eons of time past. The Lamb was present in eternity past. This heavenly-executed covenant revealed God's eternal redemption plan.

John 3:16 *For God so loved the world that he gave his ONLY BEGOTTEN SON that whosoever believeth in him should not perish but have everlasting life.*

Jesus was God's only begotten Son in the fullest meaning of the word. The Greek word for begotten is *monogenes*, *Mono* means "one" and *genes* is the Father-Son relationship or "one of a kind." There has never been anyone like Jesus and never will be. He is the one of a kind, unique Son of God: The <u>ONLY</u> begotten Son. Jesus was not "begotten" in time but in eternity past. He was not "begotten" at the time of the incarnation. He was already "the only begotten Son of God."

Christ was begotten by God outside the boundaries of time. He always has been, he is, and he always will be. Jesus Christ, the Son, like the Father, is eternal. He was already God's only-begotten Son before the incarnation.

God did not promise more than one "only begotten Son." As a believer, you are a child of God, but you are not an "only begotten, one-of-a-kind" Son of God. God's only begotten Son was born of a virgin. No one can make that claim except Jesus Christ. God's only begotten Son died for mankind's sin and was raised from the dead three days later. This resurrection was not done by any man, but by the Spirit of God (Romans 8:11). No other has made nor can make this claim of resurrection done only by the Spirit that dwelled in him. None but Jesus has ever prophesied both his own death and the time of his own resurrection (Matthew 16:21; 20:17).

It was the incarnate entrance of Jesus into Earth as human flesh that laid the foundation and revelation of the eternal redemption plan from heaven. Incarnation is the union of divinity with humanity in Jesus Christ. His birth in earth revealed God's will in heaven. Jesus' birth, life, death, resurrection, ascension and glorification all revealed the will of God and made known to man events of heaven pertaining to the plan for man's redemption.

John 1:14 *And the word became flesh and dwelt among us.*

Hebrews 1:1-2 *God, who at sundry times and in divers manners spake in times past unto the fathers by the prophets, (2) hath in these last days spoken unto us by his Son, whom he hath appointed heir of all things, by whom also he made the worlds.*

One Spirit: Same Spirit
John 1:33 *And I knew him not: but he that sent me to baptize with water, the same said unto me, upon whom thou shalt see the Spirit descending, and remaining on him, the same is he which baptizes with the Holy Ghost.*

The only begotten Son is not only the Redeemer but also the Baptizer in the Holy Spirit (John 1:33). Before Jesus assumed the position of baptizer, Holy Spirit could only be "with" man. Only after Jesus ascended and was glorified would he assume the position of Baptizer in the Holy Spirit, and only after believers are baptized in the Holy Spirit could Holy Spirit abide "in" them (John 14:17 and I Corinthians 3:19).

The very same Holy Spirit with which God anointed Jesus of Nazareth is available to you as a child of God (Acts 10:38).

Death, Hell, and the Grave
He went through death, hell, and the grave to conquer them, NOT to be held, tormented, or defeated by them. He did not go there to submit to them, but to conquer them. Jesus went through death, hell, and the grave as humanity's substitute and representative, and he overcame.

I Corinthians 15:55-57, *O death, where is thy sting? O grave, where is thy victory? (56) The sting of death is sin; and the strength of sin is the law. (57) But thanks be to God, which giveth us the victory through our Lord Jesus Christ.*

Revelation 1:18, Jesus said: *I am he that liveth, and was dead; and, behold, I am alive for evermore, Amen; and have the keys of hell and of death.*

Colossians 2:1-14-15, *Blotting out the handwriting of ordinances that was against us, which was contrary to us, and took it out of the way, nailing it to the cross; (15) And having spoiled principalities and powers, he made a show of them openly, triumphing over them in it.*

On the cross, Jesus said, "It is finished." He did NOT descend to hell because he had sin, but because he had a mission. He went to hell for two reasons. (1) He went to rescue those in Abraham's bosom who had believed in his coming while living in their bodies on earth. (2) He went to preach to the spirits in prison. These were those who had been disobedient during the days of Noah.

Ephesians 4:8, *Wherefore he saith, When he ascended up on high, he led captivity captive, and gave gifts unto men.*

I Peter 3:18-20 *For Christ also hath once suffered for sins, the just for the unjust, that he might bring us to God, being put to death in the flesh, but quickened by the Spirit: (19) by which also he went and preached unto the spirits in prison; (20) which sometime were disobedient, when once the long-suffering of God waited in the days of Noah, while the ark was a preparing, wherein few, that is, eight souls were saved by water.*

The word "preach" in verse 19 does NOT mean "to evangelize or proclaim good news." It is a Greek word that means "to announce or declare." Jesus went to make a declaration to those particular spirits in prison who were especially vile and who had maintained hope of defeating the Redeemer. All their hope was dashed against the wall whenever Jesus showed up as the victorious Savior and Lord to notify them that there was no hope left for them. Jesus had won.

Satan has never had the keys to death and hell. Jesus had/has the "key." The "key" was living in obedience to God and fulfilling the law through love. Death was given entrance into earth through the rebellion and sin of Adam and Eve. Hell was created for Satan and his angels, but after man fell, one section of hell became the holding place for those who believed in the coming Redeemer, and in a different section there was a place for the eternal destination of those who followed after Satan while they lived on earth, These refused to repent of sins and to trust in the promised Redeemer of which all had access (Matthew 25:41). Neither God nor Satan has ever directly determined whose spirit goes to hell. Humans choose their own destiny.

Jesus triumphed over death, hell, and the grave by the cross. Who did he triumph over and from whom did he take the spoils? Satan is who he triumphed over and from whom he took the spoils. What were the spoils? The spoils were the souls of those under the Old Covenant who had looked forward in faith to the coming Messiah, but upon death, they had been held in Abraham's Bosom out of the presence of God until the time of redemption. Jesus came to them in hell and unlocked the door for them. Where did Jesus take these captive spirits after he had loosed them? He took them to heaven and the presence of God.

Ephesians 4:8 *Wherefore he saith. When he ascended up on high, he led captivity captive, and gave gifts unto men.*

When man repents, Jesus provides forgiveness and gives man victory over spiritual death by opening the door to eternal life for whosoever will. By accepting Jesus Christ as one's Savior, we are 'born again' and taken out of the kingdom of darkness and placed in the kingdom of Jesus Christ (Colossians 1:13). It is because of this spiritual rebirth that believers will be raised up from the dead in the last days. Jesus died as our substitute so that we could live.

<u>Hebrews 2:9</u>, *But we see Jesus, who was made a little lower than the Angels (Elohim) for the suffering of death, crowned with glory and honor; that he by the grace of God should taste death for every man.*

<u>John 10:18</u>, *Therefore doth my Father love me, because I lay down my life that I may take it again. (18) No man taketh it from me, but I lay it down of myself. I have power to lay it down, and I have power to take it again. This commandment have I received of my Father.*

The Holy Spirit of Resurrection

The very source of all life, Jesus Christ, stooped down even to taste death for us. "Life" is an essential attribute of God who is consistently described as "the living one" over against idols and gods who are no gods at all. They are without life. They are lifeless.

Romans 8:11 *But if the Spirit of him that raised up Jesus from the dead dwell in you, he that raised up Christ from the dead shall also quicken your mortal bodies by his Spirit that dwelleth in you.*

This Scripture reveals a great fact concerning the indwelling Holy Spirit. He will be the means by which those who die in Christ shall be raised up from the dead. Notice that this is the very same Holy Spirit that was 'in Christ' and raised him up from the dead. There are not two different Holy Spirits: one for Jesus and one for believers. The same Spirit that raised Christ from the dead is the same Spirit with which God anointed Jesus of Nazareth (Acts 10:38) which is the same Spirit that "came upon" Mary at the time of the incarnational event; which is the same Holy Spirit for which Jesus told them to tarry in Jerusalem; and is the same Holy Spirit in which people continued to be baptized and speak with other tongues; which is the same Holy Spirit available today to those who ask (Luke 11:13). There is only one Holy Spirit.

One needs to have an understanding of the work of Jesus to have a clear understanding of the work of the Holy Spirit. Jesus is the baptizer in the Holy Spirit. "No baptizer" means "no baptism in the Holy Spirit." No baptism in the Holy Spirit means no empowering of the Holy Spirit. No empowering of the Holy Spirit means no ability to do the greater works that Jesus said we would do. No greater works means no witness of Jesus by believers.

Christ's Life, Death, and Resurrection Revealed God's Will in Heaven

Jesus dwelt among mankind and revealed (declared) the Father's will to humanity (John 1:1-4, 14, 18). He said, "I and the Father are one." (John 10:30). He also said, "If you have seen me, you have seen the Father." (John 14:7). In addition, he stated that he only said what he heard his Father say, and only did what he saw his Father do (John 5:19; John 12:49, 8:28; Acts 10:38). In other words, there was total unity with the Father, the Son, and Holy Spirit in the redemption of mankind. To know the will of "our Father which art in heaven" look at the life of Jesus. The things Jesus did and said were the revelation of God's will for earth because God does not change. He is the same yesterday, today, and forever.

John 1:18 No man hath seen God at any time, the only begotten Son, which is in the bosom of the Father, he hath <u>declared (revealed)</u> him.

The New Testament records the life and teachings of Jesus, as well as, revelations of his words received and recorded by writers under the inspiration of the Spirit (II Timothy 3:16-17) which agree with and further reveal the fullness of the provisions of Christ's redemptive work. The New Testament is the revelation of God's will in heaven to be manifested in earth.

In the Garden of Gethsemane, Jesus struggled, but he cried out, "... *nevertheless, not my will but thine be done*" (Luke 22:42). He was speaking to his Father in heaven. God's will can be seen in the death on the cross of his only begotten Son for the sins of the world. God's will can be seen in the resurrection, ascension, and glorification of Jesus resulting in the Holy Spirit outpouring. Each event in its proper sequence.

Part of the awesome revelation was that Jesus, the Lamb of God, was manifested in the earth at an appointed time in human history in which humans saw, heard, and touched him (I Peter 1:20, I John 1:1-4; Galatians 4:4). This Lamb of God became flesh and dwelt among them and they knew he was human (I John 1:1-4; Hebrews 2). They also knew he was God's Son (Matthew 16:16).

God Must Become Flesh
If the Lamb had already been slain in heaven, <u>why must Christ become flesh?</u> It was because man had sinned against God so it must be man who paid the penalty. However, no man in earth qualified to redeem himself much less all of mankind. If humanity was to be saved, God must come and save him. But there was a problem with that because it had been man who had sinned, not God. Therefore the penalty was man's penalty to pay, not God's.

It would be worthless, meaningless, useless, and even unjust for God to come <u>as God</u> to pay the penalty that man, himself, owed. It was mankind who had broken the covenant. Satan had gotten man in his grip through mankind's own choice so it was man's failure and man's own responsibility to pay the penalty for rebellion. God's covenant requirements for mankind were fair and just. This was proven by Jesus Christ.

Adam Broke the Law but Jesus Fulfilled the Law
To show that God's requirement of obedience was just, Jesus laid aside his rights and privileges as Deity and became fully and wholly flesh: one with humanity in all respects. He did not live on earth as God with all the rights and privileges of Deity. Jesus was the second and last Adam. He lived fully as a human as others would live under the law; and he fulfilled it perfectly. How was this done?

Matthew 5:17 *Think not that I am come to destroy the law, or the prophets; I am not come to destroy, but to fulfill.*

Romans 13:8-10 *Owe no man anything, but to love him: he that loveth another hath <u>fulfilled the law</u>. (9) For this, Thou shall not commit adultery, Thou shalt not kill, Thou shall not steal, Thou shall not bear false witness, Thou shall not covet; and if there be any other commandment, it is briefly comprehended in this saying, namely, Thou shall love thy neighbor as thyself. (10) Love worketh no ill to his neighbor: therefore, <u>love is the fulfilling of the law.</u>*

Galatians 5:14 *For all the law is fulfilled in one word, even in this: Thou shall love thy neighbor as thyself.*

Romans 10:4 *For <u>r</u>ighteousness is the end of the law for everyone that believeth.* (See also Hebrews Chapters 7-9).

Jesus, Lamb of God

Jesus fulfilled the law through love for mankind, thereby, being righteous in his life. Jesus was obedient and sinless. When Jesus died, he could die <u>for</u> sinful man as mankind's representative or substitute because there was no sin in him. *The wages of sin is death, but the gift of God is eternal life* (Romans 6:23). Since there was no sin in Jesus, death nor hell had any right to hold him nor was it able to hold him because life cannot be held by death just as light cannot be overcome (or held) by darkness (Acts 2: 24). The sinless man, Jesus, died and rescued those in Abraham's bosom who looked forward in faith to the coming Messiah (Ephesians 4:8). In addition, he defeated Satan on his own turf in hell and made an open show of him (Colossians 2:15). Then he arose from the dead by the Spirit that dwelled in him (Romans 8:11). Jesus was truly the Lamb of God who died for and in the place of fallen man. Today, whosoever believes on him and the finished work of

Calvary can be reconciled to God. We are saved by faith in the finished work of Jesus Christ.

The manifestation and understanding of Jesus as the Lamb of God in the earth (John 1:36; I Peter 1:20) was given to man in order to make clear the eternal redemption plan of Revelation 13:8b. The Lamb was the "once for all time" sacrifice for the sins of whomsoever chooses to believe (I Peter 3:18, Hebrews 9:26).

John 1:36 records a glorious revelation given to John the Baptist by God of what had been done in heaven in eternity past. John the Baptist called attention to the fact that Jesus was God's Lamb. *"Behold the Lamb of God that taketh away the sins of the world."* (Compare this scripture with Revelation 13:8b and Revelation 5:1-7.) The Lamb of God was slain from the foundation of the world. John the Baptist had not been there to see this, but God revealed it to him. *"Thy kingdom come, thy will be done in earth as it is in heaven."* God's will in heaven was revealed and accomplished on earth because of Jesus Christ, the Lamb of God.

I Peter 1:18- 20 *Forasmuch as ye know that ye were not redeemed with corruptible things, as silver and gold, from your vain conversation received by tradition from your fathers; (19) but with the precious blood of Christ, as a lamb, without blemish and without spot: (20) Who verily was foreordained before the foundation of the world, but was manifest in these last times for you.*

This heavenly covenant was revealed through the incarnational birth of the Son of God. The incarnational birth, life, death, resurrection, ascension, and glorification of Jesus Christ would prepare the way for Holy Spirit to be poured out so as to indwell believers. Believers' lives and speech could then reveal that Jesus is alive and doing what he said he would. Jesus is the Baptizer in the Holy Spirit. No baptizer = no Holy Spirit baptism for believers. No Holy Spirit baptism = no power to live in the provisions of the covenant.

<u>No man was present in heaven to witness the Lamb slain from the foundation of the world. So how would man ever know of this redemption plan? God revealed his covenant and plan through types and shadows in the Old Testament and fulfilled those types and shadows in the birth, life, death, resurrection, and ascension of his Son, Jesus, who secured our salvation. BUT he knew we would also need power to live victoriously in this world.</u>

JESUS, BAPTIZER IN HOLY SPIRIT

Before his death, Jesus revealed God's will concerning Holy Spirit's role in earth in the redemption plan (John 14:16). He said that Holy Spirit would lead believers into all truth (John 16:13) and reveal the deep things of God (John 16:3; I Corinthians 2:10-12). The Holy Spirit was promised by God. Holy Spirit baptism was the Father's will in heaven for mankind on earth. *"Thy will be done on earth as it is in heaven."*

Luke 24:49 *And behold, I send the promise of my Father upon you: but tarry ye in the city of Jerusalem, until ye be endued with power from on high.*

Acts 1:4 *And, being assembled together with them, commanded them that they should not depart from Jerusalem, but wait for the promise of the Father, which, saith he, ye have heard of me.*

After his death and resurrection, Jesus spent 40 days with the disciples teaching them and revealing mysteries of the eternal plan of redemption. He told them that he must leave them and ascend to heaven, but that he would not leave them comfortless. He would ask the Father who would send Holy Spirit to indwell those who asked (Luke 11:9-13). He informed them that though Holy Spirit had been with them, he would soon dwell in them (John 14:17). Jesus revealed a mystery: Holy Spirit will indwell mankind.

When Jesus ascended to heaven he left a commission for the church as is recorded in Matthew 28 and Mark 16. But he also commanded them to not do any work of the ministry until they returned to Jerusalem and waited for the Holy Spirit outpouring that would occur after he had been glorified. This outpouring was the time of empowering the church to do the work of the ministry (Luke 24:49; Acts 1:1-8, 2:1

Chapter Five: First Things First: Part One

Introduction

God's Will for Mankind

Overview of Events in Heaven Pertaining to Humanity in Earth

God Has a Plan: Redemption and Holy Spirit Empowerment

First Event

The First Event: Redemption through the Blood Covenant

The Blood of the Covenant

The Oath of the Covenant

The Heavenly Covenant Revealed in Types in the Old Testament

The Patterns Are in Heaven

Types and Shadows: Garden of Eden: Seed of Woman: The Plan Unfolds

Gospel in the Garden

Gospel in Genesis 3:15

Types and Shadows: Revealing the Eternal Covenant in the Passover Lamb

CHAPTER 5
First Things First: Part One

Introduction

Thus far we have been laying a foundation on which to build a sound doctrine concerning Holy Spirit baptism. We have discussed the fact of Holy Spirit being the third person of the Trinity: truly God. After having discussed and clarified the meaning of the Trinity, we moved forward to talk about the makeup of mankind as being spirit, soul, and body. Then we discussed the devastation that sin brought to all humanity. Sin is a spiritual act and it opened the door to spiritual death in man which eventually brought death to the physical body. The law of sin and death was set in motion. Man was created to dwell in a body, but sin brought in death and separation of man's spirit from his body. We revealed that because of sin, after physical death man could not ascend to heaven into the presence of a holy God. Yet humans are eternal spiritual beings and will ever exist. Until forgiveness was attained by Jesus Christ, believers on the coming Messiah were shut away in Abraham's bosom while unbelievers were shut away in torments in hell. Because of sin, man was robbed of his body on earth. Man could not pay his own penalty of death and ever live again because all the seed of Adam was corrupted and all who were born into the earth were counted under sin. We discovered that man must have a Redeemer mediator to obtain forgiveness for sin so we could once again have life, and thereby, enter into the presence of our holy God.

The next two chapters will discuss the process by which redemption was brought to man and the opportunity believers now have of the Holy Spirit himself indwelling and empowering us to walk victoriously in our personal life, as well as, to be witnesses to others of Jesus Christ as the Savior of the world. Holy Spirit enables us to boldly proclaim that sin has been dealt with on the cross and all may receive life through Jesus Christ.

Now we approach the subject of the two great events that brought salvation and power for victory to mankind. This is God's will for man.

God's Will for Mankind
Thy kingdom come, thy will be done in earth as it is in heaven. Matthew 6:10

Two great events in heaven occurring out of the sight of man were made known on earth through the incarnational birth, life, death, resurrection, ascension, glorification, and outpouring of Holy Spirit on the Day of Pentecost: (1) redemption through the covenant cut in heaven as shown in Revelation 13:8b; I Peter 1:19-20 and (2) the glorification of Jesus as revealed in Acts 3:13 that opened the door for the outpouring of Holy Spirit into the earth.

Overview of Events in Heaven Pertaining to Humanity in Earth

Events in heaven are important to us according to the prayer of Jesus: *"Thy will be done in Earth as it is in Heaven."* We can know the will of God if we know what is or has happened in heaven. We do not give that statement much attention, but it is a powerful statement full of exciting insight.

The first observation is that there are things going on in heaven. It is not a place where little angels float around on clouds strumming harps. Indeed, it is a place of great activity where the will of God is done. The book of Revelation reveals mighty worship in heaven--boisterous and active. God is seen on his throne in great majesty and awe.

Even more discovery can be made about Heaven in the book of Hebrews where we discover that there is a heavenly temple in which our High Priest, sprinkled his blood upon the mercy seat. That high priest is Jesus Christ, the Son of God and Redeemer of humankind (Hebrews 5:1-10). In addition, we see in Revelation chapters 6-19 the story of the future of Earth unfold from heaven.

The Old Testament (or Hebrew Scriptures) is historical documentation of the children of Israel and the prophecies which revealed God's will to them. These prophecies were spoken to a people with limited revelation and understanding of God's redemptive plan. Revelation of the redemptive plan was *"line upon line and precept upon precept; here a little and there a little" (Isaiah 28:10)*

The revelations were in types or shadows until the fullness of time (I Peter 1:20-21; Galatians 4:4; Ephesians 1:1-12). Types and shadows are symbols or signs of the real thing. The New Testament is a beautiful unlimited revelation of those Old Testament types and shadows.

1. The first event that occurred in heaven out of the sight or participation of humanity was the eternal blood covenant cut by God (*Elohim*: one who stands in covenant relationship ratified by an oath) in which the *"Lamb was slain from the foundation of the world"* (Genesis 1:1 *Elohim*; Revelation 13:8b; Revelation 5:6; and John 1:36).

The first event concerns the redemption of mankind through the incarnational birth of Jesus Christ. In the earthly revelation of the first event, Holy Spirit "came upon" or "hovered over" Mary in the incarnational moment of Jesus Christ. Incarnation is the union of divinity with humanity in Jesus Christ (Luke1: 26-39).

2. The second event that occurred in heaven out of the sight or participation of humanity was the glorification of Jesus after his ascension (John 7:37-39; Acts 3:13). It was only after the glorification of Jesus that the outpouring of the Holy Spirit upon all flesh could and did occur. The Trinity is seen in this event in that Jesus said he would ask the Father and the Father would send Holy Spirit.

In the second event, the Holy Spirit is poured out into the earth to indwell believers. The outpouring occurred after the ascension of Jesus. This outpouring concerns the Holy Spirit empowerment of believers who choose to receive the provision of redemption provided through Jesus Christ.

In John 20:20-22, Jesus breathed on them and said, *"Receive ye the Holy Ghost."* (There will be a deeper discussion later in the book concerning this event). However, he also said he must ascend to the Father at which time he would then ask (or "pray) the Father to send Holy Spirit to them (John 15:26). He said Holy Spirit would not come if he did not go away (John 16:7). By this we can see that the coming of the Holy Spirit in fullness to indwell and empower believers was reserved for a time after his ascension. Remember Jesus is the baptizer in the Holy Spirit and he said there would be no Holy Spirit here to indwell believers until he ascended. When Jesus breathed on those disciples, he was not baptizing them in Holy Spirit. This baptism was reserved for a time following his ascension and glorification.

For these two heavenly events to benefit humanity on earth, they had to be revealed to humanity in the earth. These two revelations began with the incarnation and ended with the outpouring of the Holy Spirit on the Day of Pentecost. These two heavenly events occurred outside of the presence and participation of humanity, but both of these events were revealed to man in earth in due time. Both of these events included the Trinity: Father, the Son, and the Holy Spirit.

The first event has to do with God's redemption plan for man. The second event has to do with equipping those who believe and receive the provision of that redemption. Both are pertinent in the redemption plan. The first has to do with eternal destination through spiritual rebirth. The second has to do with equipping believers to live victoriously in this life as a witness to Jesus Christ. The first has to do with the condition of the "wineskin," and the second has to do with the "wine" to be poured into the prepared wineskin (Matthew 9:14-17; Mark 2:21-22). Until these two heavenly events were manifested and made known in the earth, they could not profit humankind. Humanity had to know in order to participate by faith in the provisions of these two events.

God Has a Plan: Redemption and Holy Spirit Empowerment

It is important to discuss the necessary order of the redemption plan before having a deeper discussion concerning the work of Holy Spirit in the earth and in each Spirit-filled believer. Without first having Jesus' incarnational birth, life, death, resurrection, ascension, and glorification there would be no outpouring of the Holy Spirit in the sense of indwelling believers as we know today. This indwelling of the Holy Spirit is vital to victory. But it could occur only after the initial outpouring on the Day of Pentecost (Acts 2:1-4). It was only after Jesus was ascended and glorified that he baptized anyone in the Holy Spirit. Holy Spirit baptizes believers into the body of Christ (I Corinthians 12:13), and Jesus baptizes in the Holy Ghost AFTER they are born-again thereby becoming new wineskins fit to be the temple of the Holy Spirit in the earth (I Corinthians 3:16). (Refer to the chapter on "Three Baptisms" for more detailed teaching on this).

God revealed himself and revealed his will into earth through his names, covenants, prophecies, types, shadows, dreams, angelic visitations, visions, stars, etc. Then he spoke to mankind through his Son, Jesus, who brought salvation to and paved the way for Holy Spirit empowerment of believers.

Hebrews 1:1-4 *God, who at sundry times and in divers manners spake in time past unto the fathers by the prophets, (2) Hath in these last days spoken unto us by his Son, whom he appointed heir of all things, by whom also he made the worlds: (3) who being the brightness of his glory, and the express image of his person, and upholding all things by the word of his power when he had by himself purged our sins, sat down on the right hand of the Majesty on high (4) being made so much better than the Angels, as he has by inheritance obtained a more excellent name than they.*

First, through the heavenly covenant cut in heaven by God in eternity past and revealed in Revelation 13:8b *("...the lamb slain from the foundation of the world.")*, Jesus obtained and accomplished redemption and salvation for fallen humanity. By becoming flesh and living without sin, he qualified to pay the penalty for man's sin and to be raised from the dead. Forty days after his resurrection, Jesus ascended to heaven where he was glorified by the Father.

Second, Jesus was glorified and Holy Spirit was then sent forth to indwell and empower believers to walk again as sons of God equipped with power to show forth God's glory in the earth. God had breathed his own breath into man when he created Adam. Sin had perverted the intended use of that God-given breath, but through salvation and the indwelling Holy Spirit man could once again use that breath to God's glory. Order: salvation on earth and glorification in heaven before Holy Spirit outpouring on earth.

The two events mentioned above are very important to the discussion and understanding of the role of Holy Spirit in the church today. Simply put, without these two events concerning the work of Jesus in the earth and his glorification in heaven, there would be no Holy Spirit outpouring and indwelling of believers since that Day of Pentecost when Holy Spirit was poured out upon all flesh.

Holy Spirit has come to indwell believers to enable them to show forth God's image and likeness and glory in the earth. Jesus said that Holy Spirit would always be with us. He has not left planet Earth, and he is still revealing the will of the Father in earth. He is present in both the Old and the New Testaments, but whereas, in the Old Testament, Holy Spirit dwelt <u>with and came upon</u> only certain ones. In the New Testament Holy Spirit can <u>indwell and empower all believers.</u>

<u>As seen in I Corinthians 2, Holy Spirit reveals God's will in the earth.</u> Holy Spirit executes the will of the Father in the earth having been justified to do so by the finished work of Jesus Christ and his glorification. He enforces the defeat of Satan in all arenas: Heaven, Hell, and Earth.

I will clarify how the transition from "dwelling with" to "dwelling in" believers was made possible through the birth, life, death, resurrection, ascension, and glorification of the Son of God, Jesus Christ.

First Event

The first event was the revelation on earth of the fact that God (*Elohim*) had already cut an eternal covenant in heaven prior to the creation story in Genesis chapter one. No man was present to know about or participate in the heavenly covenant that was made to redeem humanity should Adam and Eve break the covenant and enter into death. However, God revealed that he was a covenant God in Genesis 1:1 when he used the name *Elohim*. *Elohim* means "one who stands in covenant relationship ratified by an oath" (Andrew Jukes, *Names of God*). God revealed by that name that he was in covenant prior to the creation of man. This was a covenant of redemption made within the godhead. That heavenly covenant was revealed on earth in types and shadows throughout the Old Testament.

God revealed the heavenly covenant by cutting covenants with men on earth, but humans were prone to break the covenant. In order to bring total redemption to man, God must have a man on earth who would walk 100% in covenant with him without sin. Even after thousands of years, no covenant-keeping man was found on earth. It was clear that man could not save himself.

Because man needed a Savior, scriptures reveal that God, himself, would come and redeem mankind: Isaiah 43:11; Isaiah 45:21; Isaiah 59:15-16; Psalms 49:7; Hosea 13:4; Micah 5:2. God must not only come to man, but he must come for and as man in order to provide a way back into a relationship with the Father.

In the first event, Jesus became flesh and paid the debt of sin so fallen man could be reconciled to God. This was accomplished through Jesus' incarnational birth, life, death and resurrection. Because he was sinless, it was impossible for him to be *"holden of death"* (Acts 2:34). Jesus was sinless and kept the covenant for all mankind. He died for mankind and rose again. It is through Jesus, the Son of God that believers are brought into that eternal covenant cut by God (by *Elohim*, with *Elohim*) in heaven in eternity past, and manifested in the earth through Jesus Christ. (Revelation 13:8b). We were "*chosen in Christ from the foundation of the world*" (Ephesians 1:4). Believers are in covenant with God through Jesus Christ, our substitute and mediator.

Because of the fall, each individual is born spiritually separated from God, but we can be "born again" by faith in Jesus Christ. We become new wineskins for Holy Spirit to indwell. Mankind was created in the image and likeness of God, but because of sin we were separated from God and were not like God. Through the new birth and the indwelling of the Holy Spirit, we are equipped to again be like God.

The First Event: Redemption through the Blood Covenant

The first event is the eternal heavenly covenant revealed in Revelation 13:8b.

And all that dwell upon the earth shall worship him, whose names are not written in the book of life of <u>the Lamb slain from the foundation of the world</u>.

The key part of this verse for our discussion concerns the revelation to John the apostle that God had cut the redemptive covenant in heaven in eons past only to be revealed in the earth in the fullness of time. The plan was in place.

This verse reveals that <u>all knees</u> will bow whether saved or unsaved. More importantly it reveals: (1) <u>the fact</u> that there was a blood covenant cut by God, (2) <u>whose own blood</u> sealed the covenant (*the slain lamb, Jesus*) See Revelation 5:6-9, (3<u>) the location</u> (heaven where John was observing) and (4) the <u>time</u> it was cut ("*before the foundation of the world.*") This heavenly covenant cut in the eons of time past had to be revealed in earth for man's benefit. John revealed that the covenant sealed by the blood of Jesus was not man's covenant but God's covenant. Man can now enter into covenant with the Father through Jesus Christ.

Covenants are about relationship. The purpose of a blood covenant is to provide a binding sense of commitment to an interpersonal relationship. One of the purposes of divine covenants is to be vehicles of God's expression of his will, purpose, and promises for humanity. In addition, there are warnings concerning penalties for not abiding by the covenant. The penalties come as a result of not obeying the things God said. God does not do these bad things to you. They are sometimes the consequences of personal sin. God knows how we are designed because he created us. He knows what will bless us and what will harm us. Also the law of sin and death entered into earth through rebellion and it remains. There are evil people who do evil things motivated by demons who are also active in the earth now as in the time of Jesus. God made covenants with mankind in order to bless and prevent the law of sin and death from overwhelming mankind. Humankind can stop the power of the law of sin and death by obeying God's word. If we do what God says, we are blessed. If we do what he says NOT to do, we get into trouble because those things will not produce a good life. Humanity needs God's word to know how to be blessed in life. God made covenant promises and spoke prophesies to mankind to reveal his plan of redemption.

During the 2016 Christmas season I asked the Lord, "Who is the baby in the manger that we are celebrating?" His answer to me was, "That baby in the manger, my Son Jesus Christ, is the guarantee and fulfillment of all the prophecies and promises of God in his covenants." That is powerful!

The Blood of the Covenant

A blood covenant is guaranteed and sealed by the shedding of blood as symbolic of what would occur if the covenant is broken. There is no stronger binding covenant than a blood covenant because the very life and existence of those involved are pledged by an oath on that blood as the assurance of faithfulness to the covenant promises. That is the significance of the "cutting" of the covenant in which blood is shed because blood is symbolic of the person's life. The shedding of blood shows that the life of the one breaking the covenant will be required. The one breaking the covenant must give up his life.

In a blood covenant an oath is sworn to guarantee both the promises of the covenant and to guarantee that the penalty of death will be enforced. Jesus guaranteed the new covenant by shedding his own sinless blood on our behalf. He did not break the covenant himself, but because he became flesh and identified wholly with mankind, he qualified to die for all mankind who had broken the covenant through Adam. Because he was a sinless man, he could take his life up again. When we accept him, we are covered by his sinless blood. Before Jesus came mankind, through Adam, had no hope.

Adam was in a blood covenant with God. We can know this because death was the penalty (Genesis 2:17). When death is the penalty, it is a blood covenant. When Adam broke the covenant, he set the "law of sin and death" into motion to perpetually reign throughout all generations. Man's spirit was separated from God and was tainted at best and depraved at worst. Spiritual death eventually brings death to all physical bodies born into earth (Hebrews 9:27; Romans 5:12; I Corinthians 15:21). In order to stop death, sin had to be dealt with.

After the fall and before Christ came, God allowed animals' blood to be shed as a substitute for mankind. Shed blood indicates that death has occurred and the penalty for breaking the covenant is paid. But this was only a temporary fix because the life in the blood of animals was not eternal life and thus was only a temporary covering for sin. It must be offered over and over and over year in and year out; day in and day out.

A new covenant was cut by Jesus because the old covenant was <u>fulfilled</u> by him and no longer had any power over those who chose the way of life through Christ. The New Covenant was sealed by the blood of Jesus (Luke 22:20). We could not give our own blood, our own lives, and ever live again. But our covenant partner, Jesus Christ, came and rescued us by dying in our place. Jesus, came and gave his life for us. Jesus fulfilled all the covenant sacrificial types of the Old Testament when he went to the cross alone and gave his life as a ransom for us guaranteeing eternal life for all who believe. He died for all mankind.

The Oath of the Covenant

In a blood covenant there is always an oath on which the blessings and curses are made. Because he could swear by no greater, God swore by himself (Hebrews 6:13). That meant that if God did not keep his word of the covenant, he was bound to destroy himself. If he would bind himself in that way to a covenant on earth with Abraham (Genesis 15) then we know that the original blood covenant cut in heaven was assured by nothing less (Revelation 13:8b).

In his blood covenant with Abram, God was promising primarily three blessings: (1) heirs, (2) land, (3) and blessings (see Genesis 12:2-3). In a blood covenant a self-maledictory oath (curse against oneself) was always spoken. No stronger guarantee could be made than this self-maledictory oath. One's own life is the most precious thing one can promise to give if he breaks the covenant.

The parties involved would walk the path between the slaughtered animals so as to say, "May this be done to me if I do not keep my oath." (Genesis 15:17-18) In Genesis 15, God alone passed through the path of the slain animals and this covenant was sealed by God alone.

At this point, nothing depended on Abram. Everything depended on God who promised to be faithful to his covenant. It was after Abram believed God and it was counted to him for righteousness that Abram became a full covenant partner (Genesis 17). In Genesis 17, we see Abram entering fully into that covenant with God through the shedding of his own blood in circumcision (Genesis 17:11, 24). Through the act of shedding of blood in circumcision, he pledged his life to God.

Hebrews 6:13-18 reveals that in this covenant with Abram, God swore by himself because he could swear by no greater. There could be no stronger guarantee to the promises of the covenant than the oath sworn by God. Here we have the blood and the Word. The covenant oath declared that God would give his own life if he broke his covenant.

The shed blood of those animals offered by Abram could never remove his or anyone's sin. The life of an animal is not a sufficient substitute for man' life (Hebrews 10:4). God had his own blood in mind when he swore the oath (Psalms 110:4; Hebrews 7:17).

God never broke the covenant, nor could he without destroying himself. However, Jesus, God's Son, did die. Why? Jesus became flesh to be able to die FOR man AS man because the penalty was mankind's penalty through Adam. By "becoming flesh" Jesus qualified to pay the debt. But he had to pay the debt justly as a man and not as God. This he did.

The types and shadows of the Old Testament covenants became a reality in Christ and were sealed with his own blood. How can the shedding of the blood of Jesus Christ give life to all who choose to believe by faith in his substitutionary death? The same way that all men were counted as being in the loins of Adam when he sinned, so too those who believe on Christ will live in Him. The difference is that in Adam we had no choice. Adam gave mankind up to death by his disobedience in the Garden of Eden. Everyone is given a choice in Christ Jesus to accept him and thereby receive eternal life, or to reject him and receive eternal death.

Ephesians 1:4 says that humanity was chosen in Christ from the foundation of the world, but ultimately we then, must each make the decision to choose Christ. When we choose him, we are choosing the one who did what we could not do i.e. pay the debt he did not owe for humankind who could not pay the debt he owed and live again. Now in Christ we live, and move, and have our being (Acts 17:28), and one day we will have a new immortal body. Fallen mankind had no way to ever have a new body after physical death until Jesus came. Jesus foiled Satan's plan to keep mankind eternally from God. God gave us assurance by the oath of the covenant.

The Heavenly Covenant Revealed in Types in the Old Testament

The eternal blood covenant in which *"the Lamb was slain"* was cut in heaven in eternity past by God—*Elohim*. *Elohim* means "One who stands in covenant relationship ratified by an oath." (Genesis 1:1; Revelation 13:8b). This covenant was cut between and among the Trinity without any human knowledge or participation. This covenant was cut prior to the creation of man. Genesis 1:1 reveals that God was already "Elohim" when he created heaven and earth prior to the creation of man.

This heavenly blood covenant was the pattern for all covenants that God cut with certain men in the journey of redemption of which the Abrahamic covenant is classic (Genesis 15). God revealed his eternal covenant on earth through types and shadows in the Old Testament. This can be seen in Genesis 3 in the Garden of Eden and in Exodus 12 in the Passover Lamb.

These types and shadows in the Old Testament were fulfilled in Christ in the New Testament.

God revealed the heavenly blood covenant in the earth by cutting covenant with men such as Abraham and Moses. God's blood covenants with men such as Abraham, and Moses represented only types or shadows of the genuine, authentic, and true covenant cut by Jesus in the fullness of time and sealed by his own blood on the cross.

A type is that which only represents the real and true. It is a copy, pattern, or model that signifies a greater reality. The real or true person, event, or thing is called the anti-type. Hebrews 10:1 declares that types are but shadows of the true image they represent. The anti-type is the revelation of the true meaning of the type.

In a blood covenant there can be an intermediary or substitute when one cannot cut the covenant themselves. Animals were allowed to be the substitute for humankind from the Garden of Eden until Jesus became flesh. Then the Son of God became flesh and died as our substitute. His pain was real. His agony was real. His death was real. He was fully human. But because he was sinless, death could not hold him, therefore, he could take up his life again. Death cannot hold life. Life trumps death every time. By what he did, he paved the way for all humanity to live by accepting and declaring Jesus to be their Redeemer and representative before God. Because the life in the blood of an animal is not eternal, those sacrifices had to be made over and over. But when Jesus came, his blood carried eternal life and therefore, had to be shed only one time (Hebrews 9:24). Before his coming, how was the plan for Redemption revealed to mankind in the earth?

The Patterns Are in Heaven

The pattern by which all covenants were made was cut by God with God in heaven in eternity past (Revelation 13:8; Genesis 1:1). Just as God revealed the heavenly temple to Moses as a pattern, (Exodus 25:40; Hebrews 8:5) in the same way, the covenant God revealed in the Garden of Eden was from the pattern of the first heavenly blood covenant (Revelation 13:8b). Just as no human built the temple in heaven, so, too, no human had any part in the making of the covenant cut in heaven. It was a 'God with God' covenant into which believers would be brought by virtue of the incarnational birth of the Son of God. God revealed that covenant in the earth through various means. We will elaborate on the initial revealing of the covenant in the Garden of Eden immediately following the fall of man, then we will look into further revelation through the covenant in the Passover Lamb.

Types and Shadows: Garden of Eden: Seed of Woman: The Plan Unfolds

Genesis 3:21 is a picture or type of "covering" for sin. This "type" was a picture of the gospel of the One to come who would "eradicate" sin and make a way back to God. God provided a way for sinful man to approach him. An animal sacrifice must be made and the blood of the sacrifice provided a temporary covering for sins. These animal sacrifices had to be offered over and over because man continually sinned and thereby, required another and another covering. These sacrifices did not change or empower man within.

Eternal life for all humanity was forfeited by Adam when he sinned out of unbelief and rebellion because all humanity was in the loins of Adam when he sinned. Adam and Eve died spiritually immediately, and as a result of that eternal spiritual death having entered, they eventually died physically. The life they gave up through rebellion was the very life given to them by God when he breathed his own breathe into that lifeless dirt form. Because of sin, both Adam and Eve would know through experience the dreadful and horrible consequences of their act of rebellion.

God's glorious will for mankind to rule and reign on earth is clearly revealed in Genesis 1 and 2. Man's rebellion against God's will and the consequences are revealed in Genesis 3. However, Chapter 3 also reveals through prophecies, types, and shadows, the eternal blood covenant that Elohim had established in heaven in eternity past (Revelation 13:8b). This heavenly covenant was the provision for man should they turn away from God's will. Humanity would suffer the consequences of their rebellion and disobedience, but God's covenant of restoration would not change. God employed his blood covenant in heaven to cut blood covenants on earth with men (Genesis 3:15, 21).

"Thy will be done in earth as it is in heaven."

After sinning through disobedience in the Garden of Eden, Adam declared that they were now "naked." The glory had lifted. (Genesis 3:7, 10, Psalms 8:5). God used the slain animal's skin in the Garden to provide a physical covering for Adam and Eve that could only symbolically replace that which had been lost through sin. The life in the blood of that animal was inferior to man's life and could not pay the penalty of eternal death and separation from

God (Genesis 2:17). The "type" must be fulfilled in the "true" for fallen humanity to be fully redeemed and restored to fellowship with God.

Gospel in the Garden

There in the Garden where man had sinned, revelation of the heavenly event of Revelation 13:8b began to be unfolded and revealed in types and shadows in the earth. God began immediately after the fall to reveal the Eternal heavenly covenant in order to give hope of redemption. God gave hope to Adam and Eve. Hope is crucial. God spoke to my heart in 2017 and said, "Hope is your vision into the future." Without hope we have no direction. Adam and Eve received hope through the visual of the slain animal in the Garden of Eden. They received hope of a future new covering to replace that which had been lost.

Genesis 3:15, 21 (15) And I will put enmity between thee and the woman, and between thy seed and her seed; it shall bruise thy head, and thou shalt bruise his heel, (21) and to Adam also and to his wife did the Lord God make coats of skin, and clothed them.

These two short sentences in Genesis show that God preached the redemptive gospel right there in the garden. God began to unfold the truth of the heavenly covenant little by little as mankind would receive it. An innocent animal was slain as a picture or type of the true innocent Lamb of God yet to be manifested in the earth. The true Lamb of God would totally redeem fallen humanity.

Gospel in Genesis 3:15

Genesis 3:15 speaking to Satan, God said:

And I will put enmity between thee and the woman, and between thy seed and her seed; it shall bruise thy head, and thou shalt bruise his heel.

- God declared the gospel to Adam and Eve. This verse reveals that:
- There is an enemy that fights to defeat mankind.
- The enemy, Satan, would have seed in the earth *("thy seed")* that continually seeks humanity's destruction (John 8:44).
- Satan would especially hate women *("I will put enmity between you and the woman")*. This enmity was not placed there by God to punish woman. Instead it would be there consequentially. God was going to use a woman to bring the supernatural seed (the redeemer) into the earth that would defeat Satan, therefore, Satan would hate women.
- God declared that the Redeemer would be born of a woman providing a human body for him which would give him all the legal rights of humanity. You must have a human body just as Adam and Eve had in order to have authority in the earth *(her seed)*.
- He was to be the *"seed of woman"* or 'miracle seed.' This required God's involvement in conception because women do not produce the seed in a conception. Therefore, the One who would be the seed of that particular woman would also be the Son of God by the miraculous incarnational birth.
- The seed of Satan would *"bruise the heel"* of the seed of woman causing suffering.

- But the seed of woman would *"bruise the head"* of Satan totally defeating him.

The words of the prophetic Gospel of Genesis 3:15 and the visual of the slain animal in Genesis 3:21 were the first glimpses on earth of the covenant that had been cut in heaven in eons past between and among the Godhead. The Lamb in heaven was slain *"from the foundation of the world"* for the salvation of all mankind revealing that God himself would die for mankind and would cloth him in his own righteousness. This slain animal in the Garden, was a "type" or a foreshadowing of the "reality" that was to come in Christ Jesus.

There in the garden, blood was shed for sin. Death manifested because there had been sin, and death follows in the wake of sin. This was a visual that clearly depicted the great cost of sin. Sin brings death. Death is separation from life.

The death of that animal right there in the Garden, revealed to Adam and Eve what had happened in the spiritual world concerning themselves when they sinned. They had separated themselves from life just as life had been separated from the animal slain in the Garden of Eden. Death resulted in both cases. They saw it. They understood what sin had done to them spiritually (i.e. Life departed, death entered.)

The visual was clear. They were immediately aware of the loss of God's covering because Adam declared, *"I was naked so I hid myself"* (Genesis 3:10). They could perhaps understand immediately by the slain animals about physical death, but the full impact of spiritual death and eternal separation from God, the source of their spiritual life, was yet to be fully realized.

Types and Shadows: Revealing the Eternal Covenant in the Passover Lamb

The heavenly covenant further unfolds in Exodus 12 when God specifically designates out of all the animals, a lamb as the innocent sacrifice. It was first called the "Passover Lamb" when the children of Israel came out of Egyptian bondage. The blood of the lamb applied to the side and upper door posts protected those inside the house from the death angel. Just as the skins of the animal slain in the Garden "covered" Adam and Eve, so too the applied blood "covered" those in the house, but it did not change or empower them. It was a "type," yet to be revealed and fulfilled.

The Passover Lamb of Exodus 12 reveals the gospel picture of redemption in a type. Jesus, the anti-type, was manifested in the earth to unveil the full reality of the type. Jesus was the true Passover Lamb manifested in the flesh to take away the sins of the world. He was *"the lamb slain."* His blood was shed for all the world's redemption and restoration to God. His blood was efficacious. His blood carried eternal life so only one sacrifice one time for all was necessary. He was God's Lamb (John 1:29). The blood of Jesus, the true once for all Passover Lamb of God, not only covers the sins of those who believe on him, but it "eradicates" believer's sins and the sin nature (II Peter 1:4; Romans 8:2). There is a difference in the life and power in the blood of an animal and the life and power in the blood of Jesus. The blood of Israel's yearly Passover lamb only "covered" the Children of Israel, but the blood of Jesus gives life.

The shed blood of an innocent lamb was only a "type" and could only "cover" sin. The shed blood of Jesus Christ, was from the sinless "Lamb of God which taketh away the sins of the world." His blood "eradicates" sin i.e. totally blots out sin as though it was never there (Isaiah 43:25; Acts 3:19; Colossians 2:14). To "blot out" means to remove or erase from record. Only sinless blood could "blot out" mankind's sin. The shed blood of Jesus Christ, the sinless Lamb of God, was the fulfillment of the Passover Lamb.

The value of the blood is equal to the quality of life that is in it. There is no higher quality of life than that which is in the blood of Jesus Christ. His blood has eternal life in it, therefore, he can be the giver of life (John 1:4; I Corinthians 15:45). This eternal blood eternally blots out the writing of ordinances against mankind.

Colossians 2:14 *Blotting out the handwriting of ordinances that was against us, which was contrary to us, and took it out of the way, nailing it to his cross.*

Through the eradication of sin, each believer is made a new creature – a new creation – capable of being a vessel for Holy Spirit indwelling (II Corinthians 5:17). We enter into that heavenly Revelation 13:8b covenant with God through faith in Jesus Christ.

Believers become new creatures in Christ Jesus (II Corinthians 5:17). We are made new wineskins (Matthew 9:17). The eradication of one's sins through faith in Jesus Christ qualifies the person to be baptized in the Holy Spirit and power.

Chapter Six: First Things First: Part Two

Introduction: Second Event

Right Order: Redemption before Holy Spirit Empowerment

Second Heavenly Event Revealed in Earth: Holy Spirit Empowerment

Old Testament Witness

New Testament Fulfillment of Holy Spirit Anointing: Jesus First

Jesus' Return to Heaven

CHAPTER 6
First Things First: Part Two

Introduction: Second Event

Because of its importance I re-state here what I stated earlier. It is needful to discuss the necessary order of redemption before having a deeper discussion concerning the work of Holy Spirit in the church and in each Spirit-filled believer. Without first having Jesus' incarnational birth, life, death, resurrection, ascension, and glorification there would be no outpouring of the Holy Spirit in the sense of indwelling believers as we know today. This indwelling of the Holy Spirit is vital to victory. It was only after Jesus was ascended and glorified that he baptized anyone in the Holy Spirit. This could only occur after the initial outpouring on the Day of Pentecost (Acts 2:1-4).

Holy Spirit baptizes believers into the body of Christ (i.e. into Christ, I Corinthians 12:13), and Jesus baptizes in the Holy Ghost AFTER they are born again and, thus, become new wineskins fit to be the temple of the Holy Spirit in the earth (I Corinthians 3:16). See chapter on "Three Baptisms.

In this chapter we will discuss the second event and thereby, discover the precipitating event of the Holy Spirit outpouring, and when that event occurred. It would be upon that particular event that Holy Spirit would come to indwell and empower believers to go forth to do the work of the ministry. We will discover this by discussing the second heavenly event revealed in the earth. The event is the heavenly glorification of Jesus which opened the door for Holy Spirit to be poured out into the earth as our source of empowerment. But <u>there was a prerequisite for Jesus to fulfill before the outpouring could occur.</u> We will discuss that prerequisite here.

Right Order: Redemption before Holy Spirit Empowerment

As stated in the last chapter, two important events in which humanity was not attendant took place in heaven. The first occurred in eternity past and the second occurred upon the ascension of Jesus. Both are crucial to mankind's eternal salvation and victory in this life. Therefore, before either heavenly event could be profitable from them, they both had to be revealed in the earth to mankind.

(1) We discussed the first event of the heavenly covenant and its revelation in the earth through Jesus Christ, the "lamb slain" for the redemption of humanity. This brought Jesus **from heaven to earth** to reveal and unfold the plan of redemption through the blood covenant.

(2) The second event, which is our present subject, is the heavenly event of the "glorification of Jesus" <u>after his ascension</u> which, as with the first event, also transpired out of the sight of mankind. This event occurred after Jesus returned **to heaven from earth.** In this glorification he would receive back that which he had had prior to "becoming flesh" (i.e. that of which he had emptied himself Philippians

2:5-11). It was this glorification event that paved the way for Holy Spirit to be poured out to empower believers.

Because of the first event (eternal blood covenant), we can receive spiritual rebirth and become wineskins prepared for the new wine of the Holy Spirit baptism (John 3:3-8). Because of the second event (glorification of Jesus in heaven upon ascension), we can receive Holy Spirit, be equipped to be witnesses of Jesus Christ, and do the work of the ministry.

Second Heavenly Event Revealed in Earth: Holy Spirit Empowerment

The second event concerns the "heavenly glorification of Jesus" as the precursor for the outpouring of the Holy Spirit into the earth. This second event of the glorification of Jesus precipitated the outpouring of the Holy Spirit on the Day of Pentecost. This outpouring was the confirmation that Jesus had ascended to the Father and had been glorified just as he had said. The outpouring of the Holy Spirit in Earth proved that he was truly the Redeemer, Son of God, and the Baptizer in the Holy Spirit (John 7:37-39). If Holy Spirit was poured out as he said then they could trust that all the other things he said were true.

The baptism in the Holy Spirit empowers believers to do the works of Jesus (just as he had said), but more importantly, Holy Spirit confirms that Jesus is truly the Only Begotten Son of Almighty God and the Redeemer of all mankind (John 16:14, 15).

Only God could redeem Mankind and only God could pour out his Spirit on all flesh. Jesus promised to pray the Father to send the same Holy Spirit with which he himself was anointed. The same Holy Spirit would dwell in and empower believers (John 14:16). The Holy Spirit power that Jesus promised to his followers manifested in healings and miracles as they went forth to share the good news of the Redeemer. This empowerment occurred on the Day of Pentecost when the Holy Spirit was poured out on all flesh resulting in supernatural evidence. First, glorification then Holy Spirit outpouring (John 7:37-39, 14:26; Acts 3:13; Acts 2:4, 16).

OLD TESTAMENT WITNESS

The Old Testament type of Holy Spirit empowerment was that He "came upon" certain ones but not on all and did not "dwell in" any. It was a temporary anointing for a specific purpose on a limited few then he would leave. He did not remain.

Holy Spirit was involved in the Old Testament story over and over. He came upon men of old such as Samson (Judges 16), Elijah, and Elisha (I and II Kings) and they did supernatural exploits. Holy Spirit was "WITH" them. These were but glimpses of a future manifestation to come of Holy Spirit indwelling believers as opposed to occasionally coming upon a select few. The Old Testament Scriptures refer to a time when Holy Spirit would come upon and empower.

Isaiah 28:11-12 *For with stammering lips and another tongue will he speak to this people. (12) To whom he said, "This [is] the rest [wherewith] ye may cause the weary to rest; and this [is] the refreshing: yet they would not hear.*

Isaiah 44:2-3 *Thus saith the Lord that made thee, and formed thee from the womb, which will help thee; fear not, O Jacob, my servant, and thou Jerusalem, whom I have chosen. (3) For I will pour water upon him that is thirsty, and floods upon the dry ground; <u>I will pour my spirit upon thy seed,</u> and my blessing upon thine offspring.*

First Samuel 16:13 *Then Samuel took the horn of oil, <u>and anointed him</u> in the midst of his brethren <u>and the Spirit of the Lord came upon David</u> from that day forward.*

Ezekiel 36:26-27 *<u>A new heart also will I give you, and a new spirit will I put within you:</u> and I will take away the stony heart out of your flesh, and I will give you an heart of flesh. (27) <u>And I will put my Spirit within you</u>, and cause you to walk in my statutes, and ye shall keep judgments, and do them.*

Joel 2:28 *And it shall come to pass in those days, that <u>I will pour out my spirit upon all flesh;</u> and your sons and your daughters shall prophesy, your old men shall dream dreams, your young men shall see visions: (29) and also upon the servants and upon the handmaids in those days will I pour out my spirit.*

These Old Testament Scriptures show that the Father promised a future abiding and permanent power source for believers to enable them to live a victorious life. While on earth, Jesus gave promises of the coming and abiding Holy Spirit power to enable them to do the things that He, himself, did. Jesus even said believers would do greater things than he did (John 14:12; Acts 1:8; Luke 24:49).

This Holy Spirit power in the Old Testament is the same Holy Spirit that Jesus had as he walked on earth as a man doing the things he did (Act 10:38). Indeed, this same Holy Spirit indwells those who receive him today. There are not two different Holy Spirits.

New Testament Fulfillment of the Holy Spirit Anointing: Jesus First

Jesus was anointed with Holy Spirit at his water baptism.

Matthew 3:16-17 *And Jesus when he was baptized, went up straightway out of the water and, lo, the heavens were opened unto him, and he saw the Spirit of God descending like a dove and lighting upon him. (17) And lo a voice from heaven, saying, This is my beloved Son, in whom I am well pleased.*

Acts 10:36-38 *The word which God sent unto the children of Israel, preaching peace by Jesus Christ: (he is Lord of all). (37) That word, I say, ye know, which was published throughout all Judea and began from Galilee, after the baptism which John preached; (38) how God anointed Jesus of Nazareth with the Holy Ghost and with power: who went about doing good, and healing all that were oppressed of the devil: for God was with him.*

Luke 4:17-19 *And there was delivered unto him the book of the prophet Esaias. And when he had opened the book, he found the place where it was written, (18) the Spirit of the Lord is upon me, because he hath anointed me to preach the gospel to the poor; he had sent me to heal the brokenhearted, to preach deliverance to the captives, and recovering of sight to the blind, to set at liberty them that are bruised, (18) to preach the acceptable year of the Lord.*

Jesus was anointed with the Holy Spirit at his water baptism. It was only after this anointing that Jesus performed any supernatural healings, deliverances, or miracles. Jesus spoke much about the coming of Holy Spirit to empower and indwell believers. The Father promised to "pour out His Spirit on all flesh" and there was a designated time for this outpouring. In addition, Jesus said Holy Spirit would abide in them – not just with them. According to John 7:37-39, this outpouring and abiding was to occur after Jesus' glorification.

John 7:37-39: *"In the last day, that great [day] of the feast, Jesus stood and cried, saying, If any man thirst, let him come unto me, and drink. (38) He that believeth on me, as the scripture hath said, Out of his belly shall flow rivers of living water. (39) (But this spake he of the Spirit, which they that believe on him should receive: for the Holy Ghost was not yet [given]; because that Jesus was not yet glorified.)"*

Jesus' Return to Heaven:

Luke 24:49-53 *And behold, I send the promise of my Father upon you: but tarry ye in the city of Jerusalem, UNTIL YOU BE ENDUED WITH POWER FROM ON HIGH. (50) And he led them out as far as to Bethany, and he lifted up his hands, and blessed them. (51) And it came to pass, while he blessed them, he was parted from them, and was carried up into heaven. (52) And they worshiped him, and returned to Jerusalem with great joy: (53) and were continually in the temple, praising and blessing God. Amen.*

Mark 16:19-20 *So then after the Lord had spoken unto them, he was received up into heaven, and sat on the right hand of God. (20) And they went forth, and preached everywhere, the Lord working with them, and confirming the word with signs following.*

Before Jesus could fulfill the role of "Baptizer in the Holy Ghost" (John 1:33), he had to return to Heaven. The giving of the gift of the Holy Spirit was contingent upon Jesus' return to heaven (John 16:7).

Even after his resurrection during the 40 days before his ascension, Jesus did not baptize anyone in the Holy Ghost. It was only after he ascended and was glorified that Holy Spirit was poured out, and it was only then that Jesus began to baptize believers in the Holy Ghost (John 1:33).

Jesus had said in John 14:16 that he would *"pray the Father, and he shall give you another Comforter, that he may abide with you forever."* The disciples did not want Jesus to go away and he was telling them that he was not going to leave them alone. Jesus' time on earth was limited, but He said that the Father would send the Holy Spirit from Heaven and that he would be with them forever. Jesus had to ascend before Holy Spirit would be poured out on all flesh. He said in Jn.14:17 that, whereas, the Holy Spirit had dwelt WITH them, (after Jesus ascended), Holy Spirit would dwell IN them. This is why Jesus said that it was expedient that he return to Heaven.

John 16:7 *"Nevertheless I tell you the truth, it is expedient for you that I go away; for if I go not away; the Comforter will not come unto you:, but if I depart, I will send him unto you."*

Expedient here means "profitable or for your good." Jesus was saying that his going away was profitable and for the good of believers because if he returned to Heaven then Holy Spirit would come and indwell them on earth. But before Holy Spirit could come, Jesus must return to the Father and be glorified. <u>While on earth even after his resurrection, Jesus did not baptize anyone in the Holy Spirit. It was only AFTER he had ascended and was glorified, that he became the "baptizer in the Holy Spirit.</u>

Chapter Seven: Holy Spirit Anointing of Jesus

Holy Spirit Anointing of Jesus at His Water Baptism

Jesus Son of Man: Holy Spirit Anointing as an Example to All Humanity

Jesus' Final Exhortation & Commandments

The Mission: Instruction

The Power: The Ability to Fulfill the Mission

Conduits of Living Water

CHAPTER 7
Holy Spirit Anointing of Jesus

Holy Spirit Anointing of Jesus at His Water Baptism

It was only after his baptismal event in which God acknowledged this to be "my beloved Son in whom I am well pleased," and in which we see "the Spirit of God descending like a dove and remaining on him" that Jesus entered into ministry. In this baptismal event, we see the presence of the Trinity. Jesus is in the water, Holy Spirit descends like a dove and remains upon him, and the Father declares out of Heaven that Jesus is his beloved Son in whom he is well pleased.

At this baptism, John the Baptist witnessed Holy Spirit "descending and remaining" on Jesus. (John 1:32-33) This was the confirmation given to John by God that Jesus was the Lamb who takes away the sins of the world and the baptizer in the Holy Ghost. Only one who is "equal to or greater than" can baptize in Holy Spirit. As God's only begotten Son, Jesus can and does bap-tize in the Holy Spirit.

After the baptismal event in which Holy Spirit descended and remained on Jesus, he was led into the wilderness by the Spirit where he was tempted by Satan after he had fasted 40 days and nights (Matthew 4:1-11). Holy Spirit sustained him. This Holy Spirit experience in the life of the man Jesus is very significant as an example to all believers. Jesus did not enter into ministry nor attempt to do any works prior to the decent of Holy Spirit upon him. Luke records the significance of Holy Spirit descending on Jesus at his water baptism in the book of Acts. God anointed his Son, Jesus, with the Holy Ghost and power at his water baptism.

Matthew 3:16-17 *And Jesus, when he was baptized, went up straightway out of the water; and, lo, the heavens were opened unto him, and he saw the Spirit of God descending like a dove, and lighting upon him. (17) And lo a voice from heaven, saying, this is my beloved Son, in whom I am well pleased.*

John 1:32-33 *And John bare record, saying, I saw the Spirit descending from heaven like a dove, and it abode upon him. (33) And I knew him not but he that sent me to baptize with water, the same said unto me, upon whom thou shalt see the Spirit <u>descending, and remaining on him</u>, the same is he which baptizeth with the Holy Ghost.*

Acts 10:36-38 *The word which God sent unto the children of Israel, preaching peace by Jesus Christ: (he is Lord of all:) (37) That word, I say you know, which was published throughout all Judea, and began from Galilee, <u>AFTER THE BAPTISM which John preached:</u> (Matt. 3:11-17 above) (38) <u>HOW GOD ANNOINTED JESUS OF NAZERETH WITH THE HOLY GHOST AND WITH POWER;</u> WHO WENT ABOUT DOING GOOD, AND HEALING ALL THAT WERE OPPRESSED OF THE DEVIL: FOR GOD WAS WITH HIM.*

Peter also delineated the water baptism of Jesus Christ as the time from which a person must have walked with Jesus to even be considered for filling the position formerly held by Judas, because it was at this baptismal event that God anointed Jesus with the Holy Ghost. The Spirit of the Lord was upon Jesus because he was anointed by the Holy Ghost (Luke 4:18).

Acts 1:21-22 *Wherefore, of these men which have companied with us all the time that the Lord Jesus went in and out among us, (22) beginning from the baptism of John, unto the same day that he was taken up from us, must one be ordained to be a witness with us of his resurrection.*

Luke 4:18-19 *The Spirit of the Lord is upon me, because he hath anointed me to preach the gospel to the poor; he had sent me to heal the brokenhearted, to preach deliverance to the captives, and recovering of sight to the blind, to set at liberty them that are bruised. (19) To preach the acceptable year of the Lord.*

"Anoint" means to pour and rub on. Holy Spirit anointing is "God on flesh doing only what God can do." Holy Spirit baptism is "the time of the coming of the special presence and power of God on flesh." The anointing of Holy Spirit makes burden-removing, yoke-destroying power available (Isaiah 10:27). Jesus began to preach the Word AFTER his water baptism by John the Baptist. Why? Because Holy Spirit descended upon him and remained from that time. Here it was that God "anointed Jesus of Nazareth with the Holy Ghost and power."

With what was Jesus anointed? The Holy Spirit and Power (Acts 10:38). Who anointed him? God himself. From this we can see that although Jesus was God incarnate, he walked on Earth fully as a man just as all humanity walked then and walks today.

He functioned by the same anointing and power of the Holy Spirit that is available to all believers. He came to earth as fully man as our example and to die as our substitute.

Jesus was adamant about the believers returning to Jerusalem following his ascension to await the coming of the Holy Spirit to anoint them to do the work of the ministry. If Jesus waited until he was anointed with the Holy Ghost and power to enter into ministry and perform the things he did, then surely those believers then and we believers today need this same empowerment. Only after having been anointed by the Holy Spirit at his water baptism in the Jordan River did Jesus move into a ministry of might and power in which healings, deliverances, raising the dead, executing authority over nature, miraculously feeding multitudes, walking on water, stilling the storms, and many other supernatural things occurred.

Jesus acknowledged that Holy Spirit anointing was the power behind the things that he did.

Luke 4:17-19 *Jesus went into the synagogue on the sabbath day. And there was delivered unto him the book of the prophet Esaias. And when he had opened the book, he found the place where it was written. (18) The Spirit of the Lord is upon me BECAUSE HE HATH ANOINTED ME to preach the gospel to the poor, he hath sent me to heal the brokenhearted, to preach deliverance to the captives, and recovering of sight to the blind, to set at liberty them that are bruised, (19) to preach the acceptable year of the Lord.*

Jesus said, "The Spirit of the Lord is upon me." Why was it on him? "...because he hath anointed me..." For what? Supernatural ministry. Holy Spirit anointed him for supernatural ministry.

When did this anointing occur? Is he speaking of the incarnational moment? No. He is speaking of the water baptismal event when Holy Spirit descended and remained on him. Luke confirms this in Acts 10:36-38 as seen above. Also, Peter confirms the significance and importance of the baptismal event of Jesus (Acts 1:21-22).

Jesus Son of Man: Holy Spirit Anointing as an Example to All Humanity

As discussed in chapter 1, Jesus is fully man and fully God. He has been, is, and forever more will be God. But he was not always man. Through the incarnational birth, Jesus "became flesh" at a particular point in the history of mankind. He became flesh. During his time on earth, he laid aside his rights and privileges of Deity, and as a result, he placed himself on the same human plane to live in the limitations of all humanity. He functioned 100% as all other humans while he walked on planet Earth; yet, through obedience, he was without sin. He was anointed with the Holy Spirit by God. He came as our example and showed us God's will.

It is God's will for us to be overcomers, and the only way that is possible is for us to be baptized in the Holy Spirit. We need Hoy Spirit permanently resident within us. First, we must receive salvation through faith in the finished work of Jesus Christ which makes us new wineskins. Second, those wineskins need to be filled with the wine of Holy Spirit who equips us to walk in the image and likeness of God and to use the very breath that God breathed into us for the purpose of bringing God glory (Genesis 1:26-28; 2:7). We belong doubly to God: (1) by creation (2) by redemption from sin, bondage, and death. Mankind was initially created by God, but through sin, death entered and man died. Jesus redeemed mankind by his blood, and now when we believe on Jesus Christ as our Savior, we become new creatures in Christ Jesus (II Corinthians 5:17; John 3:3-6).

Hebrews 5:8 says that Jesus "learned obedience by the things that he suffered." Hebrews 2:18 says that "he suffered being tempted." We too, should learn when we suffer being tempted. We do not have to succumb to temptation. We have Holy Spirit within us to empower us to be overcomers in this life just as Jesus did. We make our choices just like Jesus did. <u>Remember, being flesh does not require you to sin.</u> The devil does not make you sin. Your flesh does not make you sin. <u>To sin or not to sin is a choice made by each person.</u> Holy Spirit empowers a person to make the right choice. Jesus chose not to sin though he was tempted just as you and I are tempted.

Jesus lived in all aspects of life as human flesh with its limitations, and he provided humanity with the way to God and to victorious living. Jesus is the way, the truth, and the life (John 14:6). He opened the door for "whosoever will" to enter. The way to vic-tory for Jesus was obedience to the Father. <u>The power to obey and overcome the flesh was through the anointing of the Holy Spirit. Jesus was empowered in his humanity by Holy Spirit, and as such, he made a way for all humanity to be indwelt and empowered and anointed by the same Holy Spirit as he, himself, was empowered and anointed. There are not two different Holy Spirits.</u>

Holy Spirit empowers us to resist sin and to live holy before the Lord. He also empowers us to show forth God in the earth. Jesus said believers would do greater works than he did "because I go unto my Father." How are believers to do those greater works?

John 14: 12-17 *Verily, verily, I say unto you, he that believeth on me, the works that I do shall he do also: and <u>greater works</u> than these shall ye do: <u>BECAUSE I GO TO MY FATHER.</u> (13) And whatsoever ye shall ask in my name, that will I do, that the Father may be glorified in the Son. (14) If ye shall ask anything in my name, I will do it. (15) If ye love me, keep my commandments. (16) <u>And I will pray the Father, and he shall give you another Comforter, that he may abide with you forever. (17) Even the Spirit of truth; whom the world cannot receive, because it seeth him not, neither knoweth him; but ye know him; for he dwelleth with you but shall be in you.</u>*

Therefore, we can see that Spirit-filled believers are empowered by the same Holy Spirit by which Jesus was empowered. We also notice that Jesus said that he must return to the Father so that Holy Spirit could be poured out in a new measure.

John 15:26-27 *And when the Comforter is come, whom I will send unto you from the Father, even the Spirit of truth which proceeded from the Father, he shall testify of me: (27) and ye also shall bear witness, because you have been with me from the beginning.*

Holy Spirit is the empowering factor. Jesus knew we would need Holy Spirit in order to fulfill the privileges, rights, and responsibilities of the new covenant.

John 16:7, 13 finds Jesus reiterating the need for him to return to heaven in order for Holy Spirit to be sent to indwell believers

<u>John 16:7, 13</u>, *Nevertheless, I tell you the truth; it is expedient for you that I go away; for if I go not away, the Comforter will not come unto you; but if I depart, I will send him unto you. (13) Howbeit when he, the*

Spirit of truth, is come, he will guide you into all truth: for he shall not speak of himself; but whatsoever he shall hear, that shall he speak: and he will show you things to come.

He said he MUST depart. There was no room for choice for him to stay on earth if Holy Spirit was to come and equip believers to perpetuate the gospel message of redemption. Holy Spirit would come and believers would be witnesses through supernatural gifts and spiritual fruit demonstrating the truth of the life and teachings of Jesus Christ. By the empowering of the Holy Spirit, they would do what Jesus had done. These things are witnesses to the truth that Jesus is the Son of God.

Jesus' Final Exhortation and Commandments

The last words of a dying person or one who is leaving those he or she loves are always their most important words. Time is limited so they choose those things of utmost importance that they want to impress upon the ones they are leaving behind. The last words Jesus spoke were vitally important because they were his last instructions on earth. This would be his last opportunity to instruct his followers for victorious witness. When Jesus was gone it would be up to his followers to continue the work he had begun. If they did not continue the work, then what Jesus had done would be in vain. If Jesus was the true Son of God who had come and died for the sins of the world, then what the followers of Jesus did after he left them was crucial. I am sure many questions mixed with anxiety floated through their minds and perhaps out of their mouths.

"How can we do what he has done without him here?"

"He was the Son of God and yet he told us that we will do even greater things than he did. How can that be?"

"What of the Roman government and the Jewish sects that so oppose Jesus? How will we be able to deal with them?"

"Why is Jesus leaving us?"

"How will we know if and when Holy Spirit comes?"

"How can Holy Spirit dwell in us?"

"Are we to return to the life we lived before Jesus came into our lives?"

These questions and many other things probably went through their minds as they listened to his last words because they had never experienced the power of the Holy Spirit which Jesus said was to be poured out. Up to this time, Holy Spirit had only "come upon" judges, prophets, priest, and kings, and a select few others and that only for a short period of time and with a specific purpose. Then Holy Spirit would depart. Jesus was saying Holy Spirit would come upon them and <u>dwell in them permanently</u>, but they must return to Jerusalem and wait. They were not to attempt to do any ministry or witness until they were baptized in the Holy Spirit.

Below are Scriptures containing the last words of Jesus. We can know that these were vitally important since they were his last words to those who bore the responsibility of perpetuating the gospel that He preached. He was about to depart and ascend to heaven and they would see him no more here on earth. His work was finished here and he was leaving them alone. BUT not for long because he had a plan to equip and empower them if they would believe and obey. They were given opportunity to reveal their faith by returning to Jerussalem in obedience and waiting as Jesus said to do. Thank God they did!

<u>First,</u> comes the instructions for the mission. The instructions of Jesus for perpetuating the work he had begun were clear. <u>Then</u> Jesus instructed them as to how they were to be empowered to do the work.

The Mission: Instruction

<u>Matthew 28:18-20</u>, *(18) And Jesus came and spake unto them, saying, all power is given unto me in heaven and in earth. (19) go ye therefore, and teach all nations, baptizing them in the name of the Father, and the Son, and of the Holy Ghost: (20) teaching them to observe all things whatsoever I have commanded you: and, lo, I am with you alway, even unto the end of the world. Amen.*

<u>Mark 16:15-18</u>, *And he said unto them, Go ye into all the world, and preach the gospel to every creature. (16) He that believeth and is baptized shall be saved; but he that believeth not shall be damned. (17) And these signs shall follow them that believe; in my name they shall cast out devils; <u>they shall speak with new tongues</u>; (18) they shall take up serpents; and if they drink any deadly thing, it shall not hurt them; they shall lay hands on the sick, and they shall recover. (19) So then after the Lord had spoken unto them, he was received up into heaven, and sat on the right hand of God. (20) And they went forth, and preached everywhere, the Lord working with them, and confirming the word with signs following. Amen*

The Power: The Ability to Fulfill the Mission

<u>Acts 1:4-5, 8, 9,</u> *And, being assembled together with them, commanded them that <u>they should not depart from Jerusalem, but wait for the promise of the Father,</u> which, saith he, ye have heard of me. (5) For John truly baptized with water; but you shall be baptized with the Holy Ghost not many days hence. (8) But you shall receive power, after that the Holy Ghost is come upon you: and you shall be witnesses unto me both in Jerusalem, and in all Judea, and in Samaria, and unto the uttermost part of the earth. (9) And when he had spoken these things, while they beheld, he was taken up; and a cloud received him out of their sight.*

<u>Luke 24:46-49</u>, *And (Jesus) said unto them, thus it is written, and thus it behooved Christ to suffer, and to rise from the dead the third day; (47) and that repentance and remission of sins should be preached in his name among all nations, beginning at Jerusalem. (48) And ye are witnesses of these things. (49) And, behold, <u>I send the promise of my Father upon you; but tarry ye in the city of Jerusalem, until you be endued with power from on high.</u>*

The believers who were present were given very clear instructions by Jesus: "Do not attempt to do the work assignment until you return to Jerusalem and have been baptized in the Holy Spirit of promise not many days from now."

I am sure they encouraged one another. Perhaps John recalled to them what Jesus had said concerning Holy Spirit's coming <u>after he was ascended and glorified,</u> and how Holy Spirit would comfort, teach, lead, bring things to their remembrance, and empower them to accomplish the things Jesus had left in their charge (read and reread John Chapters 7, 12, 14-16). There is no recording of anyone attempting to go against the instructions of Jesus and on the Day of Pentecost the promised Holy Spirit was poured out to equip them for ministry.

Acts 2:1-4, *And when the day of Pentecost was fully come, they were all with one accord in one place. (2) And suddenly there came <u>a sound from heaven as of a rushing mighty wind</u>, and it filled all the house where they were sitting. (3) And there <u>appeared unto them cloven tongues</u> like as of fire, and it sat upon each of them. (4) And they were all filled with the Holy Ghost, and <u>began to speak with other tongues as the Spirit gave them utterance.</u>*

Jesus had not brought up the subject of the Holy Spirit as an afterthought after his resurrection and just before his ascension. He had taught much about Holy Spirit while he was here on earth. Holy Spirit was an active and integral part of his life even from the time of the incarnational event as recorded in Luke 1:26-38.

From Luke's account, we have seen that Holy Spirit was involved in the <u>birth</u> of Jesus Christ. Then in Matthew 3:11-17, we are shown the <u>baptismal event</u> at which time (according to Acts 10:36-38,) Jesus was anointed with the Holy Ghost and power. So Holy Spirit was the active agent in the birth and in the empowering of Jesus in the flesh. It was only after his baptism and anointing with the Holy Spirit and power that Jesus went about doing what only could be done by "God on flesh doing only what God can do" which is one definition of anointing. Therefore, we can see that (1) Jesus had a supernatural birth by the Holy Spirit and (2) Jesus received a supernatural anointing with the Holy Ghost and power to do the work of the ministry.

In the same way, we see Holy Spirit involved in the birth and empowering of the Church to do the ministry Jesus had assigned them (John 20:19-23, Acts 2:4). The Church's ministry should reflect the ministry of Jesus. This is possible only because: (1) The Church had a supernatural birth (John 3:3-6; John 20:21-23) and (2) The Church received a supernatural baptism in the Holy Ghost and power (Acts 2-4, 39).

We prevent the benefits of the anointing when we refuse it through pride, doubt, or unbelief. Even Jesus, the anointed one of God, could not do mighty works in his own hometown because of the depth of their unbelief (Matthew 13:58). Jesus did not force himself on anyone nor did he force the benefits of the anointing of the Holy Spirit that was upon him.

Scripture shows that Jesus placed great importance on Holy Spirit in the lives of believers. Jesus taught about the fact of Holy Spirit empowerment. The incident in John 7:37-38 was about six months before Christ's death. The setting was in Jerusalem at the feast of Tabernacles which every male Jew was obliged to attend. This was a weeklong event. The last day with the most distinguished and call The Great Day of the Feast.

Each day waters were drawn from the Springs of Gihon which ran into the Pool of Siloam inside the city (Isaiah 44:3). The priest drew water daily from the springs during the Feast of Tabernacles to be used to pour out on the altar on which sacrifices were made in the temple. The drawing of the water was a joyous ceremony. It was done at night, but the pouring of the water upon the altar was done the next morning. The night water-drawing ceremony was accompanied by music, song, dance, and rejoicing. The night sky was lit up by very large and very tall lamps which some say were 75 feet tall. These lamps represented the fire by night that hovered over the children of Israel. Jesus declared himself to be "the light of the world" (John 8:12).

At the time of the water-pouring (mixed with wine) upon the altar on the last day of the feast, Jesus stood and cried with a loud voice, *"If any man thirst, let him come unto me and drink and out of his belly shall flow rivers of living water"* (like the water from the Spring of Gihon). This is the time and setting, as we hear the words of Jesus in John 7:37-39.

John 7:37-39 *37 In the last day, that great day of the feast, Jesus stood and cried, saying, If any man thirst, let him come unto me, and drink. (38) He that believeth on me, as the scripture hath said, out of his belly shall flow rivers of living water. (39) <u>(But this spake he of the Spirit, which they that believe on him should receive: for the Holy Ghost was not yet given; because that Jesus was not yet glorified.)</u>*

John explains that Holy Spirit was not yet given because Jesus had not yet been glorified, but still it was possible at that time to believe on Jesus as God's son, the source of light and life (John 8:12).

Isaiah 44:3 *For I will pour water upon him that is thirsty, and floods upon the dry ground: I will <u>pour my spirit</u> upon thy seed, and my blessing upon thine offspring.*

Conduits of Living Water

Through Holy Spirit baptism, believers can be conduits of the source of the river of life, Jesus Christ. What is required to be a conduit of life? We must believe, come, and drink. Through the baptism into Jesus we are born again. Through the baptism in the Holy Spirit, we are empowered and according to Jesus out of believers' innermost being shall flow rivers of living water so others may believe, come, and drink.

Are you thirsty? Here is how you drink. You <u>believe</u> the words of Jesus, you <u>come</u> and talk with him. <u>Tell him</u> you desire to be filled with the Holy Spirit. <u>Worship him</u> for the promise because he will keep his promise to you, then as you are praising him, <u>release the rivers of living water</u> through your mouth allowing the words of the heavenly language to flow from you. You need not be afraid, because we can see from Luke 11:11-13 and Acts 2:39 that this is God's will concerning us. Paul said *"I thank God I speak in tongues more than you all* (I Corinthians 14:18). Once you are full, you can then release the Holy Spirit's wisdom and power to those around you who are in need and looking for hope.

According to Luke 11:13 we are supposed to ask God for the Holy Spirit. It does not automatically happen.

Luke 11:13 *If ye then, being evil, know how to give good gifts unto your children: how much more shall your heavenly Father give the Holy Spirit <u>to them that ask him</u>?*

Acts 2:39 *For the promise is unto you, and your children, and to all that are afar off, even as many as the Lord our God shall call.*

These verses are referring to you and me today.

Chapter Eight: Glorification

Introduction

Glorification: Definition and Timing

Transfiguration: An Earthly Glimpse of Jesus' Glorification in Heaven

John and Peter Reveal Their Glimpse of the Heavenly Glorification

Heavenly Glorification of Jesus Confirmed on Earth

Proof of Heavenly Glorification Was the Holy Spirit Outpouring on Earth

First Things First--Necessary Order

CHAPTER 8
Glorification

INTRODUCTION

THE SECOND EVENT THAT WE discussed was the ascension and "glorification of Jesus" in heaven. This glorification was revealed in the earth by the outpouring of the Holy Spirit on the Day of Pentecost. Jesus impressed upon the disciples and his followers the importance of waiting for the empowerment that would come when they were baptized in the Holy Spirit. He told them not to try to do the work of the ministry without it. His own life was an example to that. Only after his water baptism when the Holy Spirit descended and remained on him did he do any work of ministry. Acts 10:36-38 and Luke 4:16-19 are very specific that God anointed Jesus of Nazareth with the Holy Ghost and power.

They obeyed and returned to Jerusalem and waited to be indued with power. When Holy Spirit was poured out on the day of Pentecost the 120 who were waiting for the promise began to speak in tongues as the Spirit gave utterance. They were accused of being drunk, but Peter told the onlookers that these were not drunk as they supposed them to be, but that they had been baptized in the promised Holy Spirit. He preached with such authority and power that 3000 believed on the Lord Jesus Christ that day and became followers of Jesus Christ.

Jesus had told them that he must go back to heaven and be glorified before Holy Spirit could come. Therefore, since Holy Spirit was poured out, it could be correctly surmised that Jesus had ascended and had been glorified by the Father. He was truly confirmed by this Holy Spirit outpouring to truly be the Son of God. He had been glorified by the Father.

GLORIFICATION: DEFINITION AND TIMING

Strong's Exhaustive Concordance defines "glorify" in this manner: "to honor, magnify, to praise, extol, celebrate; to adorn with luster, clothe with splendor; to impart glory to something, render it excellent; to make renowned; to cause the dignity and worth of some person or thing to become manifest and acknowledged." Glorification reveals who one truly is. Glory is the exercise or display of what constitutes the distinctive excellence of the subject in which it is spoken. God's glory is the manifestation of his divine attributes of perfection. These are such a visible splendor as it indicates the possession and presence of these (Exodus 33:18 – 22; 16:7, 10; John 1:14; 2:11; II Peter 1:17, etc.). God glorified his Son when he ascended, and only after glorification did Jesus baptize believers in the Holy Spirit to empower them to be witnesses. That which Jesus had with the Father prior to his becoming flesh was restored to him.

John 17:5 *And now, O Father, glorify thou me with thine own self with the glory which I had with thee before the world was.*

That of which Jesus had emptied himself was restored to him again at the time of his glorification. Jesus stepped back into that which he had "emptied" (Philippians 2:6-8). Now, he could function not only as an intercessor for humanity (Hebrews 4:15; 7:25), but also as their Baptizer in the Holy Spirit who would equip them to be witnesses of the reality of redemption through Jesus Christ.

Peter declared they had evidence that Jesus Christ was truly the Son of God and that he had now been glorified (Acts 3:13). Proof of his glorification was that Holy Spirit had been poured out. They knew that the glorification of Jesus was the reason behind these supernatural events (John 7:36-39).

Transfiguration: An Earthy Glimpse of Jesus' Glorification in Heaven

Peter, James, and John had been present with Jesus on the mount when he was transfigured before them and they beheld his glory. This was a glimpse for them that let them know what would occur in heaven when Jesus ascended and was glorified by the Father.

Luke 9:28-36 *And it came to pass about an eight days after these sayings, he took Peter and John and James, and went up into a mountain to pray. (29) <u>And as he prayed, the fashion of his countenance was altered, and his rainment was white and glistering.</u> (30) And behold, there talked with him two men, which were Moses and Elias. (31) Who <u>appeared in glory</u>, and spake of his decease which he should accomplish at Jerusalem. (32) But Peter and they that were with him were heavy with sleep: and when they were awake, <u>they saw his glory and the two men that stood with him.</u> (33) And it came to pass, as they departed from him, Peter said unto Jesus, Master, it is good for us to be here: and let us make three tabernacles; one* *for thee, and one for Moses, and one for Elias: not knowing what he said. (34) While he thus spake, <u>there came a cloud, and overshadowed them</u>: and they feared as they entered into the cloud. (35) And there came a voice out of the cloud saying, this is my beloved Son: hear him. (36) And when the voice was past, Jesus was found alone. And they kept it close, and told no man <u>in those days</u> any of those things which they had seen. (Also see John 7:36-38).*

John and Peter Reveal Their Glimpse of the Heavenly Glorification

John 1:14 *And the Word was made flesh, and dwelt among us (and <u>we beheld his glory, the glory</u> <u>as of the only begotten of the Father</u> full of grace and truth.)*

II Peter 1:16-18 *For we have not followed cunningly devised fables, when we made known unto you the power and coming of our Lord Jesus Christ, but were <u>eyewitnesses of his majesty</u>. (17) <u>For he received from God the Father honor and glory, when there came such a voice to him from the excellent glory. This is my beloved son in whom I am well pleased.</u> (18) And this voice which came from heaven we heard, <u>when we were with him in the holy mount.</u>*

John and Peter had been present and had beheld His glory on the Mount of Transfiguration as seen in Luke 9:28-36 above. Jesus had spoken of being glorified with and by the Father.

John 12:23 *"...The hour (the time) is come that the Son of Man <u>should be glorified."</u>*

John 17:5 *And now, O Father, glorify thou me with thine own self <u>with the glory which I had with thee before the world was.</u>*

John 7:37-39: *"In the last day, that great [day] of the feast, Jesus stood and cried, saying, If any man thirst, let him come unto me, and drink. (38) He that believeth on me, as the scripture hath said, out of his belly shall flow rivers of living water. (39) (But this spake he of the Spirit, which they that believe on him should receive: for the Holy Ghost was not yet [given]; because that Jesus <u>was not yet glorified</u>.)"*

Heavenly Glorification of Jesus Confirmed on Earth

After the outpouring of Holy Spirit, Luke recorded the sermon Peter preached following the healing of the lame man at the gate called Beautiful in the Temple in which he said:

Acts 3:13 *The God of Abraham, and of Isaac, and of Jacob, the God of our fathers, <u>hath glorified</u> his Son Jesus; whom ye delivered up, and denied him in the presence of Pilate, when he was determined to let [him] go.*

Jesus was glorified in heaven. How did Peter know that Jesus had been glorified? He was not in heaven to see it. Jesus had said that he must return to heaven and be glorified before Holy Spirit would be sent (John 7:36-39; John 14:12-17). The outpouring of the Holy Spirit on the Day of Pentecost was the undeniable confirmation that Jesus had been glorified. Holy Spirit outpouring was supernatural in every way. It was an event on earth that had its roots in heaven. Just as the glory cloud had "come upon and overshadowed Peter, James, John, and Jesus on the Mount of Transfiguration, so also, Holy Spirit "came upon" those in the upper room.

Acts 1:8 *But ye shall receive power, after that the <u>Holy Ghost is come upon you</u>: and ye shall be witnesses unto me both in Jerusalem,* *and in all Judea, and in Samaria, and unto the uttermost part of the earth.*

Proof of Jesus's Heavenly Glorification was the Holy Spirit Outpouring on Earth

Acts 2:1-4, 15-18 *And when the day of Pentecost was fully come they were all with one accord in one place. (2) And suddenly there came <u>a sound from heaven as of a rushing mighty wind</u>, and it filled all the house where they were sitting. (3) And there appeared unto them <u>cloven tongues like as of fire, and it sat upon each of them</u>. <u>(4) And they were all filled with the Holy Ghost, and began to speak with other tongues, as the Spirit gave them utterance.</u> (15) For these are not drunken, as ye suppose, seeing it is but the third hour of the day. (16) But this is that which was spoken by the prophet Joel. (17) And it shall come to pass in the last days, saith God, <u>I will pour out of my Spirit upon all flesh</u>: and your sons and your daughters shall prophesy, and your young men shall see visions, and your old men shall dream dreams; (18) And on my servants and on my handmaidens I will <u>pour out in those days of my Spirit</u>: and they shall prophesy.*

The heavenly event of glorification was AFTER the finished work of redemption by Jesus on earth. This glorification of Jesus was the second heavenly event at which mankind was not present, so how were people to know that Jesus had been glorified? People were not present in Heaven to witness this glorification of Jesus any more than they had witnessed "the Lamb slain from the foundations of the world."

The first heavenly event of the eternal blood covenant had been revealed to mankind through the incarnational birth, life, death, and resurrection of Jesus Christ. BUT what would be the proof of the second heavenly event of the glorification of Jesus Christ? Would it somehow be made known in the earth?

The answer is a resounding "Yes!" Humanity would know if and when the Son had been glorified in Heaven. This confirmation of glorification would also be a confirmation that Jesus was the Son of God and baptizer in the Holy Ghost, and as such, he could do what he had promised. If Holy Spirit was indeed poured out on them as Jesus had promised, then they could be assured that Jesus was the true Redeemer sent from God, and that his words were truth. He was truly the Baptizer in the same Holy Spirit with which the Father had anointed him at this water baptism (Matthew 3:16-17, Acts 10:38). He was surely God and God cannot lie. They could trust that Holy Spirit would do what Jesus had said he would do. The very Spirit of God Almighty would dwell in them as also in us today. But when would this glorification occur and how would they know?

John 7:37-39 *In the last day, that great [day] of the feast, Jesus stood and cried, saying, If any man thirst, let him come unto me, and drink. (38) He that believeth on me, as the scripture hath said, out of his belly shall flow rivers of living water. (39) (But this spake he of the Spirit, which they that believe on him should receive: for the Holy Ghost was not yet [given]; because that Jesus <u>was not yet glorified</u>.)*

John 16:7 *Nevertheless I tell you the truth; it is <u>expedient</u> for you that I go away: for if I go not away, the comforter will not come unto you; but if I depart, I will send him unto you.*

Acts 3:12-13 *(12) Ye men of Israel, why marvel you at this? Or why look ye so earnestly on us, as though by our own power or holiness we had* *made this man to walk? (13) And when Peter saw it, he answered unto the people, The God of Abraham, and of Isaac, and of Jacob, the God of our fathers, <u>hath glorified</u> his Son Jesus; whom ye delivered up, and denied him in the presence of Pilate, when he was determined to let [him] go."*

<u>Holy Spirit baptism was the sign that God would always be present in the earth: God with us through the indwelling of the Holy Spirit.</u> He had dwelt <u>among</u> the nation of Israel in the Tabernacle and the Temple. He dwelt <u>among</u> them in Jesus Christ while he was on earth. But after the glorification of Jesus, God would dwell <u>IN</u> believers by his Holy Spirit.

John 14:17 *Even the Spirit of truth; whom the world cannot receive, because it seeth him not, neither knoweth him: but you know him; for he dwelleth with you, and shall be in you.*

Jesus had told them "*....<u>ye shall receive power, after</u> that the Holy Ghost is come upon you: And <u>you shall be witnesses</u> unto me both in Jerusalem, and in all Judea, and in Samaria, and unto the uttermost part of the earth.*" *(Acts 1:8)*

When would they receive power? <u>After the Holy Ghost came upon them.</u> When would Holy Spirit be poured out? After Jesus' ascension and glorification. The Holy Spirit outpouring confirmed the glorification of Jesus. The supernatural manifestation of the Holy Spirit outpouring on the day of Pentecost and the works done through believers after Pentecost confirmed the glorification of Jesus in heaven. Holy Spirit came to dwell in believers just as Jesus had said would occur when he ascended to heaven. There is no substitute for Holy Ghost baptism. No Holy Ghost baptism = No power.

After the Holy Spirit had been poured out, Peter and John went to the temple and there they healed a lame man. The people marveled, but Peter explained that this miracle was the result of Jesus being God's Son as he had said (Acts 3). It was through the death, burial, resurrection, ascension, and glorification of Jesus that these things had occurred.

The promises of the outpouring of God's Spirit in Joel 2, Isaiah 11:1-2; 42; 61:1 and other Old Testament scriptures, plus the promises of Jesus in John 7, 12, 14, 16, Acts 1:8, etc. had now come to pass and the initial proof was in the outpouring of the Holy Spirit on the Day of Pentecost followed by miracles. These things were a "witness" to the fact that Jesus was/is truly the Son of God and that he was/is alive and was/is now seated at the Father's right hand having been glorified (John12:16; Matthew 14:62).

In John 20:21, Jesus "breathed on them" and said "receive ye the Holy Ghost," yet, he still told them (Luke 24:49) to go to Jerusalem and tarry until they were "endued with power from on high." This breathing on them event was the revelation that there was now entry into the new covenant via spiritual new birth. The first man Adam received "birth" (i.e. life) when God breathed into his nostrils the breath of life. Jesus restored that same zoe uncreated eternal life when he breathed on the disciples. This act established Jesus Christ as the Life-giver, and his church as the spiritual entity in the earth through which life flows.

It was 40 days after Jesus breathed on them before Holy Spirit was poured out and they received the baptism in the Holy Spirit in the upper room (Acts 2:4). Therefore, we can see that Christ's breathing on them was not the same as the baptism in the Holy

Spirit. Whatever great thing that breathing on them accomplished, Jesus knew that it was still necessary that they be baptized in the Holy Spirit and endued with power to be witnesses of him. At the time of his final ascension, Jesus again instructed them to return to Jerusalem to wait for another something to occur in addition to the breath-ing on them. In other words, he desired that they should receive something more i.e. something in addition to what they received when he breathed on them. <u>The Holy Spirit would be poured out</u> subsequently.

First Things First—Necessary Order

<u>First</u>, the blood covenant was cut in heaven by God for the redemption of mankind (Revelation 13:8b.) <u>The</u> blood covenant was made manifest in the earth through the incarnational birth of Jesus Christ. Jesus declared God's will in the earth through his life, his death, his resurrection, and ascension. <u>Second</u> upon his ascension, Jesus was glorified by the Father in heaven and Holy Spirit was then poured out upon all flesh.

The finished redemptive work of Jesus Christ was complete and he sat down at the Father's right hand having been glorified (Acts 2:33). Humankind could now choose to become "born again" by faith in Christ's finished work. This spiritual rebirth changes believers into "new wineskins" for the indwelling of the Holy Spirit because he could not dwell in "old wineskins."

Mark 2:22 (*New Living Translation*) *New wine calls for new wineskins. And no one puts new wine into old wineskins. For the wine would burst the wineskins, and the wine and the skins would both be lost.*

How does Jesus make believers new wineskins? In John 3:7 Jesus said, "*Ye must be born again*" Why? Because you cannot pour new wine (Holy Spirit) into old wineskins (unregenerate mankind). AFTER Jesus had sprinkled his blood on the mercy seat in the temple in heaven, the Father glorified him and sent forth the Holy Spirit into the earth as he had promised (Hebrews 7-9). Now, Holy Spirit baptizes believers into one body, Jesus Christ (I Corinthians 12:13).

Holy Spirit baptizes believers into the body of Christ, and Jesus baptizes believers in the same Holy Spirit with which he was anointed. Holy Spirit is the baptizer into the body of Christ, and Jesus is the baptizer in the Holy Spirit. Sequence and subsequence.

I Corinthians 12:13 *For by one Spirit are we all baptized into one body, whether we be Jews or Gentiles, whether we be bond or free; and have been all made to drink into one Spirit.*

John 1:33 *And I myself did not know him, but he that sent me to baptize with water the same said unto me, Upon whom thou shalt see the Spirit descending, and remaining on him, the same is he which <u>baptizeth with the Holy Ghost</u>.*

Luke 11:9-13 *And I say unto you, <u>ask</u> and it shall be given you; <u>seek</u>, and you shall find; <u>knock</u>, and it shall be opened unto you. (10) For every one that asks receives: and he that seeks finds: and to him that knocks it shall be opened. (11) If a son should ask bread of any of you that is a father, will he give him a stone? Or if he ask for a fish, will he for a fish give him a serpent? (12) Or if he shall ask an egg, will offer him a scorpion? (13) <u>If ye then, being evil, know how to give good gifts unto your children:</u>*

how much more shall your heavenly Father give the Holy Spirit to them that ask him.

By now, you can see why it is important to discuss the necessary order of redemption before having a deeper discussion concerning the work of Holy Spirit in the church and in each Spirit-filled believer individually. Without first having understanding of Jesus' incarnational birth, life, death, resurrection, ascension, and glorification, there would be no understanding of the outpouring of the Holy Spirit in the sense of indwelling believers as we know today. This indwelling of the Holy Spirit is vital to victory. But it could occur only after Jesus was ascended and glorified. Only after his glorification could he baptize anyone in the Holy Spirit. Holy Spirit is the baptizer into the body of Christ (I Corinthians 12:13), and Jesus is the baptizer in the Holy Ghost after they are born again and become new wineskins fit to be the temple of the Holy Spirit in the earth (I Corinthians 3:16).

According to Scripture, we must ask for the Holy Spirit. God does not force Holy Spirit upon any person. Luke 11:9-13, says that we ASK for Holy Spirit baptism. When? After we are born again and are wineskins fit for the new wine of the Holy Spirit. Yes, indeed! ASK! Jesus is waiting to baptize you in the Holy Spirit.

We determined that there is a Trinity and that Jesus and Holy Spirit are indeed of that Trinity with the Father. We have shown in Scripture that Jesus was involved in the eternal Covenant of Revelation 13:8b as the slain Lamb of God. In addition, we have shown that He became flesh and dwelt among men. He was the Lamb of God who died for mankind. He was resurrected, ascended, and glorified in heaven. Upon glorification, Holy Spirit was poured out just as he had promised. Holy Spirit can now dwell in believers and is the empowerment of believers to live victoriously and reflect God in the earth through the gifts and the fruit of the Spirit. The Trinity is involved in redemption and empowerment.

Chapter Nine: Three Baptisms

Introduction

Three Christian Baptisms According to Scripture

Baptism into Christ

Baptism in Water

Three Basic Modes of Water Baptism

Six Reasons for Water Baptism

Baptism in Holy Spirit

Jesus is the Baptizer in the Holy Spirit

CHAPTER 9
Three Baptisms

INTRODUCTION

THE NEW TESTAMENT SPEAKS OF three Christian baptisms. This chapter will distinguish between the three by context and content. What is the subject of the passage of scripture being read? Does the Scriptures specify whether the subject is baptism into Christ, baptism in water, or baptism in the Holy Spirit? If not, then the reader must look at all the relevant scriptures before and after to discover the context as well as the content. Consider, for example, whether the subject is salvation through faith in Jesus Christ and the resulting baptism into the body of Christ by Holy Spirit, or whether the subject concerns water baptism, which is administered by another believer? Finally, consider if the subject is about empowerment for believers administered by the great baptizer in the Holy Spirit, Jesus Christ.

In this chapter we will give a short summary of three baptisms: baptism into Christ, baptism in water, and baptism in the Holy Spirit.

Three Christian Baptisms According to Scripture
Baptism into Christ
This baptism is administered by Holy Spirit

"Baptism into Christ" occurs when you believe in your heart and confess with your mouth the Lord Jesus Christ. It is when you repent and totally trust Jesus as Savior. This brings you into the body of Christ; into His family (Galatians 3:27; Rom. 6:3-4, 10:9; I Cor. 12:13; Eph. 2:19; Gal. 3:27-28; Eph. 2:8-9).This salvation event qualifies you for water baptism.

Baptism in water is a public confession of your total reliance on Jesus for the remission of your sins. (Matthew 28:19; 3:5-6, 11; I Peter 3:21-23; John 3:3, 5). By it, you are publicly declaring that you have made a commitment to follow Jesus Christ and his teachings. Water baptism does not save you. It is an act of obedience and a public profession of your faith in Jesus Christ who saves you. (Mt. 28:19.) This is an exercise in obedience.

The former discussion concerning the water baptism of Jesus by John is not to indicate that water baptism in any way indicates that one should expect to be baptized in Holy Spirit at the time they are baptized in water though that may occur. John's water baptism drew many Jews from all classes. Many came to repent and be baptized by John; many came to criticize. Baptisms as ritual "washings" were common as part of Jewish purification rites, and as part of the process of Gentiles becom-ing practicing Jews.

First of all, you are saved by grace through faith (Ephesians 2:8, 9) not by H2O i.e. water. There is no element anywhere in creation that can save you. Only Jesus can save you. Romans 10:9-10 says you must *"believe in your heart and confess with your mouth the Lord Jesus Christ"* to be saved.

Acts 16:31 says. *"Believe on the Lord Jesus Christ and thou shalt be saved."* The thief on the cross with Jesus was saved, but was not baptized in water (Luke 23:32-43). In Acts 19, Paul baptized about 12 men in water, but it was afterwards that he laid his hands on them and they received Holy Spirit baptism. Salvation, water baptism, and Holy Spirit baptism are three distinct events.

Three Basic Modes of Water Baptism

There are 3 basic modes of water baptism used in Christian churches and I have no objection to any of these modes: (1) Sprinkle, (2) Pour, (3) Immersion. However, the word "baptism" (Gr. *Baptizo*) indicates total immersion. Immersion displays pub-licly our identity with Christ in His death, burial, and resurrection. Water baptism illustrates the spiritual cleansing we experience when we accept Jesus as Savior. Just as water cleanses the body so Holy Spirit cleanses our hearts when we trust in Christ (Rom 6:3-7; Rom 8:16).

Six Reasons for Water Baptism

There are six reasons for water baptism.

(1) To symbolize the washing away of our sins (I Peter 3:20; Acts 22:15; Ephesians 2:8).
(2) Identification with the death, burial, and resurrection Christ.

(3) To symbolize the death of our old life and the old man, the inward regeneration of the Holy Spirit, and resurrection (Romans 6:3-6; Colossians 2:12-14).
(4) To signify our new spiritual union with the Lord.
(5) Public initiation rite into the body of Christ.
(6) Jesus commanded water baptism (Matthew 28:9-20; Mark 16:15-16; Acts 2:41; 10:47-48).

Water baptism does not save us. If one is not baptized in water that does not mean they are not saved. Such was the case with the thief who was crucified with Jesus (Lk. 23:39-43). He was saved by his confession of belief that Jesus was the Christ, but he was never baptized in water. Nothing man can do except believe and confess Jesus Christ will save him. Even the grace and faith you have are provided by God and his Word. If humankind can do anything to save themselves then what Christ did was not enough. Humankind cannot save himself so they need a Savior. Man's only part is to accept what Jesus did.

The water baptism of Jesus pinpoints the time of his Holy Spirit anointing by the Father, as well as the revelation and presentation of Jesus to Israel as their long awaited Messiah who takes away the sins of the world. That is why Acts10:36-38 and Acts 1:21-22 are important. The water baptismal event of Jesus marks an important point in time. It was from this point in time that Jesus began his public ministry by the power of the Holy Spirit anointing. It was only after this Holy Spirit anointing at his water baptism that Jesus performed miracles, taught, healed, or preached.

The point to be made concerning the water baptism of Jesus is to suggest a particular time when Jesus, fully man, was anointed by God with the Holy Spirit. Acts 10:38 tells us that God anointed Jesus with the Holy Ghost and power, and in Luke 4:18 Jesus himself acknowledges the power of that Holy Spirit anointing to preach, heal, comfort, and deliver those in need. Jesus said, "The Spirit of the Lord is upon me <u>because he has anointed me</u>..." The anointing of the Holy Spirit was for the purpose of revealing God to the world by doing the things Jesus listed in this verse.

Peter identified the water baptismal event of Jesus as the demarcation line for anyone who would be considered to replace Judas as a disciple. He said anyone to be considered must have walked with Jesus from the point in time of his water baptism. Both Acts 1:21-22 and Acts 10:36-38 pinpoint Jesus' water baptism as a very significant event. I submit to you that Peter was not saying it was the water that was important in that event, but the Holy Spirit descending and remaining on Jesus that was significant (John 1:36).

The Holy Spirit involvement in the incarnational event was to bring Jesus into the world. Holy Spirit anointing at the water baptism was to present Jesus publicly to the Jews as the Son of God and their long awaited Messiah (Matthew 3:16-17; John 1:32-33).

Baptism in the Holy Spirit. Just as water baptism does not save you neither does baptism in the Holy Spirit save you. However, both water baptism and Holy Spirit baptism are two things Jesus expects born-again Christians to do. Doing neither water baptism nor being baptized in the Holy Spirit will keep you from being a Christian, but they are both things Jesus said to do. Therefore they should not be taken lightly, but followed obediently.

Holy Spirit baptism may precede or follow water baptism. Water baptism is a public confirmation of your decision to follow

Jesus in your life. Baptism in the Holy Spirit is an empowerment to live victoriously in this life as well as to display the gifts of the Holy Spirit in power as a witness that Jesus is the Son of God. Holy Spirit baptism may follow salvation instantly or it may be separated by a period of time, but salvation must precede baptism in the Holy Spirit. Jesus taught much about the baptism in the Holy Spirit that was to come after he ascended. He called it "the promise of the Father" because it was prophesied in Joel, Isaiah, and other books of the Old Testament that there would be an outpouring of God's Spirit in the last days (Luke 24:49; Acts 1:4). Much of what Jesus taught about the baptism in the Holy Spirit can be read in John, Luke and Acts in particular.

JESUS IS THE BAPTIZER IN THE HOLY GHOST

John very specifically called Jesus the "baptizer in the Holy Ghost" (John1:29-33; see also Acts 1:5; Luke 6:13). The book of Acts records the activity of the early Church after the outpouring of the Holy Spirit on the Day of Pentecost following the ascension of Jesus (Luke 24:49; Acts 1:8; Acts 2:4, 8, 10, 19). The book of Acts also reveals the Spirit-filled Church in action. The same Holy Spirit power is available to the church today.

Of which of these three baptisms have you partaken? If not all three, why have you not? Think on this. As shown above, they are all three taught in the Scriptures. The story of Jesus washing Peter's feet might suggest an analogy for us. After Jesus corrected Peter for not wanting him to wash his feet, Peter perhaps indicated that he acknowledged Jesus as the "baptizer" and not only wanted Jesus to wash his feet (sins washed away), but that he wanted all Jesus had to offer (Holy Spirit baptism). Do you want just your feet washed or your all?

Chapter Ten: Holy Spirit Baptism vs. Fruit of the Spirit

Introduction

Holy Spirit Baptism vs. Fruit of the Spirit

"Event" versus "Process"

The Fruit and the Fire

What Does Baptism Mean?

Holy Spirit Baptism: True Change

CHAPTER 10
Holy Spirit Baptism vs. Fruit of the Spirit

INTRODUCTION

In the next few chapters we will cover the subject of "Baptism in the Holy Spirit." We will approach the biblical doctrine of the Holy Spirit baptism by: (1) differentiating between the fruit of the Spirit and Baptism in the Holy Spirit; (2) defining the term "baptism," (3) reviewing Jesus' exhortation of the importance of believers being baptized in Holy Spirit, (4) seeing Jesus as our example of Holy Spirit baptism and as baptizer in Holy Spirit and (5) by examining what Jesus had to say about Holy Spirit as recorded in the Gospel of John. By this, we will be able to see the importance that Jesus placed on Holy Spirit baptism.

We have established that Holy Spirit is the third person of the Trinity and that each person of the Trinity has specific roles, but they always act in unity in every creative act and event and in the redemption plan for humankind. The redemption plan includes (1) the Father giving the Son, (Incarnation); (2) salvation through Jesus Christ; (3) Heavenly glorification of Jesus; and (4) Holy Spirit outpouring and empowerment to enable believers to live victoriously as witnesses of the Lord Jesus Christ. Holy

Spirit baptism is the time of spiritual empowerment. It is the coming of the special presence and power of God on believers. It is God on man doing what only God can do.

We will also examine what Jesus had to say about Holy Spirit by looking at Luke's assessment in his Gospel and the book of Acts. In addition, we will look at Paul's teaching on Holy Spirit in his letter to the predominately Gentile Corinthian church. First Corinthians chapters 2, 12, 14 will be our main focus in Paul's writings. We will not enter into deep theological defense or argument. We will simply allow the scripture to speak.

Holy Spirit Baptism vs. Fruit of the Spirit

"Event" vs. "Process" It is very important to understand that the baptism in the Holy Spirit is a crisis <u>event</u>, whereas, the production of fruit is a <u>process</u>. Crisis means "in a moment."

The Fruit and the Fire

The fruit of the Spirit is proof of our "walking in the Spirit," but it is not proof of our being "baptized in the Holy Spirit." The fruit does not indicate that we have the fire of the Holy Spirit. The fruit will and should develop in a Spirit-baptized person. It is important to the completeness of a Christian's life and testimony. We need both fruit of the Spirit and Holy Spirit baptism. Salvation through faith in Jesus Christ restores the image and likeness of God in believers and the fruit of the Spirit displays that image and likeness of God before the world. Holy Spirit baptism is an empowerment to use the breath breathed into Adam's nostrils to preach the gospel and to bring glory to God as intended in Genesis 2:7. Holy Spirit baptism displays God's power and majesty before the world. Until Jesus redeemed mankind, Satan was able to use this breath to destroy the things of God. Until Jesus was glorified and Holy Spirit was poured out on the earth, the display of God's majesty and power was limited to only a few. After redemption and the outpouring of Holy Spirit, all believers can now have this empowerment.

<u>The fruit of the Spirit and the power of Holy Spirit together demonstrate to the world the full restoration of the image, likeness, and proper use of the breath of God in believers</u> (Genesis 1:26-28; 2:7). Spoken to me 11-7-14.

Holy Spirit power can accomplish much, but without godly character (i.e. fruit of the Spirit), the power in the life of the Spirit-baptized person will not be credible nor will it last. Paul and Jesus both addressed Christian character and Holy Spirit power in the lives of believers. Both righteousness and Holy Spirit empower-ment in the lives of believers are important.

Galatians 5:22-25 *(22) But the fruit of the Spirit is love, joy, peace, long-suffering, gentleness, goodness, faith, (23) meekness, temperance: against such there is no law. (24) And they that are Christ's have crucified the flesh with the affections and lusts. (25) If we live in the Spirit, let us also walk in the Spirit.*

First Corinthians 13:1-8 *Though I speak with the tongues of men and of angels, and have not charity, I am become as sounding brass, or a tinkling cymbal. (2) And though I have the gift of prophecy, and understand all mysteries, and all knowledge: and though I have all faith, so that I could remove mountains, and have not charity, I am nothing. (3) And though I bestow all my goods to feed the poor, and though I give my body to be burned, and have not charity, it profiteth me nothing. (4) Charity suffereth long, and is kind; charity envieth not: charity vaunteth not itself, is not puffed up. (5) Doth not behave itself unseemly, seeketh not her own, is not easily provoked, thinketh no evil; (6) Rejoiceth not in iniquity, but rejoiceth in the truth: (7) beareth all things, believeth all things, hopeth all things, endureth all things. (8) Love never fails...*

Acts 1:4-5, 8 After his resurrection and before his ascension, Jesus spoke with the disciples:*(4) And,* (Jesus) *being assembled together with them, commanded them that they should not depart from Jerusalem, but wait for the promise of the Father, which, saith he, ye have heard of me. (5) For John truly baptized with water: but ye shall be baptized with the Holy Ghost not many days hence. (8) But ye shall receive power, after that the Holy Ghost is come upon you: and ye shall be witnesses unto me both in Jerusalem, and in all Judea, and in Samaria, and unto the uttermost part of the earth.*

Earlier, John the Baptist had declared that though he baptized them in water, Jesus would baptize them in the Holy Spirit, thereby, emphasizing that a greater one would baptize with the greater baptism. We see that fulfilled in Acts 2:4.

What Does Baptism Mean?

The first observation is the word "baptism." What does baptism or baptize mean? The Greek word *baptizo* means to dip, sink, or submerge. It is sometimes translated "bathe or wash" (Mark 7:4; Luke 11:38).

The New American Standard (NAS) New Testament Greek Lexicon distinguishes "dipping" as *bapto,* and "baptized" as *baptizo* by giving the Greek poet, Nicander's example of making pickles. Nicander says that in order to make a pickle, the vegetable should first be "dipped" (*bapto*) into boiling water and then "baptized" (*baptizo*) in the vinegar solution. Both verbs concern the immersing of vegetables in a solution, but the first is temporary. The second, the act of "baptizing" the vegetable, produces a permanent change.

Concerning our union and identification with Christ, Mark 16:16 indicates that mere intellectual assent is not enough. There must be a union with him that produces a real change like the vegetable to the pickle i.e. "baptized." (*Bible Study Magazine*. James Montgomery Boice. May, 1989.)

Mark 16:16 *He that believeth and is baptized (baptizo) shall be saved; but he that believeth not shall be damned.*

<u>The proof of whether one truly believed is a resulting true change in the one baptized (*baptizo*).</u>

Holy Spirit Baptism: True Change

Concerning union with Holy Spirit, we are not told to be "dipped" (*bapto*) in the Holy Spirit, but to be baptized (*baptizo*). We need full immersion in the Holy Spirit. That is what Jesus was saying.

When a person is baptized in the Holy Spirit, a fire and zeal "to do" accompanies it. However, if that fire is not continually fed by spending time in God's presence, it will eventually go out. God is the source of the fire, as well as, what feeds the fire. In his presence there is fuel for the fire. Spending time in the presence of God causes one to desire to be like him (i.e. fruit of the Spirit).

Nowhere is it recorded in the Bible that the church will ever not need Holy Spirit baptism. Nowhere is it recorded in the Bible that Holy Spirit will no longer manifest himself through the supernatural evidence of tongues or the gifts of the Holy Spirit. However, in time, these spiritual manifestations decreased as the epicopate gathered to themselves more and more authority. Moved initially by fear of heresies developing in the church, and later fear of losing their power over the people and by greed, they began to forbid supernatural manifestations among the laity. It was not that Holy Spirit had ceased or had been removed by God. Church history offers evidence that a lack of faith influenced by ungodly church leadership, inhibited at best and prohibited at worst the manifestation of the Holy Spirit. Therefore, supernatural manifestations and gifts almost totally disappeared during certain time periods in the church. However, the lack of manifestations of the Holy Spirit gifts was and is no proof that Holy Spirit baptism was removed from the church and from Earth. In other words it does not confirm the cessation doctrine. It does confirm a lack of faith. Jesus always was and continues to be the baptizer in the Holy Spirit.

There has always been a remnant of believers who remained faithful to God's word concerning the availability of Holy Spirit empowerment for witness and victorious living. These remnant groups were often declared to be heretics and banished from the church.

With this knowledge, we can see how baptism in the Holy Spirit teaching and experience has had to fight for survival. This ought not be. It seems reasonable that if one is willing to believe the Word of God concerning salvation through Jesus Christ, that same person should also believe the clear teaching in the same Word of God concerning Holy Spirit baptism. In addition to the teaching of Christ himself concerning Holy Spirit, fuller revelation and understanding were given to the Church through the inspired New Testament writers who knew Jesus and his teachings. They were inspired by Holy Spirit to write, and had the personal experience of the baptism in the Holy Spirit. They were first hand witnesses.

Chapter Eleven: Holy Spirit Baptism Doctrine

Introduction

Scriptures to Prayerfully Meditate

Jesus Was Anointed for Ministry

The Church was Anointed for Ministry

Before Ascension and Glorification

After Ascension and Glorification: Holy Spirit Baptism Experiences

The Persecuted Scattered Spirit-Filled Church

Holy Spirit Baptism Followed Belief in Jesus Christ

The Story of Peter and Cornelius

Paul at Ephesus

Paul at Corinth Teaching on Spiritual Gifts and Church Order

CHAPTER 11
Holy Spirit Baptism Doctrine

INTRODUCTION

Holy Spirit baptism is the coming of the special presence and power of God. It is God on man doing only what God can do. The fruit of the Spirit is proof of our walking in the Spirit—not the proof of our being baptized in the Spirit. However, the fruit of the Spirit will/should develop in a Holy Spirit baptized person's life.

Take time to prayerfully read and meditate on the scriptures below. I have placed these here with very a few comments as seeds from God's Word to be planted in your heart to bring forth fruit of revelation.

SCRIPTURES TO PRAYERFULLY MEDITATE

Matthew 3:11-17 (John the Baptist said): *(11) I indeed baptize you with water unto repentance: but he that cometh after me is mightier than I, whose shoes I am not worthy to bear: he shall baptize you with the Holy Ghost, and [with] fire: (12) Whose fan [is] in his hand, and he will thoroughly purge his floor, and gather his wheat into the garner; but he will burn up the chaff with unquenchable fire. (13) Then cometh Jesus from Galilee to Jordan unto John, to be baptized of him. (14) But John* *forbad him, saying, I have need to be baptized of thee, and comest thou to me? (15) And Jesus answering said unto him, Suffer [it to be so] now: for thus it becometh us to fulfil all righteousness. Then he suffered him. (16) And Jesus, when he was baptized, went up straightway out of the water: and, lo, the heavens were opened unto him, and he saw the Spirit of God descending like a dove, and lighting upon him: (17) And lo a voice from heaven, saying, This is my beloved Son, in whom I am well plea*sed.

John 1:32-33 *And John bare record saying, I saw the Spirit descending from heaven like a dove and it abode upon him. (33) And I knew him not, but he that sent me to baptize with water, the same said unto me: Upon whom thou shalt see the Spirit descending and remaining on him, the same is he which baptizeth with the Holy Ghost.*

Matthew 4:1-11 (After Jesus' water baptism and anointing of the Holy Spirit) Then *was Jesus led up of the Spirit into the wilderness to be tempted of the devil. (2) And when he had fasted forty days and forty nights, he was after-ward an hungred. (3) And when the tempter came to him, he said, If thou be the Son of God, command that these stones be made bread. (4) But he answered and said, It is written, Man shall not live by bread alone, but by every word that proceedeth out of the mouth of God. (5) Then the devil taketh him up into the holy city, and setteth him on a pinnacle of the temple, (6) And saith unto him, If thou be the Son of God, cast thyself down: for it is written, He shall give his angels charge concerning thee: and in [their] hands they shall bear thee up, lest at any time thou dash thy foot against a stone. (7) Jesus said unto him,* <u>It is written again</u>, *Thou shalt not tempt the Lord thy God. (8) Again, the devil taketh him up into an exceeding high mountain, and sheweth him all the kingdoms of the world, and the glory of them; (9) And saith unto him, All these things will I give thee, if thou wilt fall down and worship me. (10) Then saith Jesus unto him, Get thee hence, Satan:* <u>*for it is*</u>

written, Thou shalt worship the Lord thy God, and him only shalt thou serve. (11) Then the devil leaveth him, and, behold, angels came and ministered unto him.

Matthew 8:16-17 (After Jesus' baptism, Holy Spirit anointing, and the temptations in the wilderness) *When the even was come, they brought unto him* (Jesus) *many that were possessed with devils: and he cast out the spirits with [his] word, and healed all that were sick: (17) That it might be fulfilled which was spoken by Esaias the prophet, saying, Himself took our infirmities, and bare [our] sicknesses.*

Jesus had the authority to give His disciples power to cast out demons and heal the sick. This was for only particular times. Later, before his ascension, he gave ALL believers authority to do the same and told them to wait for the Holy Spirit to fill and indwell them for empowerment to do the mission of the ministry.

Matthew 10:1 (to the twelve disciples) *And when he had called unto [him] his twelve disciples, he gave them power [against] unclean spirits, to cast them out, and to heal all manner of sickness and all manner of disease.*

Matthew 28:19-20 (to all believers) *(19) Go ye therefore, and teach all nations, baptizing them in the name of the Father, and of the Son, and of the Holy Ghost: (20) Teaching them to observe all things whatsoever I have commanded you: and, lo, I am with you alway, [even] unto the end of the world. Amen.*

Mark 16:15-20 (All believers) *And he said unto them, Go ye into all the world, and preach the gospel to every creature. (16) He that believeth and is baptized shall be saved; but he that believeth not shall be* damned. (17) And <u>these signs shall follow them that believe;</u> In my name shall they <u>cast out devils;</u> they shall <u>speak with new tongues;</u> (18) <u>They shall take up serpents; and if they drink any deadly thing, it shall not hurt them;</u> they shall <u>lay hands on the sick, and they shall recover.</u> (19) So then after the Lord had spoken unto them, he was received up into heaven, and sat on the right hand of God. (20) And they went forth, and preached everywhere, the Lord working with [them], and confirming the word with signs following. Amen.

JESUS WAS ANOINTED FOR MINISTRY
Luke 4:16-19 *(16) And he (Jesus) came to Nazareth, where he had been brought up: and, as his custom was, he went into the synagogue on the sabbath day, and stood up for to read. (17) And there was delivered unto him the book of the prophet Esaias. And when he had opened the book, he found the place where it was written, (18)* <u>*The Spirit of the Lord [is] upon me, because he hath anointed me*</u> *to preach the gospel to the poor; he hath sent me to heal the brokenhearted, to preach deliverance to the captives, and recovering of sight to the blind, to set at liberty them that are bruised, (19) To preach the acceptable year of the Lord.*

THE CHURCH WAS ANOINTED FOR MINISTRY
Acts 2:1-4 *and when the day of Pentecost was fully come, they were all with one accord in one place. (2) And suddenly there came a sound from heaven as of a rushing mighty wind, and it filled all the house where they were sitting. (3) And there appeared unto them cloven tongues like as of fire, and it sat upon each of them. (4)* <u>*And they were all filled with the Holy Ghost, and began to speak with other tongues, as the Spirit gave them utterance.*</u>

Luke 11:9-13 *(9) And I say unto you, Ask, and it shall be given you; seek, and ye shall find; knock, and it shall be opened unto you. (10) For every one that asketh receiveth; and he that seeketh findeth; and to him that knocketh it shall be opened. (11) If a son shall ask bread of any of you that is a father, will he give him a stone? Or if [he ask] a fish, will he for a fish give him a serpent? (12) Or if he shall ask an egg, will he offer him a scorpion? (13) <u>If ye then, being evil, know how to give good gifts unto your children: how much more shall [your] heavenly Father give the Holy Spirit to them that ask him</u>?*

Before Ascension and Glorification

John 7:37-39, *(37) In the last day, that great [day] of the feast, Jesus stood and cried, saying, If any man thirst, let him come unto me, and drink. (38) He that believeth on me, as the scripture hath said, out of his belly shall flow rivers of living water. (39) (But this spake he of the Spirit, which they that believe on him should receive: <u>for the Holy Ghost was not yet [given]; because that Jesus was not yet glorified</u>.)*

John 14:12-18, 23-26, *(12) Verily, verily, I say unto you, He that believeth on me, the works that I do shall he do also<u>; and greater [works] than these shall he do; because I go unto my Father</u>. (13) And whatsoever ye shall ask in my name, that will I do, that the Father may be glorified in the Son. (14) If ye shall ask any thing in my name, I will do [it]. (15) If ye love me, keep my commandments. (16) And <u>I will pray the Father, and he shall give you another Comforter, that he may abide with you forever;</u> (17) [Even] the <u>Spirit of truth</u>; whom the world cannot receive, because it seeth him not, neither knoweth him: but ye know him; for <u>he dwelleth with you, and shall be in you</u>. (18) I will not leave you comfortless: I will come to you. (23) Jesus answered and said unto him, If a man love me, he* will keep my words: and my Father will love him, and we will come unto him, and make our abode with him. (24) He that loveth me not keepeth not my sayings: and the word which ye hear is not mine, but the Father's which sent me. (25) These things have I spoken unto you, being [yet] present with you. (26) But the <u>Comforter, [which is] the Holy Ghost, whom the Father will send in my name, he shall teach you all things, and bring all things to your remembrance, whatsoever I have said unto you.</u>

John 15:26-27 *(26) But when the Comforter is come, whom I will send unto you from the Father, [even] the Spirit of truth, which proceedeth from the Father, <u>he shall testify of me</u>: (27) And ye also shall bear witness, because ye have been with me from the beginning.*

John 16:7, 12-14 *(7) Nevertheless I tell you the truth<u>; It is expedient for you that I go away: for if I go not away, the Comforter will not come unto you; but if I depart, I will send him unto you.</u> (12) I have yet many things to say unto you, but ye cannot bear them now. (13) Howbeit when he, the <u>Spirit of truth, is come, he will guide you into all truth</u>: for he shall not speak of himself; but whatsoever he shall hear, [that] shall he speak: and he will shew you things to come. (14) He shall glorify me: for he shall receive of mine, and shall shew [it] unto you.*

Luke 24:45-53 *(45) Then opened he their understanding, that they might understand the scriptures, (46) And said unto them, Thus it is written, and thus it behoved Christ to suffer, and to rise from the dead the third day: (47) And that repentance and remission of sins should be preached in his name among all nations, beginning at Jerusalem. (48) And ye are witnesses of these things. (49) And, behold, <u>I send the promise of my Father upon you: but tarry ye in the city of Jerusalem, until ye be endued with power from on high.</u> (50) And he led them out as far as to*

Bethany, and he lifted up his hands, and blessed them. (51) And it came to pass, while he blessed them, he was parted from them, and carried up into heaven. (52) <u>And they worshipped him, and returned to Jerusalem with great joy: (53) And were continually in the temple, praising and blessing God. Amen.</u>

After Ascension and Glorification: Holy Spirit Baptism Experiences

The book of Acts tells of the activities of the Holy Spirit baptized Church as they went forth preaching the gospel, and the gos-pel being confirmed with undeniable supernatural signs following. Since it is written in a narrative fashion, one would do well to read it in a version that would do justice to the language. I prefers the King James Version, but one might want to do a first read-through in something like the New Living Translation. The point is that the book of Acts reveals the acts of the Holy Spirit in the early church which should be a pattern for the acts of the church in any age and certainly in today's world.

Acts 1:8 *<u>But ye shall receive power, after that the Holy Ghost is come upon you</u>: and ye shall be witnesses unto me both in Jerusalem, and in all Judaea, and in Samaria, and unto the uttermost part of the earth.*

Acts 2:1-13 *(1) And when the day of Pentecost was fully come, they were all with one accord in one place. (2) And suddenly there came a sound from heaven as of a rushing mighty wind, and it filled all the house where they were sitting. (3) And there appeared unto them cloven tongues like as of fire, and it sat upon each of them. (4) And they were all <u>filled with the Holy Ghost</u>, and <u>began to speak with other tongues</u>, as the Spirit* *gave them utterance.* (5) *And there were dwelling at Jerusalem Jews, devout men, out of every nation under heaven. (6) Now when this was noised abroad, the multitude came together, and were confounded, because that every man heard them speak in his own language. (7) And they were all amazed and marveled, saying one to another, Behold, are not all these which speak Galileans? (8) And how hear we every man in our own tongue, wherein we were born? (9) Parthians, and Medes, and Elamites, and the dwellers in Mesopotamia, and in Judaea, and Cappadocia, in Pontus, and Asia, (10) Phrygia, and Pamphylia, in Egypt, and in the parts of Libya about Cyrene, and strangers of Rome, Jews and proselytes, (11) Cretes and Arabians, we do hear them speak in our tongues the wonderful works of God. (12) And they were all amazed, and were in doubt, saying one to another, What meaneth this? (13) Others mocking said, These men are full of new wine.*

Acts 2 records the first occurrence of the heavenly language of "tongues." Speaking in "tongues" was the unique factor of all the occurrences of early church Holy Spirit baptisms recorded in Acts 8, 10, and 19. All the other spiritual gifts had occurred throughout the Old Testament period except tongues and interpretation. In Acts 2, the people in the upper room appeared to be drunk. Notice that no one prior to this outpouring who had ever prophesied, healed, had a word of knowledge or wisdom, performed miracles, showed great faith, or discerned spirits were ever accused of being drunk. It was not those things that made the onlookers say they were drunk. They appeared drunk and sounded drunk because the language of the Spirit is not of this world. Unknown tongues was a new, unique, visual, and audial occurrence. People heard them speak in their own language, but that was not why they said they were drunk. That was amazing, but it was not a drunken behavior. The accusation of drunkenness was based on other things. A drunk can sound like they are jabbering non-sense syllables and they stagger. But they are not accused of being drunk when they speak another language and their speech is understood. Therefore, the behavior that caused that accusation of drunkenness was unusual. They heard them speak in tongues! All the other supernatural things that occurred such as prophesying or boldness was not new phenomenon, but speaking in tongues was not only new, but highly strange!

It was the fulfillment of Old Testament prophesies and promises. This is still for you today. Nothing has changed.

Many people speak more than one human language. That is not unusual. The languages foreigners heard at Pentecost were truly theirs, but there was more than languages of men as is confirmed in subsequent scriptures such as I Corinthians 12 and 14 when Paul exhorted the people to speak to each other in their common language rather than tongues which others could not understand. Speaking in tongues is for speaking directly to God or for Holy Spirit speaking to the church with interpretations. I Corinthians 14:1-4 says when one speaks in tongues no man un-derstands him/her. This is referring to tongues that is received at the time of baptism in the Holy Spirit as well as the spiritual gift that must be accompanied by interpretation. Paul also says in that same scripture that when we speak in tongues, we are speaking to God!

Your "prayer" language or the language of your spirit is spoken directly to God. I Corinthians 14:2 says *"For he that speaketh in an unknown tongue speaketh not unto men but unto God..."*, and vese14 says, *"When you pray in tongues, your spirit prayeth."*

Praying in tongues is the language of one's Holy Spirit-baptized tongue. It is the language of one's spirit by the Holy Spirit. James said that no MAN (i.e. person) can tame the tongue, but Holy Spirit can. According to one scientific study, this spoken heavenly language bypasses the brain and human reason. It is of the spirit.

THE PERSECUTED SCATTERED SPIRIT- FILLED CHURCH

The following Scriptures are clear examples of the early church experiencing unknown tongues as evidence of Holy Spirit baptism.

Acts 8:1-8, 14-17 *(1) And Saul was consenting unto his (Stephen) death. And at that time there was <u>a great persecution against the church which was at Jerusalem; and they were all scattered abroad throughout the regions of Judaea and Samaria, except the apostles.</u> (2) And devout men carried Stephen [to his burial], and made great lamentation over him. (3) As for Saul, he made havoc of the church, entering into every house, and haling men and women committed [them] to prison. (4) <u>Therefore they that were scattered abroad went everywhere preaching the word.</u> (5)Then <u>Philip went down to the city of Samaria, and preached Christ unto them.</u> (6) And the <u>people with one accord gave heed</u> unto those things which Philip spake, hearing and seeing the <u>miracles</u> which he did. (7) For <u>unclean spirits, crying with loud voice, came out of many</u> that were possessed [with them]: and many taken with palsies, and that were lame, were healed. (8) And there was <u>great joy in that city</u>. (14) Now when the apostles which were at Jerusalem heard that Samaria had received the word of God, they <u>sent unto them Peter and John: (15) Who, when they were come down, prayed for them, that they might receive the Holy Ghost: (16) (For as yet he was fallen upon none of them: only they* *were baptized in the name of the Lord Jesus.) (17) Then laid they [their] hands on them, and they received the Holy Ghost.*

HOLY SPIRIT BAPTISM FOLLOWED BELIEF ON JESUS CHRIST.

It was <u>after</u> the revival in Samaria, and <u>after</u> people became believers that Peter and John went to Samaria and prayed for them to receive Holy Spirit baptism. These believers had been baptized in water unto repentance. What did Philip preach to the Samaritan? He preached Christ to them (v.5). Subsequently, Peter and John came and <u>laid hands on those believers and they received the Holy Spirit. Right order: salvation then baptism in the Holy Spirit.</u>

THE STORY OF PETER AND CORNELIUS

Acts 10:44-46 *While Peter yet spake these words, the Holy Ghost fell on all them which heard the word. (45) And they of the circumcision which believed were astonished, as many as came with Peter, because that on the Gentiles also was poured out the gift of the Holy Ghost. (46) For they heard them speak with tongues and magnify God. Then answered Peter, (47) Can any man forbid water, that these should not be baptized, which have received the Holy Ghost as well as we? (48) And he commanded them to be baptized in the name of the Lord.*

PAUL AT EPHESUS

Acts 19:1-6 *(1) And it came to pass, that, while Apollos was at Corinth, Paul having passed through the upper coasts came to Ephesus: and <u>finding certain disciples</u>, (2) He said unto them, <u>Have ye received the Holy</u>*

<u>Ghost since ye believed?</u> *And they said unto him, We have not so much as heard whether there be any Holy Ghost. (3) And he said unto them, Unto what then were ye baptized? And they said, Unto John's baptism. (4) Then said Paul, John verily baptized with the baptism of repentance, saying unto the people, that they should believe on him which should come after him, that is, on Christ Jesus. (5) When they heard [this], they were <u>baptized in the name of the Lord Jesus. (6) And when Paul had laid [his] hands upon them, the Holy Ghost came on them: and they spake with tongues, and prophesied.</u>*

John's baptism was unto repentance and was not done in the name of Jesus because Jesus had not yet been revealed to Israel. At the water baptism of Jesus, he was revealed to Israel as the Messiah. God declared Jesus to be the Messiah at his water baptism as recorded in John 1:32-33. John saw the Holy Spirit descend and remain on Jesus which was the confirmation to John that this was the Messiah. This was the one who would baptize in the Holy Spirit. This was the one that John the Baptist said was mightier than him because John only baptized in water, but the Messiah would baptize in the Holy Spirit. The Ephesian disciples had only heard John's message of baptism unto repentance, but no one had brought the message to them concerning the manifestation of Jesus the Messiah and the availability of Holy Spirit baptism. When they heard, they received. Have you received since you believed?

PAUL AT CORINTH TEACHING ON SPIRITUAL GIFTS AND CHURCH ORDER

I Corinthians 12 *(1) Now concerning spiritual [gifts], brethren, I would not have you ignorant. (2) Ye know that ye were Gentiles, carried away unto these dumb idols, even as ye were led. (3) Wherefore I give you to understand, that no man speaking by the Spirit of God calleth Jesus accursed: and [that] no man can say that Jesus is the Lord, but by the Holy Ghost. (4) Now there are diversities of gifts, but the same Spirit. (5) And there are differences of administrations, but the same Lord. (6) And there are diversities of operations, but it is the same God which worketh all in all. (7) But the manifestation of the Spirit is given to every man to profit withal. (8) For to one is given by the Spirit the word of wisdom; to another the word of knowledge by the same Spirit; (9) To another faith by the same Spirit; to another the gifts of healing by the same Spirit; (10) To another the working of miracles; to another prophecy; to another discerning of spirits; to another [divers] kinds of tongues; to another the interpretation of tongues: (11) But all these worketh that one and the selfsame Spirit, dividing to every man severally as he will. (12) For as the body is one, and hath many members, and all the members of that one body, being many, are one body: so also [is] Christ. (13) For by one Spirit are we all baptized into one body, whether [we be] Jews or Gentiles, whether [we be] bond or free; and have been all made to drink into one Spirit. (14) For the body is not one member, but many. (15) If the foot shall say, Because I am not the hand, I am not of the body; is it therefore not of the body? (16) And if the ear shall say, Because I am not the eye, I am not of the body; is it therefore not of the body? (17) If the whole body [were] an eye, where [were] the hearing? If the whole [were] hearing, where [were] the smelling? (18) But now hath God set the members every one of them in the body, as it hath pleased him. (19) And if they were all one member, where [were] the body? (20) But now [are they] many members, yet but one body. (21) And the eye cannot say unto the hand, I have no need of thee: nor again the head to the feet, I have no need of you. (22) Nay, much more those members of the body, which seem to be more feeble, are necessary: (23) And those [members] of the body, which we think to be less honorable, upon these we bestow more abundant honor; and our uncomely* *[parts] have more abundant comeliness. (24) For our comely [parts] have no need: but God hath tempered the body together, having given more abundant honor to that [part] which lacked: (25) That there should be no schism in the body; but [that] the members should have the same care one for another. (26) And whether one member suffer, all the members suffer with it; or one member be honored, all the members rejoice with it. (27) Now ye are the body of Christ, and members in particular. (28) And God hath set some in the church, first apostles, secondarily prophets, thirdly teachers, after that miracles, then gifts of healings, helps, governments, diversities of tongues. 2(9) [Are] all apostles? [Are] all prophets? [Are] all teachers? [Are] all workers of miracles? (30) Have all the gifts of healing? Do all speak with tongues? (*Bring messages by the gift of tongues to the church?) *Do all interpret? (31) But covet earnestly the best gifts: and yet shew I unto you a more excellent way.*

Paul said he would show them a more excellent way than just coveting the gifts. Love opens the door to the manifestation of these gifts. Galatians 5:6 says faith works and is moved forward by love. Paul did not mean that the gifts were to be forfeited in lieu of love, but that love should be the motivation for the manifestation of any gifts of the Holy Spirit. Love displaces the possibility of pride.

I Corinthians 13:1-4 *Though I speak with the tongues of men and of angels, and have not charity, I am become as sounding brass, or a tinkling cymbal. (2) and though I have the gift of prophecy, and understand all mysteries, and all knowledge; and though I have all faith, so that I could remove mountains, and have not charity, I am nothing. (3) and though I bestow all my goods to feed the poor, and though I give my body to be burned, and have not charity, it profiteth at me nothing. (4) Charity suffereth long, and is kind; charity enveyth not; charity vaulteth not itself, is not puffed up.*

1 Corinthians 14:1-4, 14 *(1) Follow after charity, <u>and desire spiritual [gifts]</u>, but rather that ye may prophesy. (2) For he that speaketh in an [unknown] tongue speaketh not unto men, but unto God: for no man understandeth [him]; howbeit in the spirit he speaketh mysteries. (3) But he that prophesieth speaketh unto men [to] edification, and exhortation, and comfort. (4) He that speaketh in an [unknown] tongue edifieth himself; but he that prophesieth edifieth the church. (14) For if I pray in an [unknown] tongue, my spirit prayeth, but my understanding is unfruitful.*

In this chapter, Paul deals with order in the church. Paul's intention is not to stop the use of tongues in church, but to teach how tongues as a prayer language edifies the speaker because they are speaking directly to God, but also tongues as the manifestation of the gift of tongues can profit and edify the church when accompanied by interpretation. Without interpretation, tongues spoken to the church have no value. In I Corinthians 14:1-6, Paul informed them that speaking in tongues is good and profitable for the church body when accompanied by the gift of interpretation. Together they profit and edify the church as does prophecy.

Paul distinguished between the gift of tongues that requires the gift of interpretation, and a person's personal prayer language that he/she uses in speaking directly to God. Verse two of that chapter says you speak directly to God when you speak in tongues. This is your prayer language. This is the language of your spirit. This is a good thing. Verse 14 says when you pray in unknown tongues your spirit is praying. Remember, you are not speaking to man when you are praying in tongues. You are speaking directly to God. This does not require the gift of interpretation. This is your prayer language to God. When you are speaking in tongues in prayer to God, you are speaking mysteries according this scripture. These mysteries are not mysteries that God does not understand. These are mysteries that you give voice to by the Holy Spirit and mysteries that Holy Spirit reveals to you according to I Corinthians 2:9-12.

First Corinthians 2:9-12 *But as it is written, Eye hath not seen, nor ear heard, neither have entered into the heart of man, the things which God hath prepared for them that love him. (10) <u>But God hath revealed them unto us by his Spirit</u>: for the Spirit searches all things, yea the deep things of God. (11) For what man knoweth the things of a man save the spirit of man that is in him? <u>Even so</u> the things of God know what no man, but the spirit of God. (12) Now we have received, not the spirit of the world, but the spirit which is of God; <u>that we might know the things that are freely given to us of God.</u>*

John 16:13 *Howbeit when he, the Spirit of truth, is come, he will guide you into all truth: for he shall not speak of himself; but whatsoever he shall hear, that shall he speak: and he will show you things to come.*

Have you received since you believed? If not, why not? Have you spoken in tongues since being baptized in Holy Spirit? If not, why not? Ask and you shall receive

Chapter Twelve: The Unique Role of Holy Spirit Baptism

The Unique Roles of Father, Son, and Holy Spirit

The Unique Role of Holy Spirit

Who is Holy Spirit?

Jesus' Relationship with Holy Spirit on Earth

Jesus: God's Son Whom God Anointed with the Holy Ghost

Promise to Believers

Fulfillment of the Promise

CHAPTER 12
The Unique Role of Holy Spirit Baptism

THE UNIQUE ROLES OF FATHER, SON, AND HOLY SPIRIT

The Father DID NOT come to indwell man. He is the one who sent Jesus to redeem mankind and the one from whom the Holy Spirit is generated. Those roles are unique to the Father. The Father is the source of begetting the Son and of the procession of the Holy Spirit.

John 3:16 *For God so loved the world that he gave his only-begotten son that whosoever believe a thin him should not perish but should have everlasting life.*

John 14:16 *And I will pray the Father, and he shall give you another comforter, that he may abide with you forever.*

Jesus, the Son of God DID NOT come to indwell man in the literal sense that Holy Spirit indwells. Jesus lives in us by faith, but he is now literally in heaven seated at the right hand of the Father as our mediator and intercessor.

Acts 2:33 *Therefore being by the right hand of God exalted, and having received of the Father the promise of the Holy Ghost, he hath shed forth this, which you now see and hear.*

Ephesians 1:20 *Which he wrought in Christ, when he raised him from the dead, and sat him at his own right hand in the heavenly places.*

Hebrews 7:25 *Wherefore he is able also to save them to the uttermost that come unto God by him, seeing he ever liveth to make intercession for them.*

Hebrews 7:8 *And here men that die receive tithes; but there he receiveth them, of whom it is witnessed that he liveth.*

Jesus was made flesh and dwelt among us. He came to reveal the Father and to redeem all mankind. (Jn. 1:14, 18) Jesus is the only way to God, but he does not indwell us in the sense that Holy Spirit does. The Father chose humanity, Jesus redeemed humanity, and Holy Spirit draws humanity to God (Hebrews 1). Even though God chose all humanity for redemption through Christ Jesus, the decision as to whether to choose Christ is left up to each individual.

Holy Spirit DOES come to indwell believers: He comes to teach, guide, lead, and draw all mankind to Jesus Christ. He had been "with" man, now He is "in" those who ask and receive Him. He is the new wine who has been "poured out" to us, upon us, and lives in us. John chapters 12-16 reveals that Holy Spirit leads, teaches, reveals, counsels, comforts, convicts and draws us to the Father God. In I Corinthians chapters 12-14, Paul tells us that Holy Spirit empowers, gives gifts to edify the church, instructs, heals, reveals, and does what man alone cannot do.

Who is Holy Spirit?

He is God: one with the Father and the Son. The Father is not the Son or the Holy Spirit. The Son is not the Father or the Holy Spirit. Holy Spirit is not the Father or the Son.

The interworking and interaction among the Father, Son, and Holy Spirit is a term referring to the relationship to, with, and among the three persons of the Trinity. This shows interaction and interworking in the Godhead. This is called "*circumincession*" or "*perichoresis*" which is: *"The theological concept, affirming that the divine essence is shared by each of the three persons of the Trinity in a manner that avoids blurring the distinctions among them. By extension, this idea suggests that any essential characteristic that belongs to one of the three is shared by the others. Circumincession or perichoresis also affirms that the action of one of the persons of the Trinity is also fully the action of the other two persons."* (Definition from *"Pocket Dictionary of Theological Terms"* by Stanley J. Grenz, David Guretzki and Cherith Fee Nordling)

While there is interaction in and among the Trinity in perfect unity, still each one's role is unique in their relations with humanity.

Holy Spirit is and always has been because He is eternal in existence. He is one with the Father and the Son. He is God. The Father sent (gave) Jesus, His Son, to be the Redeemer of the world. He then promised that the Holy Spirit would come. Through Jesus Christ, the Father sent Holy Spirit to reside with and in humankind.

"Who is Holy Spirit?" He is God. He is that one who indwells believers on earth connecting us to the new covenant and to heaven. He is the one who empowers us to do the things Jesus did and greater than those things would we do according to Jesus (John 14:12). He is the giver of the supernatural gifts (I Corinthians 12). He is the developer of the godly character within us called "fruit of the Spirit." He is the one who gives the utterances spoken by those who are baptized in the Holy Spirit.

Jesus' Relationship with Holy Spirit on Earth

Jesus' authority and power over every realm is demonstrated in Luke 4:14-9:50. In this section of Scripture his authority and power over demons, disease, nature, the effects of sin, tradition, and all people is presented as a prelude to his diverse ministry of preaching, teaching, healing, etc. When he walked on earth as a man, Jesus' authority was from the Father and his power was from the Holy Spirit. Christ worked and taught "through the Holy Spirit."

> "While he was on earth in the flesh, Christ was totally dependent upon the Holy Spirit. He had to surrender himself and make himself available to the Spirit. If Christ was so dependent upon the Spirit of God, how much more are we? How much more do we need to make ourselves available to the Holy Spirit, his gifts, and his power? Jesus did not cease to be God, but he walked 100% human as man while on earth. He worked within the boundaries of humanity as we do. Whatever he told us to do, we can do it in our humanity baptized in the same Holy Spirit with which Christ was baptized." (David Dories, Ph.D. *Spirit Filled Christology*).

See: Acts 10:34-38; Luke 3:21-22; Mt. 3:16-17; Jn. 1:29-36; Lk. 4:14-6:49. Hebrews 9:14

Jesus: God's Son Whom God Anointed with the Holy Ghost

Matthew 3:13-17 *Then cometh Jesus from Galilee to Jordan unto John, to be baptized of him. (14) But John forbad him, saying, I have need to be baptized of thee, and comest thou to me? (15) And Jesus answering said unto him, Suffer [it to be so] now: for thus it becometh us to fulfil all righteousness. Then he suffered him. (16) And Jesus, when he was baptized, went up straightway out of the water: and, lo, the heavens were opened unto him, and he saw the <u>Spirit of God descending like a dove, and lighting upon him:</u> (17) And lo a voice from heaven, saying, This is <u>my beloved Son</u>, in whom I am well pleased.*

As <u>Jesus</u> was baptized by John in the Jordan River, the <u>Holy Spirit</u> descended, the <u>Father</u> spoke. This shows the manifestation of the Trinity: plurality in unity and unity in plurality.

John 1:26-34 *John answered them, saying, I baptize with water: but there standeth one among you, whom ye know not; (27) He it is, who coming after me is preferred before me, whose shoe's latchet I am not worthy to unloose. (28) These things were done in Bethabara beyond Jordan, where John was baptizing. (29) The next day John seeth Jesus coming unto him, and saith, <u>Behold the Lamb of God</u>, which taketh away the sin of the world. (30) This is he of whom I said, After me cometh a man which is preferred before me: for he was before me. (31) And I knew him not: but that he should be made manifest to Israel, therefore am I come baptizing with water. (32) And John bare record, saying, <u>I saw the Spirit</u>*

descending from heaven like a dove, and it abode upon him. (33) And I knew him not: but he that sent me to baptize with water, the same said unto me, Upon whom thou shalt see the Spirit descending, and remaining on him, the same is he which baptizeth with the Holy Ghost. (34) And I saw, and bare record that this is the Son of God.

Acts 10:34-38 (at Ephesus) *Then Peter opened [his] mouth, and said, Of a truth I perceive that God is no respecter of persons: (35) But in every nation he that feareth him, and worketh righteousness, is accepted with him. (36) The word which [God] sent unto the children of Israel, preaching peace by Jesus Christ: (he is Lord of all) (37) That word, [I say], ye know, which was published throughout all Judaea, and <u>began from Galilee, after the baptism which John preached; (38) How God anointed Jesus of Nazareth with the Holy Ghost and with power: who went about doing good, and healing all that were oppressed of the devil; for God was with him.</u>*

Luke 4:18 *The Spirit of the Lord is upon me, <u>because he hath anointed me</u> to preach the gospel to the poor; he hath sent me to heal the brokenhearted, to preach deliverance to the captives, and recovering of sight to the blind, to set at liberty them that are bruised.*

Promise to Believers

God anointed His Son, Jesus, with the Holy Spirit and power. This is the same Holy Spirit and power in which believers today are baptized. Jesus left believers promises concerning their empowerment by the same Holy Spirit with which he was anointed. **There are not two different Holy Spirits: one for the anointing of Jesus and a different one for anointing the Church. They are one and the same. The same Holy Spirit that**

empowered Jesus is the same Holy Spirit in which Jesus baptizes believers.

John 7:37-39 *In the last day, that great day of the feast, Jesus stood and cried, saying, if any man thirst, let him come unto me, and drink. (38) He that believeth upon me, as the scripture hath said, out of his belly shall flow rivers of living water. (39) (But this spake he of the Spirit, which they that believe on him should receive: for the Holy Ghost was not yet given; because that Jesus was not yet glorified.)*

John 14:12-16 *(12) Verily, verily, I say unto you, He that believeth on me, the works that I do shall he do also; and <u>greater [works] than these shall he do; because I go unto my Father</u>. (13) And whatsoever ye shall ask in my name, that will I do, that the Father may be glorified in the Son. (14) If ye shall ask any thing in my name, I will do [it]. (15) If ye love me, keep my commandments. (16) <u>And I will pray the Father, and he shall give you another Comforter, that he may abide with you forever</u>.*

John 16:7 *Nevertheless I tell you the truth; it is expedient for you that I go away: for if I go not away, the Comforter will not come unto you; <u>but if I depart, I will send him unto you.</u>*

Acts 1:8 *You shall receive power <u>after</u> that the Holy Ghost is come upon you....*

Fulfillment of the Promise

The disciples knew that certain things were to occur before the Father would/could pour out Holy Spirit on all flesh. Many prophecies concerning the birth, life, death, burial, and resurrection had to be fulfilled prior to the Holy Spirit outpouring.

There would be an incarnational birth of God's Son through a virgin. He would grow up and present himself to Israel as the Passover Lamb who would take away not only their sins but the sins of the whole world. He would be rejected, crucified, and buried, and on the third day he would be resurrected. Satan was defeated in heaven (Revelation12), earth (Matthew 28:18-20), and finally in hell (Col 2:15) by "the Seed of woman" just as God had spoken that it would be (Genesis 3:15). When Jesus arose from the dead, he ascended to heaven where he sprinkled his blood on the mercy seat (Hebrews 9). Then salvation was guaranteed for whosoever will believe.

After his physical resurrection, Jesus remained for 40 days teaching, training, and revealing truth to the disciples. At his ascension, he told them to not attempt to do any kind of ministry until they were endued with power from on high. He then sent them to Jerusalem to wait for the promise of the Father that he would ask the Father to send. They waited and 10 days later Holy Spirit was poured out. That out-pouring confirmed that: (1) Jesus was who he said he was. (2) Jesus had truly returned to heaven. (3) Jesus had been glorified. Truly, out of their bellies (innermost being) flowed rivers of living water in fulfillment of Jesus's words (John 7:37-39).

Chapter Thirteen: The Unique Sign: Sounds from Heaven

Unknown Tongues: Sounds from Heaven

Spread of Holy Spirit Baptism Accompanied by Tongues: Acts 8, 11, 19

Man's Tongue

The Tongue: A Creative Force

Holy Ghost Power Can Tame the Tongue

Let's Think About It

CHAPTER 13
The Unique Sign: Sounds from Heaven

Unknown Tongues: Sounds from Heaven

Isaiah 28:11-13 *For with stammering lips and another tongue will he speak to this people. (12) To whom he said, This [is] the rest [wherewith] ye may cause the weary to rest; and this [is] the refreshing: yet they would not hear. (13) But the word of the LORD was unto them precept upon precept, precept upon precept; line upon line, line upon line; here a little, [and] there a little; that they might go, and fall backward, and be broken, and snared, and taken.*

When Holy Spirit was "poured out" on the Day of Pentecost, they did speak with "stammering lips and another tongue" just as Isaiah had prophesied.

Joel 2:28 *And it shall come to pass afterward, that I will pour out my Spirit upon all flesh; and your sons and your daughters shall prophesy, your old men shall dream dreams, your young men shall see visions*

Acts 2:4 *And they were all filled with the Holy Ghost, and began to speak with other tongues, as the Spirit gave them utterance....*

Peter said, *"This is that which was promised by the prophet Joel"* (Acts 2:16). God had revealed to Joel that he would pour out His Spirit upon all flesh in the last days. Peter was saying that this which the people were seeing and hearing was that Holy Spirit outpouring. This outpouring marked the beginning of the "last days. According to Peter, this Acts 2 scene is what it can look like when God pours out His Spirit.

What were they doing? They were speaking in tongues and they appeared to be drunk. They were perhaps staggering and their speech appeared to be slurred or gibberish because people did not understand the words being spoken. This was confirmation of the Holy Spirit being poured out as was promised. These same manifestations confirmed that Cornelius's household was baptized in the Holy Spirit. Peter pointed out that because those in Cornelius' gathering spoke in tongues, that was the confirmation that they had received the same Holy Spirit (Acts 10:44-46) as was received by those in the upper room.

Some would say that something other than tongues is the sign that one is baptized in the Holy Spirit, but Peter said tongues was the evidence that Cornelius's household had received just like those in the upper room on the Day of Pentecost. Tongues was the only manifestation that was unique to the initial outpouring, and they continued to be made manifest with each Holy Spirit baptism event recorded in Acts and in I Corinthians. All the other gifts had occurred prior to this day, but not tongues. Tongues was unique to the Day of Pentecost outpouring of the Holy Spirit.

In the Old Testament there had been words of wisdom, words of knowledge, faith, gifts of healings, working of miracles, prophecy, discerning of spirits, but NEVER had there been unknown tongues. In Jesus' ministry all the other gifts were seen, but not tongues because they were reserved for the confirmation of Holy Spirit baptism on the day of Pentecost. Tongues was unique to this time. Jesus, the Redeemer, had come and had accomplished the work of salvation. Now the Church must be equipped with the same power and authority Jesus had.

Jesus is the baptizer in the Holy Spirit. If there is a baptism in the Holy Spirit then there has to be one of equal status to be the baptizer. Only God could send and only God could baptize in Holy Spirit because Holy Spirit is one with the Father and the Son. No lesser one could baptize in Holy Spirit. That Jesus was God's Son and baptizer in Holy Spirit was proven by the outpouring that Jesus had promised before he ascended, and it occurred exactly as he said it would. Jesus said that Holy Spirit baptism would equip them to do what he did and greater things. God saved the best until last.

This reminds one of the first miracle of Jesus where he turned the water into wine. John 2:9-10 says *"... when the ruler of the feast had tasted the water that was made wine, and knew not whence it was: (but the servants which drew the water knew;) the governor of the feast called the bridegroom, (10) And saith unto him, Every man at the beginning doth set forth good wine; and when men have well drunk, then that which is worse: but <u>thou hast kept the good wine until now</u>."*

In the same way, the good wine of the Holy Spirit was saved until the last days... until now. Joel 2 was being fulfilled right before their eyes. The Spirit of God was poured out upon all flesh, but at that point, only those in the upper room had received it. As

Luke 11:11-14 and Acts 2:39 say <u>Holy Spirit Baptism is available to whosoever asks even those of us who are "afar off." Have you asked him for the Holy Spirit?</u>

For the promise is unto you, and to your children, and to all that are afar off, even as many as the Lord our God shall call. Acts 2:39

Boldness and confidence resulted from being baptized in Holy Spirit that day and also today.

John 14: 16-17 (16) And I will pray the Father, and he shall give you another Comforter, that he may abide with you forever: (17) Even the Spirit of truth whom the world cannot receive, because it seeth him not, neither knoweth him: but you shall know him: for he dwelleth with you and shall be in you.

John 15:26 But when the Comforter is come, whom I will send unto you from the Father, even the Spirit of truth, which proceeded from the Father, he shall testify of me.

John 16:7, 13 (7) Nevertheless I tell you the truth: it is expedient for you that I go away: for <u>if I go not away, the Comforter will not come unto you:</u> But if I depart, I will send him and unto you. (13) Howbeit, when he, the Spirit of truth is come, he will guide you into all truth: for he shall not speak of himself: but whatsoever he shall hear, that shall he speak: and he will show you things to come.

Acts 2:12-18 *(12) "And they were all amazed, and were in doubt, saying one to another, what meaneth this? (13)Others mocking said, These men are full of new wine. (14)But Peter standing up with the eleven, Lifted up his voice, and said to them, Ye men of Judea, And* *all you that dwell at Jerusalem, be this known unto you, and hearken to my words (15) For these men are not drunk, as you suppose, seeing it is but the third hour of the day. (16) <u>But this is that which was spoken by the prophet Joel.</u> (17) <u>And it shall come to pass in the last days, saith God, I will pour out of my Spirit upon all flesh: and your son and your daughters shall prophesy, and your young men shall see visions, and your old men shall dream dreams: (18) And on my servants and on my handmaidens I will pour out in those days of my Spirit: And they shall prophesy.</u>*

Spread of Holy Spirit Baptism Accompanied By Tongues: Acts 8, 11, 19

Acts 8:14-19 (Samaria): *(14) Now when the apostles which were at Jerusalem heard that Samaria had received the word of God, they sent unto them Peter and John: (15) Who, when they were come down, prayed for them, that they might receive the Holy Ghost: (16) (For as yet he was fallen upon none of them: only they were baptized in the name of the Lord Jesus.) (17) <u>Then</u> laid they [their] hands on them, and they <u>received the Holy Ghost.</u> (18) And when Simon <u>saw</u> that through laying on of the apostles' hands the Holy Ghost was given, he offered them money, (19) Saying, Give me also this power, that on whomsoever I lay hands, he may receive the Holy Ghost.*

There is good reason to believe that the thing Simon saw that day was the very same manifestation of tongues as occurred earlier: Holy Spirit manifestation of tongues.

Acts: 19:1-6 (*1) And it came to pass, that, while Apollos was at Corinth, Paul having passed through the upper coasts came to Ephesus: and <u>finding certain disciples,</u> (2) He said unto them, <u>Have ye received the Holy Ghost since ye believed?</u> And they said unto him, We have not* *so much as heard whether there be any Holy Ghost. (3) And he said unto them, Unto what then were ye baptized? And they said, Unto John's baptism. (4) Then said Paul, John verily baptized with the baptism of repentance, saying unto the people, that they should believe on him which should come after him, that is, on Christ Jesus. (5) When they heard [this], <u>they were baptized</u> in the name of the Lord Jesus. (6) And when Paul had <u>laid [his] hands upon them, the Holy Ghost came on them; and they spake with tongues, and prophesied</u>.*

Paul said in I Corinthians 14:5 that *"I would that ye all spake with <u>tongues</u>...."* Therefore, we can be sure that Paul taught about Holy Spirit baptism and tongues for all. He also said in I Corinthians 14:18, *"I thank my God, I speak with tongues more than ye all."* Paul knew the power and the value of speaking in tongues much and often. We will discuss this in more detail in a later chapter. In I Corinthians 14:39, Paul says to *covet to prophesy and <u>forbid not to speak in tongues</u>.*

Man's Tongue

There is much said concerning the tongue and words in the Bible, therefore, words are important. Sounds going forth from our mouths create life or death. Our tongues reveal our hearts. Jesus said in Matthew 12:34, *"O generation of vipers, how can ye, being evil, speak good things? <u>For out of the abundance of the heart the mouth speaketh.</u>"*

God created man in His own image. God created as only God can do. God spoke and there was. Mankind also allows or disallows life by his/her words. Phrases like "I hate you" create evil.

Phrases like "I love you" creates good. Our tongue determines our destiny. Proverbs and James instruct us to learn how to live and speak from God's wisdom and knowledge.

James 3:1-8 *My brethren, be not many masters, knowing that we shall receive the greater condemnation. (2) For in many things we offend all. If any man offend not in word, the same [is] a perfect man, [and] able also to bridle the whole body. (3) Behold, we put bits in the horses' mouths that they may obey us; and we turn about their whole body. (4) Behold also the ships, which though [they be] so great, and [are] driven of fierce winds, yet are they turned about with a very small helm, whithersoever the governor listeth. (5) Even so <u>the tongue</u> is a little member, and boasteth great things. Behold, how great a matter a little fire kindleth! (6) And <u>the tongue</u> [is] a fire, a world of iniquity: so is the tongue among our members, that it defileth the whole body, and setteth on fire the course of nature; and it is set on fire of hell. (7) For every kind of beasts, and of birds, and of serpents, and of things in the sea, is tamed, and hath been tamed of mankind: (8) <u>But the tongue can no man tame</u>; [it is] an unruly evil, full of deadly poison.*

THE TONGUE: A CREATIVE FORCE

Proverbs 4:23 *Keep thy heart with all diligence; for out of it [are] the <u>issues</u> of life."*

Proverbs 18:21 *Death and life [are] in the power of the tongue: and they that love it shall eat the fruit thereof.*

James 1:26-27 *If any man among you seem to be religious, and bridleth not his tongue, but deceiveth his own heart, this man's religion [is] vain.*

Holy Spirit Power Can Tame the Tongue

From the very beginning in Genesis 1, we can see that our creator God is a talking/speaking God. He spoke all creation into being. He had conversation with the only part of creation made in his image and likeness: mankind. Words are a vital part of our relationship with the creator God. Mankind is made in God's image and likeness. We are speaking beings. We speak to humans and other living things. Our words contain life or death. We speak to God to praise and worship Him, to petition, and to intercede for others. Our God is a mighty God. He is the ALL Powerful One.

Use your <u>earthly language</u> to bring life to those around you just like your heavenly Father. Use your <u>heavenly language</u> of the Spirit to build yourself up and to pray the perfect will of God. The utterances given by Holy Spirit are not gibberish or foolishness. They are the sounds of heaven. (I Corinthians 14:1; Jude 21 and Romans 8:26.) (See Chapter on "The Value of Tongues"). God breathed his own breath into Adam (i.e. passed on to all humanity), but when sin entered, man's nature was corrupted and he began to use his breath to create death and destruction by his words and corresponding actions. After redemption through Christ Jesus, that breath is again empowered to bring life.

When you are baptized in the Holy Spirit, you should covet or earnestly desire the gifts of the Spirit. When you speak in tongues to the church, there needs to be an interpretation in order for the church and you to be edified. When you pray in tongues, you are not bringing a message to the church, and it does not require interpretation. You are edified, built up, charged up like a battery as Jude 20-21 tells us because you are speaking directly to God who reveals to you the mysteries you are speaking by the Holy Spirit (I Corinthians 2; 14:1-4).

Let's Think About It

God preserved a unique manifestation for the entry of the Holy Spirit into the Earth and the Church in particular. He reserved for that time something that had not previously been revealed or manifested in the earth (i.e. the heavenly language of the Spirit/ speaking in other tongues). This language is for believers in Jesus Christ. It is a sign to and of this new "company of believers" (Terry Mize, 2014). This is for the Body of Christ. Baptism in the Holy Spirit is so much more than tongues, but it is through tongues that God edifies each individual believer and it is through the gift of tongues with interpretation that he edifies the Church. (I Corinthians 14). Holy Spirit is the one who gives "utterance" to the person speaking in tongues (Acts 2:4). He indwells those who ask him (Luke 11:9-13). Let us breathe out life into the earth by preaching the good news of Jesus Christ by the empowerment of the Holy Spirit.

Chapter Fourteen: The Value of Tongues

Introduction

The Power of the Tongue and Unity: Babel and Pentecost

What is the Value of Speaking in Tongues?

Speaking in Tongues is the Confirmation of Baptism in the Holy Spirit

When You Speak in Tongues You Speak Directly to God

Speaking in Tongues Edifies the Speaker

Speaking in Tongues Makes One Conscience of His Presence

Speaking in Tongues Stimulates Faith

Speaking in Tongue Brings Spiritual Refreshing

Speaking in Tongues Assists with Prayer Life

Speaking in Tongues Helps One to Give Thanks Well

Speaking in Tongues Reveals Your Heart

Speaking in Tongues is a Sign for the Unbeliever

Speaking in Tongues Brings Revelation & Understanding

You Have Received the Spirit of God Who Reveals the Mysteries

Mysteries Are Not Meant to Remain Mysteries

Love Is the Key

CHAPTER 14
The Value of Tongues

INTRODUCTION

THERE ARE MANY ASPECTS AND truths to discuss concerning Holy Spirit, but the one thing most associated with differences of opinions has to do with speaking in tongues. The Church was birthed speaking in tongues and moving in Holy Ghost power. The early church was a Charismatic church and there is no reason we should think it needs to change. We need the same power that they needed.

Though birthed in power, between 400-700 A.D. most supernatural manifestations such as healing, miracles, and tongues, had been gathered under the strict direction of the episcopate and had mostly disappeared. The episcopate saw the manifestation of the gifts of prophecy and speaking in tongues among lay people as troublesome. In spite of that, throughout church history one sees Holy Spirit baptism manifesting in groups of believers. Most of the time these groups and manifestations were dealt with as heresies by the church officials. This was the norm from about 500AD and western theology moved toward the doctrine of cessation. The doctrine of cessation says that spiritual gifts such as speaking in tongues, prophecy, and healing ceased with the apostolic age.

Though it is not biblically based, the cessationist belief was basically unchallenged in the western church until the 1700s and early 1800s in England and Scotland, and then in the early 1900s in North America. The hold of cessationism was challenged by Holy Spirit revival.

The modern world was introduced and exposed to Holy Spirit baptism and "tongues" as a biblical supernatural manifestation of the Holy Spirit beginning with Edward Irving's revival in London and the West of Scotland Revival in the 1830s, the Azusa Street Revival in Los Angeles, California with William Seymour in ear-ly 1900s, plus succeeding revivals. According to the Pew Forum analysis, today, about 600 million people speak with tongues hav-ing been baptized in the Holy Spirit. Pentecostal and Charismatic Christians together make up about 27% of all Christians and more than 8% of the world's total population. Who is this Holy Spirit from whom this heavenly language flows? He is the third person of the Trinity. He is God.

The Holy Spirit is in the world to equip believers to carry on the business of God initiated by Jesus Christ. This business is done by the empowered church. The Gospels present Jesus as spending 75% of His time healing and ministering to the sick and casting out demons. Healing was never a side issue with Jesus nor should it be with the empowered church. Jesus healed by the same Holy Spirit in which he baptizes the Church.

Matthew 8:16-17 *When the even was come, they brought unto him many that were possessed with devils: and <u>he cast out the spirits with his word, and healed all</u> that were sick: (17) that it might be fulfilled which was spoken by Esaias the prophet, saying, Himself took our infirmities, and bare our sicknesses.*

Luke 4:18 *The Spirit of the Lord is upon me, because he hath anointed me to preach the gospel to the poor; he hath sent me to heal the brokenhearted, to preach deliverance to the captives, and recovering of sight to the blind, to set at liberty them that are bruised.*

Today, almost everyone knows someone who speaks in tongues, and certainly they have heard tongues spoken. But what is the value of speaking in tongues? Why did God pour out that HolySpirit gift to mankind on the Day of Pentecost?

Life and death are in the power of the tongue. That makes what you say important. You must guard your heart with all diligence because out of it are the issues of life. In other words, you set the boundaries on your life by the words you speak.

Faith-filled words appropriate what God said you could have. You are saved by the words of your mouth (Romans 10: 9-10). You are healed and you are blessed in the same way.

1 Peter 2:24, "*Who his own self bare our sins in his own body on the tree that we, being dead to sins, should live unto righ-teousness: by whose stripes ye were healed.*"

You speak your faith as recorded in Mark 11:23, "*For verily I say unto you, That whosoever shall say unto this mountain, Be thou removed, and be thou cast into the sea; and shall not doubt in his heart, but shall believe that those things which he saith shall come to pass; he shall have whatsoever he saith.*"

Jude 20 But *ye, beloved, building up yourselves on your most holy faith, praying in the Holy Ghost.*

The Power of the Tongue and Unity: Babel and Pentecost

Genesis 11:1-9 tells us that these people were <u>all in accord and all saying the same thing for evil</u>. Then God said, "L*et us go down and confuse their language.*" God confused their words and their communication with each other because their intentions and hearts were evil. The intention of the Babel event was to create evil in the earth.

> *And <u>the whole earth was of one language, and of one speech</u>. (2) And it came to pass, as they journeyed from the east, that they found a plain in the land of Shinar; and they dwelt there. (3) And they said one to another, Go to, let us make brick, and burn them thoroughly. And they had brick for stone, and slime had they for mortar. (4) And they said, Go to, let us build us a city and a tower, whose top [may reach] unto heaven; and <u>let us make us a name</u>, lest we be scattered abroad upon the face of the whole earth. (5) And the LORD came down to see the city and the tower, which the children of men builded. (6) <u>And the LORD said, Behold, the people [is] one, and they have all one language; and this they begin to do: and <u>now nothing will be restrained from them, which they have imagined to do.</u> (7) Go to, let us go down, and there confound their language, that they may not understand one another's speech. (8) So the LORD scattered them abroad from thence upon the face of all the earth: and they left off to build the city. (9) Therefore is the name of it called Babel; because the LORD did there <u>confound the language of all the earth: and from thence did the LORD scatter them abroad upon the face of all the earth.</u>"*

The intention of the upper room Holy Spirit event was to create good and life. Luke tells us in Acts 2 that on the Day of Pentecost they were **<u>all in</u> <u>one accord, saying the same thing for good,</u>** God said, let us go down and **<u>unite</u>** their language. This heavenly language unites and equips the church to do mighty things for God. <u>Unknown tongues is the language of the born-again spirit of man. It is truly sounds from Heaven.</u>

Acts 2:1 *And when the Day of Pentecost was fully come, they were all with one accord in one place.*

Luke tells us in Acts 2 that on the Day of Pentecost <u>they were all</u> <u>in one accord, saying the same thing for good</u>. In essence, God said, "Let us go down and <u>unite</u> their language." Jesus had much to say about being baptized in the Holy Spirit. Jesus said come unto Him and drink and "rivers of <u>living water</u> will flow from your innermost being (spirit)." As a result of Holy Spirit outpouring, gifts of the Holy Spirit flowed; prophecy flowed; healing and deliverance flowed. These are mani-festations of the presence of "rivers of living waters," but tongues was the unique confirmation that they had received a baptism in the Holy Spirit. Tongues flowed from their innermost being for the first time on the Day of Pentecost. But why tongues? What is the value?

WHAT IS THE VALUE OF SPEAKING IN TONGUES?
Speaking in Tongues is the Confirmation of Baptism in the Holy Spirit.
Speaking in tongues was the unique sign on the Day of Pentecost that Holy Spirit had been poured out and speaking in tongues has been received and repeated by millions upon millions since that Day. What was the first occurrence like? Acts 2:4 *And <u>they were all</u>* <u>*filled with the Holy Ghost, and began to speak with other tongues, as*</u> <u>*the Spirit gave them utterance.*</u>

When You Speak in Tongues You Speak Directly to God. 1 Corinthians 14:1-2 *"Follow after charity, and desire spiritual [gifts], but rather that ye may prophesy. (2) <u>For he that speaketh in an [unknown] tongue speaketh not</u> unto men, but unto God: for no man understandeth [him]; howbeit in the spirit <u>he speaketh mysteries</u>.*

After teaching on the gifts of the Spirit in I Corinthians 12, Paul teaches about the importance of love in the manifestation of these gifts in chapter 13. Paul encourages his readers to be sure that charity is the moving force behind the manifestation of these gifts. Then he goes on to encourage them to desire spirituals or spiritual gifts. Paul emphasized that they should desire to prophesy instead of just speaking in unknown tongues in the gatherings (I Corinthians 14:1). Remember that chapter 12 is a foundational teaching on Holy Spirit gifts. Paul explains that all the gifts are administered by the Holy Spirit. His goal is to bring balance and order to the church at Corinth concerning the operation of the gifts of the Spirit. His goal is not to keep them from speaking in tongues, but to bring understanding of the gifts in order to not only edify themselves, but to also edify the church as a whole. We know from I Corinthians 1:7 that the church at Corinth did not lack any of the spiritual gifts.

We see from I Corinthians 1, that there were some who came from "Chloe's household" to advise Paul of the condition of the church and to seek answers and guidance for the church gather-ings. This group informed Paul that there were quarrels among some of the church members. Paul addressed this issue and moved forward answering questions concerning the times of commu-nion when the church gathered together (I Corinthians 10). Then we read his discourse on spiritual gifts in the church in chapters

12-14. Chapter 14 reveals the crux of a major problem which was order in the service when the church came together.

Paul does a great balancing act as he walks a tight rope between order and manifestation of the gifts of the Spirit in the church. One of the major problems was that each and all of the Spirit-filled believers were eager to speak in tongues or bring messages in tongues which were perhaps not always interpreted. There are two reasons why tongues are not always interpreted: (1) there was no interpreter or perhaps no one was brave enough to interpret. It is one thing to bring a message in an unknown tongue and quite another to interpret that message into the language that people understand. The responsibility is tremendous. (2) Then again, perhaps not every utterance in tongues was/is the manifestation of the "gift of tongues" that requires an interpreter.

What do I mean by the second reason? There is a "gift" of tongues in which a message is uttered through the Spirit-filled believer by the Holy Spirit <u>to the church</u>. This requires the gift of interpretation to be complete and to be understandable in order to edify or instruct the church. Not every spirit-filled tongue-talking believer brings a message to the church through the gift of tongues, yet they may all pray in tongues, sing in tongues, and worship in tongues. The point is that just because one speaks in tongues does not mean that he/she is bringing a message to the church that needs interpretation. It is sometimes difficult for a novice to know the difference.

NOTICE: A person's prayer language is used for speaking directly to God, but when it is a message by the Holy Spirit gift of tongues, it is God speaking to the church and this requires the gift of interpertion.

When you are baptized in the Holy Spirit, you should covet or earnestly desire the gifts of the Spirit. When you speak in tongues to the church, there needs to be an interpretation in order for the church and you to be edified. When you pray in tongues, you are not bringing a message to the church, and it does not require interpretation. You, yourself, are edified, built up, charged up like a battery as Jude 20-21 tells us because you are speaking directly to God who reveals to you the mysteries you are speaking by the Holy Spirit (I Corinthians 2; 14:1-4).

Pray in Tongues. When you pray in tongues your spirit prays, you are edified, you are "built-up," made strong on your most holy faith. You speak directly with God. It brings your tongue under control and reminds you of the Spirit's indwelling just to name a few reasons to speak in tongues.

Seeking, asking and knocking is the key to experiencing the power of God through the Baptism in the Holy Spirit.

Ask God to bring a hungering and thirsting for a renewal and revival to yourself and to the Church so you and the Church may be blessed and profit from it.

Paul refers to tongues as a <u>personal communion and communication with God</u> in I Corinthians 14:2 which says *"For he who speaks in an unknown tongue speaks not to man, but to God."* This is a good thing. It is an excellent thing. Speaking the language of the Spirit, is a personal intimate communion with God. Paul emphasizes that this tongue has nothing to do with speaking to man. This is man speaking directly to God by the Spirit of God. Paul goes on to enlighten the church concerning <u>the gift of tongues</u>

which is God speaking to his church by his Spirit through a Spirit filled believer. This gift of tongues in bringing a message to the church, needs the gift of interpretation to be complete.

So we can see that there is <u>(1) a personal prayer language in tongues</u> through which Spirit-filled believers speak directly to God, and <u>(2) there is the gift of tongues</u> by which God speaks to his church. This gift of tongues requires an interpreter.

*Speaking in Tongues Edifies the Speaker. 1 Corinthians 14:4 *"He that speaketh in an [unknown] tongue edifieth himself; but he that prophesieth edifieth the church."*

Edify means to build up or charge up like a battery. There are times in the lives of people when they experience lack of joy or peace. There are times when there is a dreadful foreboding feeling or depression that comes to drain a person of their joy. God has given us the answer. The answer is to pray in tongues until we are encouraged and built up in faith. Praying in tongues is a choice of your will after you have been baptized in the Holy Spirit. It is not something that is only available occasionally. Tongues is a tool used by the Holy Spirit to edify you at any time.

*Speaking in Tongues Makes One Conscience of His Presence. <u>Acts 10:46</u>, *"For they heard them speak with tongues, and magnify God…"*

Praying in tongues declares that you know that God is present with you, and that he is alive in you.

*Speaking in Tongues Stimulates Faith. <u>Jude 20</u> *"But ye, be-loved, building up yourselves on your most holy faith, <u>praying in the Holy Ghost</u>."*

<u>1 Corinthians 14:14-15</u>, says *(14) For if I pray in an [unknown] tongue, my spirit prayeth, but my understanding is unfruitful. (15) What is it then? <u>I will pray with the spirit</u>, and I will pray with the understanding also: <u>I will sing with the spirit</u>, and I will sing with the understanding also.*

Jude was encouraging the church by teaching them how to build themselves up on their most holy faith. Very simply he said: pray in the Holy Ghost. Paul clarifies this when he says that it is our spirit that prays when we speak in tongues (I Corinthians 14:14). That is a great encouragement and revelation. Think about it. When you pray in tongues, it is not just out of your mouth or out of your head, or out of your mind, it is right out of your spirit which is filled with Holy Spirit himself who knows the deep things of God and reveals them to us according to I Corinthians 2:10.

*Speaking in Tongues Brings a Spiritual Refreshing. <u>Isaiah</u> <u>28:11-12</u>, *(11) <u>For with stammering lips and another tongue will he speak to this people.</u> (12) To whom he said, <u>This [is] the rest</u> [wherewith] ye may cause the weary to rest; and <u>this [is] the refreshing</u>: <u>yet they would</u> <u>not hear</u>*

We see from this that even though <u>God speaks to us by stammering lips and another tongue</u> there are those who will still refuse to hear him because it is unusual and different and many are not willing to be identified with supernatural tongues. That is because it does not seem logical. However, as we are seeing in this list of the value of tongues, God has imparted to us a tremendous gift in Holy Spirit and unknown tongues is the voice of Holy Spirit.

Spirit-filled believers have no room or reason for complaining because God has supplied us with everything we need through Holy Spirit that abides within. We can be refreshed and enter into rest through this heavenly language of the Spirit. This is a very good reason to be Spirit-filled and speak in tongues.

*Speaking in Tongues Assists with Prayer Life. Romans 8:26, "*Likewise the Spirit also helpeth our infirmities: for we know not what we should pray for as we ought: but the Spirit itself maketh intercession for us with groanings which cannot be uttered.*"

Everyone has had situations in which they needed God to be involved, but they did not know how to pray concerning the need. That is the time to allow Holy Spirit to use our vocal cords to make intercession with groanings that cannot be translated into words.

*Speaking in Tongues Helps One to Give Thanks Well. First Corinthians 14:16-17 *Else when thou shalt bless with the spirit how shall he that occupies the room of the unlearned say Amen at thy giving of thanks, seeing he understandeth not what thou sayest? (17) For thou verily givest thanks well but the other is not edified.*

Paul did not say giving thanks in tongues was a bad thing. He was telling the people that when we are speaking in tongues it is (1) spoken directly to God, or (2) it is for binging a message to those present. When it is for the church, it is spoken aloud to the congregation and an interpretation should follow. Praying or praising God in tongues can be spoken out loud in unison with the congregation, but it is not addressing any person because this is to God alone. Any earthly language falls short of giving God thanks perfectly, but this scripture says that <u>Holy Spirit enables us to give thanks well to the God</u> who has given us all things through Jesus Christ.

∗Speaking in Tongues Reveals Your Heart. <u>Matthew 12:34</u>, *O generation of vipers, how can ye, being evil, speak good things? For out of the abundance of the heart the mouth speaketh.*

No matter what language a person speaks when they open their mouth, what is in them is revealed. In the same way when we speak in heavenly tongues, our hearts are revealed to God.

∗Speaking in Tongues Is a Sign for the Unbeliever. <u>1 Corinthians 14:22</u> *Wherefore tongues are for a sign, not to them that believe, but to them that believe not: but prophesying [serveth] not for them that believe not, but for them which believe.*

Acts 8:14-19 *(14) Now when the apostles which were at Jerusalem heard that Samaria had received the word of God, they sent unto them Peter and John: (15) Who, when they were come down, prayed for them, that they might receive the Holy Ghost: (16) (For as yet he was fallen upon none of them: only they were baptized in the name of the Lord Jesus.) (17) Then laid they [their] hands on them, and they received the Holy Ghost. (18) And when Simon saw that through laying on of the apostles' hands the Holy Ghost was given, he offered them money, (19) Saying, Give me also this power, that on whomsoever I lay hands, he may receive the Holy Ghost.*

There was a physical manifestation resulting from hands being laid on them for receiving the baptism in the Holy Spirit. Simon saw the power of God manifested. There is no reason to believe that what he saw was any different from the other instances such as Acts 19:1-6 when Paul laid hands on those in Ephesus to receive the same Holy Spirit baptism.

Acts 10: 44-46 *(44) While Peter yet spake these words, the Holy Ghost fell on all them which heard the word. (45) And they of the circumcision which believed were astonished, as many as came with Peter, because that on the Gentiles also was poured out the gift of the Holy Ghost. (46)* <u>*For they heard them speak with tongues*</u>*, and magnify God.*

Acts 19:1-6 *(1) And it came to pass, that, while Apollos was at Corinth, Paul having passed through the upper coasts came to Ephesus: and finding certain disciples, (2) He said unto them, Have ye received the Holy Ghost since ye believed? And they said unto him, We have not so much as heard whether there be any Holy Ghost. (3) And he said unto them, Unto what then were ye baptized? And they said, Unto John's baptism. (4) Then said Paul, John verily baptized with the baptism of repentance, saying unto the people, that they should* <u>*believe on him which should come after him, that is, on Christ Jesus.*</u> *(5) When they heard [this], they were baptized in the name of the Lord Jesus. (6) And when Paul had laid [his] hands upon them, the Holy Ghost came on them;* <u>*and they spake with tongues, and prophesied.*</u>

*Speaking in Tongues Brings Revelation and Understanding. Ephesians 1:17. *That the God of our Lord Jesus Christ, the Father of glory, may give unto you the spirit of wisdom and revelation in the knowledge of him.*

The word 'revelation" is from the Greek word *apokalupsis*. It means something that has been veiled or hidden for a long time and then suddenly, almost instantaneously, becomes clear and visible to the mind or eye. Sometime we need direction and guidance beyond our own human understanding. This is the time to pray in the spirit for wisdom and revelation.

*You Have Received the Spirit of God Who Reveals the Mysteries. First Corinthians 2:9-12 *But as it is written, eye hath not seen, nor ear heard, neither have entered into the heart of man, the things which God hath prepared for them that love him. (10) But <u>God hath revealed them unto us by his Spirit: for the Spirit searches all things, yea, the deep things of God.</u> (11) For what man knoweth the things of a man, save the spirit of man which is in him? Even so the things of God knoweth no man, but the Spirit of God. (12) <u>Now we have received not the spirit of the world, but the Spirit which is of</u> God; <u>that we might know the things that are freely given to us of God.</u>*

*<u>Mysteries Are Not Meant to Remain Mysteries.</u> In I Corinthians 2:4, Paul says he comes to the church in "demonstra-tion of the power of God." He goes on to say that he comes speak-ing the wisdom of God to the perfect (mature) Saints. The world does not understand the wisdom of God, but believers can know it. The wisdom of God is in a mystery, but <u>God reveals these myster-ies to believers by his Spirit as we can see clearly in I Corinthians 2:7-12. No revelation or understanding of any mystery will ever</u> conflict with the written word of God. Instead it should confirm the Word of God.

In all these wonderful blessings that we receive from being baptized in the Holy Spirit, we must always remain humble, loving, kind, and ever caring for others. We must never be puffed up or prideful. This blessing is for whosoever will and not for just an elite group of people.

*Love is the Key
Love is the key to sowing or reaping the most benefits from being baptized in the Holy Spirit.

First Corinthians 13:1-3 *Though I speak with the tongues of men and of angels, and have not charity, I am become as sounding brass, or a tinkling cymbal. (2) And though I have the gift of prophecy and understand all mysteries, and all knowledge; and though I have all faith, so that I could remove mountains, and have not charity, I am nothing. (3) And though I bestow all my goods to feed the poor, and though I give my body to be burned, and have not charity, if profiteth me nothing.*

1 John 4:7-8. *(7) Beloved, let us love one another: for love is of God; and every one that loveth is born of God, and knoweth God. (8) He that loveth not knoweth not God; for God is love.*

Chapter Fifteen: Love Is the Key to Power

Introduction

Love Fulfills the Law

The Truth Will Make You Free

Love: A Way of Life

Priorities

Beloved, Let Us Love One Another

Love: The Conduit of Holy Spirit Power

CHAPTER 15
Love Is the Key to Power

> First Corinthians 13:1-4 *Though I speak with the tongues of men and of angels, and have not charity, I am become as sounding brass, or a tinkling cymbal. (2) And though I have the gift of prophecy, and understand all mysteries, and all knowledge; and though I have all faith, so that I could remove mountains, and have not charity, I am nothing. (3) and though I bestow all my goods to feed the poor, and though I give my body to be burned, and have not charity, it profiteth at me nothing. (4) Charity suffereth long, and is kind; charity envyeth not; charity vaulteth not itself, is not puffed up.*

THIS PASSAGE OF SCRIPTURE IS speaking of what is called *agape* love. Agape is a Greco-Christian term referring to the highest form of love. It is considered to be the love originating from God or Christ for mankind. As can be seen above it is selfless and sacrificing. Without this kind of love the gifts of the Holy Spirit, according to Paul, are nothing.

Introduction

When one is truly converted, positive changes should occur in their hearts and lives. The changes should look like the fruit of the Spirit (Galatians 5:22-24). Both the fruit and the gifts of the Spirit are important to the testimony of Jesus Christ today. Too often, we think of God only in terms of power, but we need to look deeper to find the foundation upon which this power is released. The Bible says "God is love" not "God is power." He <u>has</u> all power, but he <u>is</u> love. He is the Almighty one, but without love, power can be destructive.

While we are seeking God for Holy Spirit power, let us realize that Holy Spirit empowers us to do what is right in our lives and to fulfill the law by love instead of worrying about the law or fretting about what part the law plays in our holiness before God. We fulfill the law when we love God and love our neighbor.

Love Fulfills the Law

John 3:16 and I John 4:8 shows us that God is love and that love flows from him. God expresses his love in more than words. God expressed his love through his giving. He gave his best--his Only Begotten Son. There was no greater gift to be given. Jesus came in love to suffer and to die for us.

God's plan was revealed in the covenants, but Adam broke the covenant in the Garden of Eden that thrust all humanity into a fallen nature away from God. God explained that covenant clearly to Adam and Eve prior to their sinning. He told them of their blessings and then he told him of the penalty for breaking the covenant through disobedience. They would surely die. Death is the penalty for breaking a blood covenant. This death was not just physical, but also spiritual death. Adam understood what was at stake. Spiritual death is the eternal separation from a life of any quality (i.e. forever).

Man is spirit, soul, and body. To be separated from life (bios) in the body results in the body returning to the dust. Though the body returns to the dust, the spiritual part of man is an eternal ever-existent entity. Therefore, a person will never cease to be. In other words you will never "not be."

Life in this body is limited because the body has its origins in the earth and through Adam's sin, every human body is touched by death causing the body upon death to return to the dust. While you are alive in this mortal body on earth, you can believe on the Lord Jesus Christ and your spirit is born-again. One day those who are born-again spiritually, will receive a new body which will be immortal. That which is eternal (spirit and soul) is not of this physical realm. That which is spiritual (soul and spirit) is uncreated. You will not get a new spirit or a new soul after death.

God's plan was for mankind to live in a body that would never die. Our bodies are our earth suits. It is through the body that we connect with the physical world through our five senses: hearing, sight, touch, taste, and smell. These physical senses alert us to danger and they also provide us with joy in living. Mankind makes choices and decisions based on their senses.

The soul is who we uniquely are. Man became "a living soul." Our souls express our personalities. A person expresses who they are through their reasoning, mind, choices, will, values, emotions, intents, thoughts, actions and reactions, attitudes, passions, intellect, etc. This is the personal you. You will always be you. People often ask themselves, "Who am I?" Look inside yourself and see. This part of us can be shaped into whatever mold we choose. We can choose whether to be good or bad. We can choose to follow Jesus or not. We can choose to develop the fruit of the Spirit or to live by the lust of the flesh.

The Truth Will Make You Free

Your spirit is that eternal part that receives your perception of truth. We live by that which we receive as truth. Our "truth" guides our souls to make the choices that confirm that which we believe. We can believe that God is good or that God is unforgiving. We can believe that God heals or that God puts sickness on us. Whatever we receive as truth is what we live by. It is what we base our decisions on. What we believe to be truth is crucial. So what is truth?

Jesus came to reveal truth. He said, *"I am the way, the truth, and the life"* (John 14:6). He also said in his prayer to the Father, *"Thy word is truth, Oh Lord"* (John 17:17). If we receive Christ as Savior, we have access to truth. Why do we need truth? *The truth will make you free* (John 8:32).

The world would tell you that there is no absolute truth, but Jesus did not agree with that. He said that you can know the truth, and the truth will make you free. The truth you know and practice determines the quality of life you live. This quality of life is not about how much money or how much stuff you accumulate.

Instead, it is how much joy, peace, and love you live in. It is about how you share that love, joy, and peace with others. It is about all the fruit of the Spirit including temperance, self-discipline or self-control. It is about long-suffering (patience), goodness, meekness, and other such traits (Galatians 5:22-23). Love is the key because God is love, and if you walk in love, all the other fruit will be desired and developed in you.

Love: A Way of life
As love is exercised as a way of life, all of the fruit of the Spirit will show forth in our lives. The fruit of the Spirit is listed in Galatians 5:22-23: *love, joy, peace, long-suffering, gentleness, goodness, faith, meekness, and temperance.* Against these there is no law.

When these fruit are developed in our lives, they support the gifts of the Holy Spirit as being from God. How do you display these fruit in your relationships, at home, at work, raising children, in public, and in private? When these gifts are developed in our lives, they display the wisdom of God. Have you picked and chosen to whom or with whom you will practice these fruit or are they such a part of your life that you live this way with everyone all the time? Even your enemies.

Priorities
How much time do you spend praying for power to overcome your shortcomings in these fruit of the Spirit areas compared to how much time you spend praying for power to heal? We definitely

need to move in the gifts of the Spirit, but we also need to conform our way of life to show forth the fruit of the Spirit.

When one's character is established in the fruit of the Spirit, the gifts of the Spirit will flow out over love for those in need. Jesus was moved by compassion which is love flowing from the innermost parts (Matthew 9:36; Luke 7:13). We must also be moved by this love.

First Corinthians 13:1-3 is often overlooked or is less preferred than versus 4-8. However, the first three verses declare that the gifts of the Spirit are nothing without love being the motivating force behind the working of those gifts in our lives. Furthermore, Galatians 5:6 says that faith is moved along by or expresses itself in love. The fruit of the Spirit is the foundation on which the gifts function.

Galatians 5:14 *For the law is fulfilled in this one word, thou shall love thy neighbor as thyself.*

Romans 13:8-10 *Owe no man anything, but to love one another: for he that loveth another hath fulfilled the law.* (9) *For this, Thou shall not commit adultery, thou shall not kill, thou shall not steal, thou shall not bear false witness, thou shall not covet; and if there be any other commandment, it is briefly comprehended in this saying, namely, thou shall love thy neighbor as thyself.* (10) *Love worketh no ill to his neighbor, therefore love is the fulfilling of the law.*

First John 4:7-8 *Beloved, let us love one another, for love is of God and every one that loveth is born of God and knoweth God. He that loveth not, knoweth not God for God is love.*

Beloved, Let Us Love One Another.

The Bible does not say that moving in the gifts is a sign that they know God, but it says those who love, know God. Love is the foundation of all the other fruit and love is the foundation on which the gifts should be ministered forth. Beloved, let us love one another.

Do not hear what I am not saying. I am not discounting the gifts of the Holy Spirit or saying they are second to anything. What I am saying is that Spirit-filled Christians need to present Christ in their day to day life to be a witness through the gifts. The fruit of the Spirit is that witness.

Love: The Conduit of Holy Spirit Power

On March 20, 2004, the Lord spoke to me and said, "The Trinity is that which is given to you to know and experience of the totality of God." The Trinity is the Father, Son, and Holy Spirit. Often sermons are preached concerning the love of God the Father, or the grace of God the Father, and many other subjects concerning the Father. And, of course, we hear sermons concerning Jesus Christ: his birth, his life, his death, his resurrection, his ascension, and his present ministry as High Priest of the Church. But sometimes we fail to remember that Jesus said He would not leave us here on earth comfortless, but that He would send one to be with us and empower us.

Jesus sent Holy Spirit. In fact, Holy Spirit empowers us to develop the fruit of the Spirit in our lives so as to be an example of love to the world. Jesus told the disciples right before He ascended to the Father that they should go back to Jerusalem and wait until they were endued with "power from on high" before going out to do what He had instructed them to do as recorded in Mark 16:15-20. The power of love can heal the brokenhearted just as the power of the gifts can heal the physically ill. Both are important.

He had spoken clearly and specifically to the disciples and the people concerning the "promise of the Father" (Joel 2 and Isaiah 28) being sent upon them to enable them to not only live full of might and power as witnesses to the fact that Jesus Christ truly was and is the Son of God who died for mankind and is risen from the dead (Acts 4:33), but also to live holy before God and man (I Peter 1:15-17). The fruit of the Spirit depicts holy living.

Jesus was emphatic about the importance of the Holy Spirit in the lives of believers. We are followers of Jesus; yet, we often discount what He said about the Holy Spirit. As Spirit-filled believers, we often fail to come into the lives of people demonstrating the power of God as Paul did in I Corinthians 2:4, or to come into the lives of people demonstrating love. We talk a good talk but <u>where is the power? Where is the love?</u> Acts 1:8 says "Ye shall receive power after the Holy Ghost has come upon you and you shall be witnesses...." I John 4:7-8 tells us that God is love. If we are of God then we should love as God loves. Beloved let us love one another.

Have you asked for this Holy Ghost visitation from God as Jesus instructed us to do? If not, now is the time. You will know his power and you will know his love. Only after you know his love and power can you give to others that which they need. Jesus is waiting for you. All you have to do is ask.

Luke 11:11-13 says: *(11) If a son shall* ask *bread of any of you that is a father, will he give him a stone? Or if he* ask *a fish, will he for a fish give him a serpent? (12) Or if he shall* ask *an egg, will he offer him a scorpion? (13) If ye then, being evil, know how to give good gifts unto your children:* how much more shall your heavenly Father give the Holy Spirit to them that ask him?

Ask and you shall receive. God only gives good gifts. James 1:17 says: *Every good gift and every perfect gift is from above, and cometh down from the Father of lights, with whom is no variableness, neither shadow of turning.*

As Christians and followers of Christ, our main purpose is to bring people to him for salvation. However, too often, we try to do this without the anointing of the Holy Spirit or the display of the fruit of the Spirit in our lives. We read in the Word of God that we shall lay hands on the sick and they shall recover, or as Jesus said in John 14:12 *"Verily, verily, I say unto you, He that believeth on me, the works that I do shall he do also; and greater than these shall he do; because I go unto my Father."* Where are these greater works? It is also taught and preached that our words are full of creative power, yet, the manifestations of these things evade us.

Brothers and sisters, this ought not to be. What is lacking? Where has the Church missed it? I don't mean one local church, I mean the Body of Christ. Where have we missed it? Perhaps you individually have not missed it. I pray that is true. But, if indeed we're not walking in the love and power of God (fruit and gifts), we have missed it. We have missed out on being witnesses to the fact that Jesus Christ truly was and is the <u>only-begotten Son</u> of God, who not only died for us, but was raised up by the Spirit of God on the third day. He asked the Father to send Holy Spirit to empower us to live a life of love displaying the presence of God in power. Both are essential.

Acts 4:33 says: *And with great power gave the apostles witness of the resurrection of the Lord Jesus: and great grace was upon them all.*

Without love, none of the other fruit can develop correctly in our lives. Perhaps we have forgotten to develop the fruit of the Spirit that paves the way to be a conduit for Holy Spirit power.

Chapter Sixteen: Holy Spirit Empowerment

Introduction

The Trinity Distinctions

Holy Spirit Baptism is a Gift

Holy Spirit Baptism: Special Presence and Power of God on Man

How to Receive Baptism in Holy Spirit

CHAPTER 16
Holy Spirit Empowerment

Introduction

E<small>SSENCE</small> IS THE FUNDAMENTAL NATURE *of something apart from which the thing would not be what it is. It is the core of what makes something what it is without it being something else.*

God had a plan. Humanity would always be flesh. They would never be God because mankind was created and God is the creator. Man was made in God's image and likeness and was created without sin. Sin corrupted man and opened the door to death when he disobeyed God. Man sinned. Man died. The plan did not stop there. God gave his son Jesus who became flesh and lived as man on earth, but Jesus was also fully God though he laid aside the unique abilities and attributes of his deity while he walked on earth. When Jesus arose from the dead, he said that all power (i.e. all *exousia* authority) had been given to him in heaven and earth.

He also said that he must return to heaven so that Holy Spirit could come and indwell those who would believe on him. Holy Spirit is the third person in the Trinity, He is God. Jesus made the way for Holy Spirit to come and dwell in believers. Jesus not only had a human flesh and blood body prepared for him when he came to earth as Savior, but we see Holy Spirit also comes to indwell the Body of Christ today through indwelling each member. Paul told the Corinthian church that our bodies are the temple of the Holy Ghost. That was part of the plan. First, redemption guaranteeing man eternal life (i.e. eternity with the highest quality of existence in the presence of God). Second, just as Jesus was anointed by the Holy Spirit, so too Jesus made the way for Holy Spirit to indwell and empower believers to be victorious over sin just as he had been. Holy Spirit indwelling also guarantees resurrection for believers. <u>This insures believers an immortal body.</u> Death will be defeated forevermore. That is the value of Holy Spirit to you.

Although humans are not God, believers can have Holy Spirit resident within them always. Thus the problem was solved. God would dwell in believers who would then be equipped to do all things needful for the kingdom of God just as Jesus had done. Holy Spirit would empower and equip believers so they could present Jesus in their victorious life and in the power of the Spirit. Holy Spirit was sent to indwell believers after the glorification of Jesus Christ, and believers could be united with God in power. We now have full access to the Father in heaven through Jesus Christ, and we have the ability of God by the indwelling Holy Spirit. And because the same Spirit that raised Christ from the dead dwells in believers, he shall quicken our mortal bodies (Romans 8:11). Holy Spirit dwells in believers' bodies (I Corinthians 6:19).

THE TRINITY DISTINCTIONS

There are things particular to each of the Persons of the Godhead yet they work together in everything as one. That which is particular to <u>each</u> "person of the Trinity, <u>when combined</u>, defines

Trinity. The Trinity is the Father, Son, and the Holy Spirit. "The Trinity is that which God has given us to know and experience of the totality of God" (Spoken to my heart by God in 2004),

The Father has a Son of equal and same essence as Himself. The Father is the sender of the Son, the giver of the Son, the receiver of the Sacrifice of the Son, sender and giver of the Holy Ghost to humankind. He is the source of begetting and sending. It is from the Father through the Son that the Holy Spirit proceeds.

The Son has particulars peculiar to himself. He is Son, Mediator, Savior, Restorer, God Incarnate. The Incarnate Son made the way for the Holy Spirit to indwell humankind. The Son was the Sacrifice. He is the Redeemer, High Priest, Holy Spirit Baptizer, and the Word of God.

Holy Spirit is the Spirit of the Father and the Son. He is not just a "part" of each of the other two; he is God within His own right: separate from, but working in conjunction with them just as they work in conjunction with the Holy Spirit and each other. I Corinthians 2 tells us that Holy Spirit is the revealer of truth and the deep things of God. He abides (lives) in believers who receive Christ's completed work by faith. He is the enabler of man to call Jesus Christ the Son of God, and to call out, "Abba, Father."

Galatians 4:6 *And because ye are sons, God hath sent forth the Spirit of his Son into your hearts, crying, Abba, Father."*

First Corinthians 12:3 *Wherefore I give you to understand, that no man speaking by the Spirit of God calleth Jesus accursed: and that no man can say that Jesus is the Lord, but by the Holy Ghost.*

He is the teacher and comforter. He is the one who empowers the sons and daughters of God to do the work of the Church as recorded in Matthew 28, Mark 16, Luke 24, John 21, and Acts 1:1-8.

Acts 1:4-8, Jesus commanded them that they should not depart from Jerusalem, but *wait for the promise of the Father, which, [saith he], ye have heard of me. (5) For John truly baptized with water; but ye shall be baptized with the Holy Ghost not many days hence. (6) When they therefore were come together, they asked of him, saying, Lord, wilt thou at this time restore again the kingdom to Israel? (7) And he said unto them, It is not for you to know the times or the seasons, which the Father hath put in his own power. (8) But ye shall receive power, after that the Holy Ghost is come upon you: and ye shall be witnesses unto me both in Jerusalem, and in all Judea, and in Samaria, and unto the uttermost part of the earth.*

Without Holy Spirit enablement, we are incapable of doing these tasks.

The Holy Spirit is that of the Godhead which can be imparted to not only dwell WITH mankind, but to dwell IN mankind. He enables and empowers humanity to be restored to the pre-fall condition of humanity (Genesis 1:26-28) and to reign in life with Christ (Romans 5:17). Jesus Christ provided our resurrection and Holy Spirit is the guarantor of resurrection. The Father did not come to inhabit us; the Son did not come to inhabit us. **It is Holy Spirit who inhab-its believers.** God spoke one day and said to me, "The Trinity is that which has been given to man to know and experience of the TOTALITY of God: Father, Son, and Holy Spirit." If you are not experiencing the Holy Spirit, you are not experiencing all God has for you.

John 14:17 *Even the Spirit of truth; whom the world cannot receive, because it seeth him not, neither knoweth him: but ye know him; for he dwelleth with you, and shall be in you.*

<u>The Father is God</u>
<u>The Son is God</u>
<u>AND</u>
<u>The Holy Spirit is God</u>

They are one in essence and one in unity. Each is involved in the plan for all creation and redemption. How can we experience the Father? How can we experience Jesus? How can we experience Holy Spirit? Every person can experience God in all his creation. But there is a deeper understanding for believers. Believers actually experience God personally when they accept Jesus as God's only begotten Son who died for the sins of the world. Believers experience God in his Word in a way that unbelievers cannot. You experience God in prayer and praise, and every breath you take. You experience God as you meditate on his Word and listen for his voice. And you surely experience God when he speaks to your heart.

I said to the Lord: "Lord, fill this place with your glory." God said to me, "Fill this place with praise and I will come. Where I am is my glory; therefore, my glory will fill this place when you praise because I inhabit your praise. I am manifested when you praise. Where praise is—-I am." God is in the place where we praise Him. In praise, we experience God.

Augustine said, "God loves, Jesus is the lover, Holy Spirit reveals the love and the lover to the loved one." Holy Spirit is not some afterthought, but has a very important and necessary part in salvation and victorious living for the redeemed. He is God as the Father is God and as the Son is God. Holy Spirit helps us to pray, praise, and worship God. He is the "living water" that flows out of a believer's spirit.

Holy Spirit Baptism is a Gift

Holy Spirit Baptism is a gift as sure as salvation, healing, and deliverance are gifts. God has provided for total victory and restoration through redemption by Jesus Christ and through the presence and power of the Holy Spirit in believers. The last words Jesus spoke before His ascension had to do with the church being empowered by the Holy Spirit. Acts 1:8, *"Ye shall receive **POWER** after that the Holy Ghost is come upon you."*

Luke records much about Holy Spirit Baptism: Acts 8:1-8, 14, 17; 11:1-18; 19:1-6. Paul wrote concerning Holy Spirit in First Corinthians 2; 3:16; 6; 19; Chapters 12, 13, and 14; Second Corinthians 6:16.

Holy Spirit Baptism: Special Presence and Power of God on Man

Holy Spirit Baptism is the coming to mankind of the special presence and power of God. It is God's power imparted to man. Why? To draw people to God. Wherever Jesus went, multitudes gathered as they were drawn by healings, miracles, signs, and wonders. Then Jesus would teach them. We should do the same.

Until Jesus came and redeemed mankind, they were not able to receive Holy Spirit to dwell in them because one cannot put new wine in old wineskins. After Jesus provided the way to life, then Holy Spirit could come to indwell. Paul reminded the Corinthian church that our bodies are the temple of the Holy Ghost (I Corinthians 6:19).

Among other things, Holy Spirit baptism is for power to overcome the flesh, thereby, developing the fruit of the Spirit and moving in the supernatural gifts of the Holy Spirit. The gifts of the Holy Spirit are listed in I Corinthians 12 and the Fruit of the Spirit is listed in Galatians 5:22. The fruit of the Spirit will and should develop in a Holy Spirit baptized person. The fruit of the Spirit is proof of our <u>walking</u> in the Spirit. It is <u>not</u> the proof of our being <u>baptized</u> in the Holy Spirit.

The effects of Holy Spirit Baptism are great love, fullness of joy, sharing, continuing praise of God, holy impulses and aspirations, as well as the fruit of the Spirit, and manifestations of the nine gifts as recorded in I Corinthians 12 (*...as the Spirit wills*). Holy Spirit wills to do the will of the Father just as Jesus did. Jesus only did what pleased the Father. Jesus Himself said in John 5:18-20, "*I only say what I hear my Father say and only do what I see the Father do.*" Jesus did it <u>THEN because it was the will of the Father. We do it NOW because it is STILL</u> the will of the Father.

<u>I Corinthians 2:1-5</u> tells us that Paul came in the demonstration of the power of God. Shall we do less? What did Paul do? He imitated Jesus. What are we to do? Imitate Jesus as Paul did. Where does this power for demonstration come from? It comes from the Holy Spirit Baptism the same as it did on the Day of Pentecost. Jesus did the work of the ministry by the same power of the Holy Spirit that was poured out on the Day

of Pentecost and this Holy Spirit baptism is available to you and to me. All believers have access to it (Acts 2:39).

<u>Acts 10:34-38</u>, *Then Peter opened [his] mouth, and said, Of a truth I perceive that God is no respecter of persons: (35) But in every nation he that feareth him, and worketh righteousness, is accepted with him. (36) The word which [God] sent unto the children of Israel, preaching peace by Jesus Christ: (he is Lord of all:) (37) That word, [I say], ye know, which was published throughout all Judaea, <u>and began from Galilee, after the baptism which John preached; (38) How God anointed Jesus of Nazareth with the Holy Ghost and with power: who went about doing good, and healing all that were oppressed of the devil; for God was with him.</u>*

Jesus said, "...*greater things than these shall you do.*" (John 14:12). How can we ever do the things he did? By the same Holy Spirit by which He was anointed by the Father. What can we do? Whatever Jesus did, we can do. If He healed by the Holy Spirit then we can heal by the same Holy Spirit power. If He cast out demons by the Holy Spirit, we can also cast out demons by the same Holy Spirit. This is possible because the Holy Spirit is Divine just as Jesus is Divine.

Why did Jesus need to be baptized in the Holy Spirit if he, himself, was God? The answer is that Jesus came to earth <u>as a **HUMAN**</u> to redeem humankind. He came to show us the way and, as our example, of necessity he must be anointed with the same Holy Spirit to do the work of the ministry. His life showed us what we can and should do. The Word became flesh. He did not cease to be the Word, but at the same time, the Word **BECAME** flesh. He was still God, but He did not function as God. He came to earth and functioned as a human just like you or me. He had to lay aside His God abilities and become truly human in order to walk as a truly human with all its limitations. He had to be tested, tempted, and tried as a human like us. Through it all, he did not sin. He did not have "one up" on us because he was God in the flesh. Instead, he emptied himself or incapacitated his abilities (as God) by his will. He could have called ten thousand angels down, but he chose not to *(Matthew 26:53).

Paul recorded this in Philippians 2: 6-8: *Who, being in the form of God, thought it not robbery to be equal with God: (7) But made himself of no reputation, and took upon him the form of a servant, and was made in the likeness of men: (8) And being found in fashion as a man,* <u>*he humbled himself, and became obedient unto death,*</u> *even the death of the cross.*

Our equipping is by the same Holy Spirit that came upon and remained on Jesus at his water baptism. It is the same Holy Spirit with which God anointed Jesus (Acts 10:38 and Luke 4:18). Read and meditate on these scriptures: Matthew 4:15-17; John 1:29-36; Acts 10:34-38.

Jesus could tell believers to go and do these things because he knew we could. He would baptize us in the same Holy Spirit with which he was anointed by the Father. It was only after Jesus was anointed with the Holy Ghost that he began to do miracles and signs. We need that same anointing to empower us to do his work in the earth as a testimony that Jesus is alive today seated at the right hand of the Father.

Matthew 28:18-20; Mark 16:15-20; Luke 4: 18-29, Acts 1:8; 10:38

We know how Paul could say, *"And my speech and my preaching was not with enticing words of man's wisdom, but in demonstration of the Spirit and of power* (1 Corinthians 2:4)

We can walk in the same power that Jesus walked in. The power that delivers and heals. The right and might to come boldly into the presence of God, sit in God's presence, hear God's voice, be blessed, set totally free, and be empowered to walk in freedom from bondage. This power will sustain us at all times as we make ourselves available to the totality of God: Father, Son, and Holy Spirit. He has come to lead us into all truth, to teach us the truth, to empower us to overcome, and to be more than conquerors in Christ Jesus. Holy Spirit has come to empower us to produce fruit in our lives as we abide in the vine (John 15).

So what are you going to do with the Holy Spirit in your life? He is the active one in the earth today just as Jesus was active and the focal point when He came to earth. Remember Jesus said in John 16:7, *"It is expedient for me to go away because if I go not away the Holy Spirit will not come."* He went away and Holy Spirit was poured out on the Day of Pentecost and has not left since. He is still empowering, equipping, teaching, revealing, leading, and drawing people to Jesus. Are you experiencing Him personally? Do you feel His presence even now? He is real and He is right where you are right now. Each time you praise and worship God, you will sense His presence.

If you are not baptized in the Holy Spirit, you can be. God wants you to be. All you have to do is ask and receive. Jesus told us how to receive.

Luke: 11:9-13, *And I say unto you, Ask, and it shall be given you; seek, and ye shall find; knock, and it shall be opened unto you. (10) For every one that asketh receiveth; and he that seeketh findeth; and to him that knocketh it shall be opened. (11) If a son shall ask bread of any of you that is a father, will he give him a stone? Or if [he ask] a fish, will he for a fish give him a serpent? (12) Or if he shall ask an egg, will he offer him a scorpion? (13) If ye then, being evil, know how to give good gifts unto your children:* **<u>how much more shall your heavenly Father give the Holy Spirit to them that ask him?</u>**

It is that simple. It is when you ask, seek and knock that you receive. The true sense of verse 9 is "ask and keep on asking; seek and keep on seeking; knock and keep on knocking." We continue to persevere until we have prayed the "effectual fervent prayer" that gets results (James 5:16). The word "prayer" in James 5:16, is supplication which means "to plead humbly." The word "effectual" means "that which has an effect on the one praying to bring them into line with God's word." In other words, your praying should have an effect on you. It should be in line with God's word, and God's word should have an effect on your spirit man to bring you into line with truth. The word "fervent" means "hot to boil." This type of prayer accomplishes much. It is dynamic in its working and makes tremendous power available.

How to Receive Baptism in Holy Spirit

In this book, you have read God's word concerning Holy Spirit's work in the earth, his involvement in redemption, and the fact of being empowered when you are baptized in the Holy Spirit that Jesus taught about. Think on what you have read. Think on the many scriptures you have as a witness to the truths shared in this book. Ask God to reveal his word to you. When you see what his word plainly teaches, your faith will rise and courage will come. Then you are ready to release the utterances coming up in you. These utterances are not your native tongue or any language of man so they sound like "non-sense syllables." Begin to speak them over your tongue, from your mouth and your breath. This is the language of Heaven; the language of the Spirit. Continue. When you stop speaking in tongues, realize that this language is available at any moment you choose to speak it. Do it again right away. Then repeat it often. Return to the chapter on the value of tongues and reread it. These are the reasons that God gave you his precious Holy Spirit to indwell you every moment of everyday.

Chapter Seventeen: Victory in the Holy Spirit

Introduction

Scripture References

They Did Not Already Have That Power

They Were Not to Move Without It

This Empowering Would be A Unique Experience

Two Lasting Deposits: Proof of Holy Spirit Permanency

Deposit Number One Was "Power"

Deposit Number Two Was "Tongues"

Holy Ghost Power Has Come

CHAPTER 17
Victory in the Holy Spirit

Introduction

God's Word, his presence, and his anointing renew, refresh, and empower your spirit with life and victory. Anointed with what? The Holy Ghost. Anointing is God on flesh doing only what God can do. Another way to speak about the anointing is that it is the empowering hand of God on a person's life, equipping him for a task. Therefore, to live in the anointing is to live daily in the awareness and adventure of the empowering and equipping of Holy Spirit. After being born again, believers should seek to be baptized in the Holy Spirit.

Scriptures References

<u>Isaiah 10:27</u>, *And it shall come to pass in that day, [that] his burden shall be taken away from off thy shoulder, and his yoke from off thy neck, and the yoke shall be destroyed because of the anointing.*

<u>Acts 10:36-38</u>, *(36) The word which [God] sent unto the children of Israel, preaching peace by Jesus Christ: (he is Lord of all:) (37) That word, [I say], ye know, which was published throughout all Judaea, and began from Galilee, after the baptism which John preached; (38) How*

God anointed Jesus of Nazareth with the Holy Ghost and with power: who went about doing good, and healing all that were oppressed of the devil; for God was with him.

Luke 24:48-49 *And ye are witnesses of these things. (49) And, behold, I send the promise of my father upon you: but tarry ye in Jerusalem until you be endued with power from on high.*

Mark 16:15-20, *(15) And he said unto them, Go ye into all the world, and preach the gospel to every creature. (16) He that believeth and is baptized shall be saved; but he that believeth not shall be damned. (17) And these signs shall follow them that believe; In my name shall they cast out devils; they shall speak with new tongues; (18) They shall take up serpents; and if they drink any deadly thing, it shall not hurt them; they shall lay hands on the sick, and they shall recover. (19) So then after the Lord had spoken unto them, he was received up into heaven, and sat on the right hand of God. (20) And they went forth, and preached everywhere, the Lord working with [them], and confirming the word with signs following. Amen*

John 7:37-39, *(37) In the last day, that great [day] of the feast, Jesus stood and cried, saying, If any man thirst, let him come unto me, and drink. (38) He that believeth on me, as the scripture hath said, out of his belly shall flow rivers of living water. (39) (But this spake he of the Spirit, which they that believe on him should receive: for the Holy Ghost was not yet [given]; because that Jesus was not yet glorified.)*

Acts 1:5-8, *(5) For John truly baptized with water; but ye shall be baptized with the Holy Ghost not many days hence. (6) When they therefore were come together, they asked of him, saying, Lord, wilt thou at this time restore again the kingdom to Israel? (7) And he said unto them, It is not for you to know the times or the seasons, which the Father hath put in his own power. (8) But ye shall receive power, after that the Holy Ghost is come upon you: and ye shall be witnesses unto me both in Jerusalem, and in all Judaea, and in Samaria, and unto the uttermost part of the earth.*

<u>Joel 2:28</u>, *And it shall come to pass afterward, [that] I will pour out my spirit upon all flesh; and your sons and your daughters shall prophesy, your old men shall dream dreams, your young men shall see visions:*

Much of the information below is from an article shared with me by a classmate several years ago and the name of the author was not on the paper. I have no way of tracing it to its origin, but it contains some insight that will be profitable to consider. I have interjected my own comments and Scripture for the reader's consideration.

Let's look at <u>Luke 24:49</u>: *And, behold, I send the promise of my Father upon you: but tarry ye in the city of Jerusalem, until ye be endued with power from on high.*

There are three observations we can infer about Holy Spirit baptism from this passage of scripture:

They Did Not Already Have That Power.

They had already performed acts of power as described in Luke 10:17-19 when Jesus sent the seventy out two by two, but Jesus said there was a <u>promise not yet fulfilled</u> which indicated that it was a promise <u>they had not yet experienced</u>. What had they experienced? They had known a <u>temporary anointing</u> from God in order to function as necessary. This anointing or empowering was no different from any other Old Testament anointing that came upon people equipping them for a specific task. Elijah in 1 Kings and Samson in Judges 14:6 give examples of *"The Spirit of the Lord came upon..."*

Similarly, in the New Testament, Jesus empowered the disciples in order for them to function as required at a specific time. Matthew 10:1 and Luke 9:1-2 give examples where Jesus gave His twelve disciples power over unclean spirits, to cast them out and heal all kinds of sickness and disease. Until they were specifically given power, they could not function. Their enabling came through the releasing of power and authority at specific times. They did not move in power every day but only as often as they were empowered to do so. However, that was to change.

They Were Not To Move Without It

Whatever this power was that He was telling them to go to Jerusalem and wait for, Jesus implied that it was vital to their future life and ministry.

NOTICE: All their previous empowering and anointing had been specifically given "by Jesus personally" but He was about to leave them and ascend to the Father. So now, He was stressing the importance of not attempting to function without another source of power.

Many have made the mistake of attempting to function independent of God's power. The seven sons of Sceva as recorded in Acts 19:13-17, found they did not have the power or authority to cast demons out of people's lives. Jesus came to make this available to those who trusted in Him. Judges 16:4-21 tells the story of Samson who after disobeying God, presumptuously attempted to move in the power of the Spirit only to find that the power was no longer there. Sadly, the enemy overcame him.

By instructing the disciples to remain in Jerusalem until they had been clothed with power, Jesus was not imposing a restrictive command. Rather, He was protecting them from any potential failure that would have been experienced by attempting to function without the necessary empowering and anointing of God. In fact, Jesus was simply telling them to begin their ministry in exactly the same way He had begun His own ministry.

Before Jesus began His ministry, He had an encounter with the Holy Spirit that resulted in His being empowered to fulfill His ministry. After

Luke 4:14-21, *(14) And Jesus returned in the power of the Spirit into Galilee: and there went out a fame of him through all the region round about. (15) And he taught in their synagogues, being glorified of all. (16) And he came to Nazareth, where he had been brought up: and, as his custom was, he went into the synagogue on the Sabbath day, and stood up for to read. (17) And there was delivered unto him the book of the prophet Esaias. And when he had opened the book, he found the place where it was written, (18) The Spirit of the Lord [is] upon me, because he hath anointed me to preach the gospel to the poor; he hath sent me to heal the brokenhearted, to preach deliverance to the captives, and recovering of sight to the blind, to set at liberty them that are bruised, (19) To preach the acceptable year of the Lord. (20) And he closed the book, and he gave [it] again to the minister, and sat down. And the eyes of all them that were in the synagogue were fastened on* him. (21) And he began to say unto them, This day is this scripture fulfilled in your ears.

Mark 1:9-11, (9) And it came to pass in those days, that Jesus came from Nazareth of Galilee, and was baptized of John in Jordan. (10) And straightway coming up out of the water, he saw the heavens opened, and the Spirit like a dove descending upon him: (11) And there came a voice from heaven, [saying], Thou art my beloved Son, in whom I am well pleased.

Acts 10:38, (38) How God anointed Jesus of Nazareth with the Holy Ghost and with power: who went about doing good, and healing all that were oppressed of the devil; for God was with him.

Matthew 3:11, 16-17, (11) I indeed baptize you with water unto repentance: but he that cometh after me is mightier than I, whose shoes I am not worthy to bear: he shall baptize you with the Holy Ghost, and [with] fire. (16) And Jesus, when he was baptized, went up straightway out of the water: and, lo, the heavens were opened unto him, and he saw the Spirit of God descending like a dove, and lighting upon him: (17) And lo a voice from heaven, saying, This is my beloved Son, in whom I am well pleased.

John 1:25-36 (25) And they asked him, and said unto him, Why baptizest thou then, if thou be not that Christ, nor Elias, neither that prophet? (26) John answered them, saying, I baptize with water: but there standeth one among you, whom ye know not; (27) He it is, who coming after me is preferred before me, whose shoe's latchet I am not worthy to unloose. (28) These things were done in Bethabara beyond Jordan, where John was baptizing. (29) The next day John seeth Jesus *coming unto him, and saith, <u>Behold the Lamb of God, which taketh away the sin of the world.</u> (30) This is he of whom I said, After me cometh a man which is preferred before me: for he was before me. (31) And I knew him not: <u>but that he should be made manifest to Israel, therefore am I come baptizing with water.</u> (32) And John bare record, saying, I saw the Spirit descending from heaven like a dove, and it abode upon him. (33) And I knew him not: but he that sent me to baptize with water, the same said unto me, <u>Upon whom thou shalt see the Spirit descending, and remaining on him, the same is he which baptizeth with the Holy Ghost. (34) And I saw, and bare record that this is the Son of God. (35) Again the next day after John stood, and two of his disciples; (36) And looking upon Jesus as he walked, he saith, Behold the Lamb of God!*

Jesus was not equipped to move forward without the Holy Spirit anointing and empowering. Similarly, Jesus instructed the disciples to wait to minister until they received Holy Spirit baptism. Why should we be different? This was to be a life-changing experience, and it was.

This empowering was different from that which Jesus had given in Matthew 10 to the disciples. That had been limited and temporary. The outpouring of Holy Spirit was a specific fulfillment of a long-standing promise. What was that promise? Joel 2:28-29 says that the Holy Spirit would be, *"poured out on all flesh..."* John the Baptist declared the same promise in a different way, but now it was even more specific as recorded in <u>Matthew 3:11</u>. John the Baptist named the one through whom this outpour-ing would be administered. *I indeed baptize you with water unto re-pentance: but he that cometh after me is mightier than I, whose shoes I* am not worthy to bear: he shall baptize you with the Holy Ghost, and [with] fire.

Jesus, Himself, also referred to the promise when he said in Luke 24:49. And, *behold, I send the promise of my Father upon you: but tarry ye in the city of Jerusalem, until ye be endued with power from on high.* Later, Jesus reiterated the command and promise just before He ascended to heaven.

He also gave an indication of how near the fulfillment of the promise was as recorded in Acts 1:4-5, *(4) And, being assembled together with [them], commanded them that they should not depart from Jerusalem, but wait for the promise of the Father, which, [saith he], ye have heard of me. (5) For John truly baptized with water; but ye shall be baptized with the Holy Ghost not many days hence.*

From our position in time, we can see exactly how all the pieces fit together. However, to those living at that time, it was not so clear. There was no apparent connection between (1) Joel's Old Testament prophesy, (2) John the Baptist's declaration in Matthew 3:11, and (3) Jesus' command to go to Jerusalem and tarry until they were endued with power.

However, with the fulfillment of the promise in Acts 2, there came an explanation of what the promises and command meant. The manifestation of Holy Spirit outpouring was confirmation that it was indeed the long-awaited promise. Now the picture was complete and clear for all to see that "*...this is that which was spoken by the prophet Joel*" (Acts 2:16).

This Empowering would be A Unique Experience

This empowerment was not only different because it was a specific fulfillment of long-standing promises, but also, because it was to be a unique experience. The experience in Acts 2 was unique compared to all the other previous encounters with the Holy Spirit.

Two Lasting Deposit: Proof of the Holy Spirit Permanency

Now the Spirit was given permanently, and to prove its permanency two lasting deposits were left with each recipient of the Spirit: Power and Tongues.

Deposit Number One Was "Power"

This is resident power not temporary power. As we have seen, power was given at various times for specific tasks. In fulfillment of Jesus' prophecy in Acts 1:8, those who tarried, received power and never lost it. Nowhere do you find the disciples praying for power. Instead, we have a catalogue of powerful manifestations performed by men who knew this power was resident within them. There is a differ-ence between me allowing you to borrow my car occasionally and giving you the keys to my car and saying, "use it anytime you like." From the day of Pentecost onwards, those disciples never required a subsidiary power source. They now had their own personal built-in generator from which they could draw power constantly. True, they asked God to perform miracles, signs, and wonders—but the miracles performed came through them.

Deposit Number Two Was "Tongues"

The second deposit to prove the Spirit's permanency was "tongues." The first lasting deposit was power resident within and the second lasting deposit proving the Spirit's permanency was tongues. Tongues were and are a unique and continuing sign of the Baptism in the Spirit. **Tongues were unique simply because no one had ever spoken in tongues prior to Acts 2.** They were a sign in the sense that they pointed to the fulfillment of the promise of the Holy Spirit.

Why Tongues? Simply because there are instances in the Old Testament of all the other manifestations listed in 1 Corinthians 12:7-11 *{(7) But the manifestation of the Spirit is given to every man to profit withal. (8) For to one is given by the Spirit the word of wisdom; to another the word of knowledge by the same Spirit; (9) To another faith by the same Spirit; to another the gifts of healing by the same Spirit; (10) To another the working of miracles; to another prophecy; to another discerning of spirits; to another [divers] kinds of tongues; to another the interpretation of tongues: (11) But all these worketh that one and the selfsame Spirit, dividing to every man severally as he wills.*

All of the gifts listed here EXCEPT tongues and their accompanying interpretation had been manifested before both in the Old Testament, as well as, in the life of Christ and those he empowered such as in Matthew 11. Had God used any manifestation of the Spirit that had occurred prior to the day of Pentecost after the resurrection of Jesus, there would have been no noticeable difference in the outpouring in Acts chapter two.

God withheld supernatural tongues knowing in His eternal plan and purpose that a day was coming when He would, in a unique way, pour out His Spirit on all flesh. He also knew that He would accompany that unique outpouring with an equally unique sign.

The miracle of tongues had the desired effect as recorded in Acts 2:5-12, *(5) And there were dwelling at Jerusalem Jews, devout men, out of every nation under heaven. (6) Now when this was noised abroad, the multitude came together, and were confounded, because that every man heard them speak in his own language. (7) And they were all amazed and marvelled, saying one to another, Behold, are not all these which speak Galileans? (8) And how hear we every man in our own tongue, wherein we were born? (9) Parthians, and Medes, and Elamites, and the dwellers in Mesopotamia, and in Judaea, and Cappadocia, in Pontus, and Asia, (10) Phrygia, and Pamphylia, in Egypt, and in the parts of Libya about Cyrene, and strangers of Rome, Jews and proselytes, (11) Cretes and Arabians, we do hear them speak in our tongues the wonderful works of God. (12) And they were all amazed, and were in doubt, saying one to another, What meaneth this?*

This caused the amazed and perplexed onlookers to exclaim, "What does this mean?" to which Peter replied, "Let me explain this to you. This is that spoken by the prophet Joel." On that day, 3,000 people were born again.

In 1 Corinthians 14:22, Paul emphasized that tongues were a supernatural sign to the unbelievers that may cause one to conclude a number of things. He may even conclude you are mad as Paul states in 1 Corinthians 14:23: *"If therefore the whole church be come together into one place, and all speak with tongues, and there come in [those that are] unlearned, or unbelievers, will they not say that ye are mad?"* They accused Peter and the others of being drunk on the day of Pentecost, BUT they also asked, "What does this mean?"

The fact is they knew it had meaning! It was a sign that pointed to something even more significant. Three thousand people believed on Jesus Christ that day because of tongues and the demonstration of those who were baptized in the Holy Spirit.

Tongues were also helpful in allowing the Apostles to conclude whether or not someone was baptized in the Spirit. Acts 10:1-48 records the story of Peter being politely interrupted by the Holy Spirit filling his hearers while he was preaching at the house of Cornelius. Peter had to conclude that the unbelievable had really happened, that is, the Gentiles had received the Spirit just as the Jewish converts had. What caused Peter to be able to conclude this was the fact that he <u>heard</u> them speak in tongues (Acts 10:47).

Holy Ghost Power Has Come

The power that Jesus said they should wait for has now come. A "clothing" from on high had truly been their experience and for the first time in their lives, they were completely wrapped around and filled with the Holy Spirit and with power. God clothed them with a suit of power inside and out. This time (as opposed to the prophets and judges in the Old Testament) this Holy Spirit power suit was not on loan. Holy Spirit now dwells within. This indwell-ing is permanent. They continued daily to enjoy the benefit of the provision. That empowering from on high became the gateway to living in the anointing. It was a permanent deposit, and it can be yours permanently also.

That power is still available today to believers. The power to produce events that draw people to God: to heal, to speak in tongues, to perform miracles, to deliver, to heal the broken

hearted, to set the captives free, to know things supernaturally, to demonstrate all that the gifts of the Holy Spirit make available to believers.

If you are a believer in Jesus Christ, obey Him as the first Christians did and be baptized in the Holy Ghost and power for His service and stop trying to do things in your own power. The power of the Holy Spirit will help you overcome and to live victoriously. He will cause you to feel and know the love of Almighty God and bring a desire to please Him. He will deliver you from bondages, habits, and hang-ups; heal and bind up your wounds, and heal your broken heart. That is what He can and will do. He will prosper and meet your every need as you serve Him with your whole heart. God has a plan for you. We serve that God. The God who loves us so much that He literally comes to live within us by his Holy Spirit if you ask Him in. Ask Him right now.

Chapter Eighteen: Fully Persuaded

Of What Are You Fully Persuaded?

When is a Person Fully Persuaded?

Persuaded

How do You Become Fully Persuaded?

CHAPTER 18
Fully Persuaded

> Romans 4:20b *And being fully persuaded that, what he had promised, he was able also to perform. And therefore it was imputed to him for righteousness*

> Romans 8:38-39 *For I am persuaded, that neither death, nor life, nor angels, nor principalities, nor powers, nor things present, nor things to come, (39) Nor height, nor depth, nor any other creature, shall be able to separate us from the love of God, which is in Christ Jesus our Lord.*

OF WHAT ARE YOU FULLY PERSUADED?

DO YOU TRUST IN GOD's integrity, faithfulness, commitment, and Word that He wants the best for you? Do you believe Darwin's Evolution, Islamic Allah, or the Creator God of the Bible? What do you put your faith in? What are you betting your life on?

Everyone has a final authority. It may be one's own self, another person, a philosophy, a theory, a book. What is your final author-ity? Again, I ask what are you betting your life on as the thing that is truth? Science or God? Bible or Quran? Man's knowledge or God's knowledge? Evolution or creation?

The God of the Bible is the only God with whom you can have a living relationship. He is a God full of mercy, grace, and love. Who is your God? The God of the Bible is a personal living God, There is no other "God" who has a personal living present relationship with his or her followers. Only the God of the Bible; the Father of our Lord Jesus Christ: the creator of humanity and all things. God is for real. He is alive! So we could know who he is and what he is like, Jesus came to reveal God to us. You can know what God is like.

<u>God is love (I John 4:8)</u>. <u>He doesn't lie</u>, (Numbers 23:190, <u>He doesn't change</u> (James 1:17, Hebrews 13:8), and <u>He is no respecter of persons</u> (Acts 10:34).

We can personally know God by experience. We can know that the Bible is God's revelation of himself to man, and a revelation of man's beginning and destiny. We have confidence that this is true because of history and the fulfillment of many hundreds of prophecies that could not possibly be foretold and come to pass without supernatural intervention. The Bible alone will not convince you or persuade you, but the God of the Bible through his presence, power, and love can totally convince your heart and mind.

Are you fully persuaded of these things? Persuaded means that you <u>believe</u>, are <u>convinced</u>, <u>assured</u>, and <u>fully trusting</u>. It is knowing that you know without doubt to the point that you act on what you are persuaded of with full confidence in the end result. Totally convinced- unmovable. Eve, was <u>not</u> totally convinced of God's word (Gen. 3:1-3, 6).

Romans 4:16-20, *Therefore it is of faith, that it might be by grace; to the end the promise might be sure to all the seed; not to that only which is of the law, but to that also which is of the faith of Abraham; who is the father of us all, (As it is written, I have made thee a father of many nations,) <u>before him whom he believed, even God, who quickeneth the dead, and calleth those things which be not as though they were.</u> Who against <u>hope believed in hope</u>, that he might become the father of many nations, according to that which was spoken, So shall thy seed be. And <u>being not weak in faith</u>, he considered not his own body now dead, when he was about an hundred years old, neither yet the deadness of Sarah's womb: He <u>staggered not at the promise of God through unbelief;</u> but was <u>strong in faith</u>, giving glory to God; And **being fully persuaded that, what he had promised, he was able also to perform. And therefore it was imputed to him for righteousness.***

Abraham was fully persuaded. He believed, was convinced, totally assured, fully trusting. A person does half a job and is not committed when they are not fully persuaded. Hebrews 11:17-19, records the Hall of Faith. All these people were fully persuaded. This is a showcase of those who were totally convinced, assured, and fully trusting in God's word.

Romans 4:20a: *Abraham staggered not at the promise of God through unbelief; but was strong in faith, giving glory to God.*

Romans 8:11, 37-39 (11) *But if the Spirit of him that raised up Jesus from the dead dwell in you, he that raised up Christ from the dead shall also quicken your mortal bodies by his Spirit that dwelleth in you. (37) Nay, in all these things we are more than conquerors through him that* *loved us. (38) <u>For I am persuaded</u>, that neither death, nor life, nor angels, nor principalities, nor powers, nor things present, nor things to come, (39) Nor height, nor depth, nor any other creature, shall be able to separate us from the love of God, which is in Christ Jesus our Lord.*

What was Paul fully persuaded of here? He was convinced that the God of Abraham is no respecter of person; that he does not change; does not lie; and that God is love. When we believe these things about God then we can become fully persuaded. Often we try to have great faith for great things before we are ever convinced of these elementary but crucial facts about God. Abraham believed that God was not only able to keep his promises, but that God would keep his promises to him.

In II Timothy 1:12, Paul said to Timothy, *"For I know in whom I have believed."* For Paul there was no doubt or turning. He believed God would keep his word just as Abraham had believed God's word. The word "know" here is *oida* which means to know inwardly, without effort, to understand. It means to know without outward evidence. In other words, Paul was fully persuaded.

In Romans 12:1-3, we are told to present our bodies a living sacrifice and to renew our minds to think like God. Unless we are fully persuaded that God is love, doesn't lie, doesn't change, is no respecter of persons, and that the Bible is God's revelation of himself and of man, we will not do this. But when we are fully persuaded of these things, it is with joy that we conform our thoughts to the Word of God because we know that God loves us and what he tells us to do will bless and benefit us. You will never commit to God if you are not fully persuaded that God is love, doesn't lie, doesn't change, is no respecter of persons, and that the Bible is God's word to you.

When is a Person Fully Persuaded?
One is fully persuaded when he is fully, totally, without reservation, assured, convinced, and without doubt, totally trusting even when there are great risks. Here are some examples.
- Abel obeyed God because he was fully persuaded that he had access to God.
- Noah built an Ark inland because he was fully persuaded that God was sending a flood.
- Abraham sacrificed Isaac in his heart and mind because he was fully persuaded that God would raise him up because God had said the Messiah (seed) would come through Isaac (Hebrews 11:17-19).
- Isaac sowed in famine. He was fully persuaded because God said He would increase his seed sown.
- Enoch walked with God and was not because he was fully persuaded that God was God.
- The three Hebrew children were delivered from the fiery furnace declaring their God would deliver them because they were fully persuaded that God was the one true God.
- Daniel was delivered from the lion's den because he was fully persuaded that what he did was right and therefore God would deliver him. He believed God was his protector.
- The men on the road to Damascus declared, "Did not our hearts burn within us as he spoke with us?" They were fully persuaded that this was the risen Savior.
- Ten of the disciples after the resurrection were fully persuaded when they saw him, and later Thomas was fully persuaded when Jesus told him to touch him for assurance. They all were fully persuaded this was the Jesus who had died and rose again.

- <u>120 waited in the upper room</u> because they believed they would be endued with power from on high because they were fully persuaded the risen Lord Jesus Christ was truly God's own son.
- <u>Paul on the road to Damascus</u> was fully persuaded because he met Jesus and never turned away no matter what he went through.
- <u>John was exiled to the Isle of Patmos</u> for preaching Jesus. He knew what would happen, yet he preached because he was fully persuaded that Jesus was God's Son and Redeemer who died for the sins of the world. He knew his message was truth.

There was a reward for all those who were fully persuaded then and there is a reward now for being fully persuaded. The reward is eternal as well as many blessing here in this life.

In II Corinthians 4:7-9 Paul said he was *"hard pressed on every side, <u>but not</u> crushed; perplexed, <u>but not</u> in despair; persecuted, <u>but not</u> abandoned; struck down, <u>but not</u> destroyed."* Though those things happened to Paul, STILL he continued to fulfill the call of God on his life because he was fully persuaded that <u>God not only "could" but "would" keep him in all circumstances</u>.

Are you fully persuaded of the Word of God concerning you and concerning the Trinity, of Jesus being God's only begotten Son and Savior of the world, of the Holy Spirit indwelling and empowering believers, and of the value of tongues? How can you know when you are fully persuaded?

Persuaded
It is through words, actions, and attitudes that persuasion can be seen.

- Words will be in agreement with that of which you are fully persuaded.
- Attitudes of peace and control because you know the end from the beginning.
- Actions line up with that of which you are fully persuaded; of that of which you are fully convinced.
- There will be no fear of the outcome when you are fully persuaded that God is a covenant-keeping God who wants only good for you.
- Boldness and confidence become a way of life concerning those things of which you are persuaded.

Are you fully persuaded about the Word of God? When we are not fully persuaded we are tossed about to and fro. When we are not fully persuaded, we are double-minded and our double mindedness shows up in our words, attitudes, and actions. Sometime people act when they are not fully persuaded. It is much better to wait until you are fully persuaded than to act and be disappointed because you are not yet fully convinced that God will keep his word to you. Faith works mightily when you are fully persuaded.

How do We Become Fully Persuaded?
The answer is that we must spend time with God getting acquainted with him, knowing him, learning to trust him and his

love. Until you are fully persuaded of his love for you, you will not have faith to receive the things that he has promised. If you are baptized in the Holy Spirit, pray much in the Spirit and let God reveal himself to you.

Personal time alone with God and with his word is vital so do not discount it. Right now take a moment to think about how much time you are giving God. How much time during the day is he your total focal point? Perhaps you are busy and it is hard to find time to spend with God, but even when you are busy, fill your heart and mind with the Word of God and with praise and worship for God.

You can be fully persuaded and you can walk in the blessings of God. You can see great victories. You can receive your prayers answered, but as with all relationships it takes time spent together and commitment to be fully persuaded of God's love and faithfulness to you.

There are two joint avenues through which one can gain truth about God: (1) his written word, (2) prayer. God's word is his bond. He does not lie. The written word tells us of his promises, activities, and actions in the past. By these things we see examples of his power, authority, justice, and love. We are instructed and are given examples of reading, meditating, believing, and obeying the Word of God. We are shown examples of people who obeyed and also examples of dis-obedience to God's word. We are told of the blessings God has for us, and his promises to fulfill those blessings. These include salvation, healing, deliverance, provision, protection, wisdom, peace, power, etc.

Praying to God declares that we believe he is and that he is a rewarder of those who diligently seek him (Hebrews 11:6). In our prayers, we use his Word as a basis for our requests. His Word and prayers are tightly woven together because his Word reveals what he has promised. Because he does not lie, we know we have what he has promised.

Does his Word lie about Jesus being God's son? Does it lie about Jesus dying, and rising again on the third day? Does it lie when it says that Jesus' death, burial and resurrection were so all could be eternally saved? The Word declares that <u>this same Jesus</u> told his followers that he would ask the Father to send his promised <u>Holy Spirit</u> to not only dwell with them, but be resident within them. This occurred and the result was that they all spoke in tongues. This repeated on other occasions in Acts 8, 10, 19, and in I Corinthians. For example. We have God's promise of Holy Spirit through the teachings of Jesus, the manifestations and perpetua-tion of the outpouring of Holy Spirit, and the words in Acts 2:39 that this Holy Spirit experience is for all who are afar off. We are "afar off" and Holy Spirit baptism is for us today.

Holy Spirit baptism brings a power source that enables us to live in victory with the expectation that whatever Jesus did, we can do through the same Holy Spirit. As we spend time in prayer and God's word, our faith will increase and the impossible becomes possible.

The question remains: Are you fully persuaded? When you are fully persuaded that God is love; He does not lie (His Word is true); He is no respecter of persons (if He did things for and through Paul, Peter, etc. He will do it for and through you), and he does not change (whatever he has ever done, he will do it again) then your life will reflect it.

Read and think on the Bible verses given to you in this book, and read others from your Bible. Spend time talking to God about them. Then when you are fully persuaded that God desires and needs believers to have this Holy Spirit experience. Yield your lips, tongue, breath, and vocal cords to him. Praise him in the heavenly language of the Spirit. God expects you to make the sounds because God gave that breathe and intends you to use it. He will not make those sounds for you or use your breath for you, but he will give it life and utterance. It is your breath, tongue, mouth, lips, but it is His life in it. Yield them to Holy Spirit.

Let the Scriptures speak to you. As you pray and speak to God about his word, he will confirm their truth to you.

Luke 11:13 *"If you then being evil, know how to give good gifts unto your children: how much more shall your heavenly Father give the Holy Spirit to them that ask him"*? Ask and you shall receive, knock and it shall be opened. Seek and you shall find.

Acts 1:3- Presented himself alive after His suffering by many convincing, fully persuasive proofs.

The book of Acts is the design for the New Testament Spirit-filled Church. (I Cor. 15:5-7) In Acts you see signs, wonders, miracles, various gifts of the Holy Spirit.

What have you seen and heard concerning God? Are you boldly sharing it with others as Peter did on the day of Pentecost? You will boldly share, show, and shine forth that of which you are fully persuaded. What is it that you are bold to speak of? You can trust God's Word and Holy Spirit who is to teach, reveal, and guide born-again Christians. The Bible contains truth, and Holy Spirit reveals that truth to those who ask. Read the Word concerning Holy Spirit in the New Testament. What did Jesus say? Whatever He said has not changed. Holy Spirit is still in the earth doing the same things for believers today as from the beginning. His Word is truth. God does not change. If God changes He is not trustworthy and the foolish saying, "you just never know what God is going to do" would be true.

You can know what God is going to do if you read the Bible. His blood covenant was cut and sealed through Jesus Christ and the Word of the covenant can be trusted. He will do exactly what He says He will do. Holy Spirit has been sent to lead, guide, teach and reveal the covenant promises, and the power of the Holy Spirit is more than enough to execute the promises of God in your life. Reread chapter one and see that Holy Spirit is the third person of the Trinity. The Father is God. The Son is God. Holy Spirit is God. Amen. He is no respecter of persons. He does not lie. God is alive. Are you fully persuaded of these things about God? Read His written Word and talk to God about it. Listen and he will speak to your heart personally and He will never speak contrary to His written Word.

Holy Spirit Doctrine Scriptures
LIST OF SCRIPTURES CONCERNING HOLY SPIRIT DOCTRINE

John 7:37-39 with Acts 3: 13
John 14:12 – 18, 23-26
John 15:26 – 27

John 16:7, 12-14
Acts 1:1 -8
Acts 2:1-4
Acts 8:1-8, 14-17
Acts 11:1-18
Acts 19:1-6
John 1:30-34
Matthew 3:11, 13:11
Luke 24:46-49
Matthew 28:16-20
Mark 16:15-18
First Corinthians 2:9ff
First Corinthians 12
First Corinthians 14
Babel vs Day of Pentecost both events dealt with language. In both, man spoke words. Babel created division into many languages. The supernatural language of God tames the tongue that no man can tame. James 3:1-8
Our tongues govern our lives. Proverbs 4:2
Babel was in rebellion to God. Pentecost was in obedience to God

About the Author

Dr. Betty Gilliam earned a *BSE in secondary education and MS in secondary counseling from the University of Central Arkansas, an MA in Pastoral Ministry from Oral Roberts University and a Psy.D from Graduate Theological Foundation. She has successfully completed the course work for a PhD in Renewal Church History at Regent University. She studied at Oxford University, Christ Church several summers.*

Dr. Gilliam taught in the Cabot, Arkansas public school district for a number of years and was the middle school counselor when she resigned to help found Faith Christian Center with her husband, Gene. She has co-pastored Faith Christian Center Church in Jacksonville, Arkansas with her husband since 1984. She is the President of Central Arkansas Bible College and co-founder of Word Churches International. Dr. Gilliam has taught in several Bible colleges and was the first person to teach a college counseling course in any University in Bulgaria after they were freed from communism.

Made in the USA
San Bernardino, CA
17 April 2018